THE CALCRAFTS

— OF —

REMPSTONE HALL

THE INTRIGUING HISTORY OF A DORSET DYNASTY

Richard D. Ryder

HALSGROVE

First published in Great Britain in 2005

British Library Cataloguing-in-Publication Data.
A CIP record for this title is available from the British Library.

ISBN 1 84114 456 8

HALSGROVE

Halsgrove House
Lower Moor Way
Tiverton, Devon EX16 6SS
Tel: 01884 243242
Fax: 01884 243325
email: sales@halsgrove.com
website: www.halsgrove.com

Printed and bound in Great Britain by The Cromwell Press, Trowbridge

CONTENTS

Acknowledgements   *4*

Preface   *5*

Maps and Calcraft Family Tree   *6*

1   Sex and Magic   7

2   John Calcraft MP (1726–1772) and Elizabeth Bride   19

3   John Calcraft MP and Georgiana Bellamy   43

4   Rt Hon. John Calcraft (the Younger) (1765–1831)   60

5   Sir Granby Thomas Calcraft (1766–1820)   76

6   John Hales Calcraft MP (1796–1880)

    and Lady Caroline   81

7   Sir Henry Calcraft (1836–1896)   103

8   William Montagu Calcraft (1834–1901)   111

9   The Twentieth Century: After the Dynasty   116

Addendum   *169*

Short Bibliography   *170*

Index   *171*

ACKNOWLEDGEMENTS

I would like to thank all descendants of the Calcraft family for their help in preparing this book, also the Hamilton-Fletchers, Professor John Cannon, the Duke of Hamilton, Dr Robert Oxlade, Simon and Anna Butler, Penelope Merrett, Liliana and Nick Mack, Rachel Trethewey, Jan Martin, Andrew Parsons, Susan Inge, Audrey Ryder, Charlotte Odgers, and Lady Cook. Photographs by Simon Butler, Joey Osborne, Henry Ryder and Vanessa Ryder.

THE ISLE OF PURBECK
(inset left) Dorset County

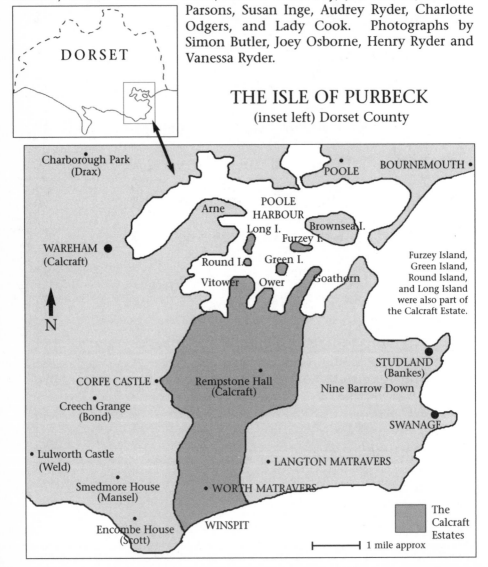

DORSET

Charborough Park
(Drax)

POOLE

BOURNEMOUTH

POOLE HARBOUR

Arne

Long I.

Brownsea I.

Furzey I.

WAREHAM
(Calcraft)

Round I.

Green I.

Vitower   Ower   Goathorn

Furzey Island, Green Island, Round Island, and Long Island were also part of the Calcraft Estate.

N

STUDLAND
(Bankes)

CORFE CASTLE

Rempstone Hall
(Calcraft)

Nine Barrow Down

Creech Grange
(Bond)

SWANAGE

Lulworth Castle
(Weld)

LANGTON MATRAVERS

Smedmore House
(Mansel)

WORTH MATRAVERS

Encombe House
(Scott)

WINSPIT

The Calcraft Estates

1 mile approx

PREFACE

There is something intriguing about a dynasty. Like an individual, a dynasty is born, grows to maturity and then declines. It is possible to see dynasties as living things in themselves. They are rather like empires: they live and die. This book is about one such dynasty. A dynasty that has almost been forgotten but one that, in its day, had influence not only upon the West Country, but also nationally and internationally.

When looking at the history of a family from a distance in time certain trends appear. Patterns emerge over the course of five or six generations. First, there is the continuation of family traditions. Then, one can see the opposite tendency: the reaction of a succeeding generation against its parents' values. Finally, there emerges a tendency for children to try to realise the frustrated ambitions of their parents. All three of these patterns appear in the case of the Calcrafts of Rempstone.

The heart of the book is about the political lives of the Calcrafts. But I hope it is far more fun than just this. It looks at personal motives, scandals and the climates of the times. It is also about that baffling thing – the British class system. It is about a lineage and not about an extended family: it concentrates upon the Squires of Rempstone and their ladies. The book is, however, on several levels, ranging from the racy to the very serious. Because half a dozen of my sources are currently almost unobtainable to scholars, I have quoted from them at considerable length.

In order to reduce their confusion, readers should note that the first three Calcraft Squires of Rempstone were all called John: John Calcraft MP (1726–1772) who was also called Honest Jack and Crafterio; his son the Rt Hon. John Calcraft MP (1765–1831), called 'the Younger'; and the latter's son John Hales Calcraft MP (1796–1880). The first John has two chapters (Chapters 2 and 3) devoted largely to himself, whereas John the Younger and John Hales Calcraft have one chapter each (Chapters 4 and 6 respectively).

Richard D. Ryder
Rempstone 2005

THE SQUIRES OF REMPSTONE

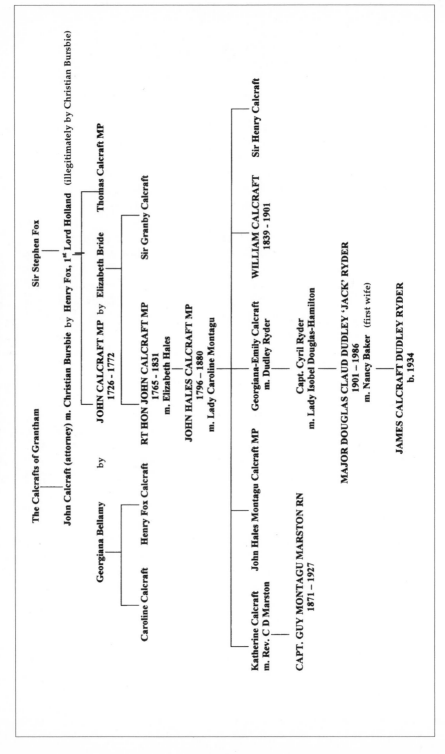

The Calcrafts of Grantham

Sir Stephen Fox

John Calcraft (attorney) m. Christian Bursbie by Henry Fox, 1ˢᵗ Lord Holland (illegitimately by Christian Bursbie)

Georgiana Bellamy   by   Thomas Calcraft MP

JOHN CALCRAFT MP by Elizabeth Bride
1726 - 1772

Caroline Calcraft   Henry Fox Calcraft

RT HON JOHN CALCRAFT MP
1765 - 1831
m. Elizabeth Hales

Sir Granby Calcraft

JOHN HALES CALCRAFT MP
1796 – 1880
m. Lady Caroline Montagu

John Hales Montagu Calcraft MP

Georgiana-Emily Calcraft
m. Dudley Ryder

WILLIAM CALCRAFT
1839 - 1901

Sir Henry Calcraft

Katherine Calcraft
m. Rev. C D Marston

CAPT. GUY MONTAGU MARSTON RN
1871 – 1927

Capt. Cyril Ryder
m. Lady Isobel Douglas-Hamilton

MAJOR DOUGLAS CLAUD DUDLEY 'JACK' RYDER
1901 – 1986
m. Nancy Baker (first wife)

JAMES CALCRAFT DUDLEY RYDER
b. 1934

1

SEX AND MAGIC

Like many politicians, the Calcrafts of Rempstone Hall had an active sex life and, to an extent, it is sex that powers their story: sex repressed, sex concealed and sex indulgently enjoyed. To this day, the heart of Rempstone throbs with a sexual magic – both beautiful and sinister – that has haunted, quite literally, the members of the Calcraft dynasty; a political and landed dynasty that began in 1726 and lasted until the death of the last male Calcraft in 1901.

Long before Rempstone became an ancient manor and hamlet, and then a farmhouse in the sixteenth century, it was a place of mystery. In the woods at the end of its eastern driveway lie the remains of a Bronze Age stone circle, partly destroyed by clay workings in the middle ages. Nine great iron-stones still stand half hidden among the trees where, to this day, offerings of money and flowers are often anonymously laid. Riders tell stories as to how their horses have shied or refused to pass this pagan site.

In the twentieth century archeologists discovered that Rempstone Heath, two thousand years ago, was one of the greatest industrial sites in Europe – exporting from Ower and the islands of Poole Harbour, goods of shale and pottery as well as iron. Across the southern side of Rempstone Hall runs the chalk escarpment of Nine Barrow Down – the burial place of ancient tribal chieftains and, in the shadow of its northern slope, there have been found the traces of a prehistoric ceremonial trackway running from the Stone Circle westwards, past the house, and towards Corfe Castle. On the hills directly opposite the house are two circular earthworks of unknown date and purpose, one planted with Maritime pines by Lady Caroline Calcraft in the 1870s and the other confining a strangely twisted clump of hawthorne. A quarter of a mile to the west of Rempstone Hall are the remains of a Roman villa and the whole of Rempstone and its wild heathland are crossed by medieval roadways which, for centuries, carried the Purbeck stone and marble down from Worth Matravers to the harbour.

Today, as for the last few hundred years, Rempstone Hall is an isolated house two and a half miles from the nearest villages at Corfe and Studland. To the east lies the farm of Kingswood and to the west those of Rollington and Brenscombe. Rempstone Hall itself remains shrouded in its own dark woodlands full of oak, chestnut, larch and massive pines planted around the year 1790. The plantations' names are evocative: Nelson's, Foxground, Strength and the Gwyle. In the eighteenth and nineteenth centuries the

Rempstone estate ran all the way across the Isle of Purbeck from the islands and southern shores of Poole Harbour to include Worth Matravers and the storm battered cliffs of Winspit. That territory, some eleven square miles, together with most of the houses in Wareham, were bought by the founder of the dynasty, John Calcraft MP (1726–1772) *[see Plate 1]*, in the mid eighteenth century. After the First World War, the southern part of the estate was sold – although it is unclear for what reason. Today, John Calcraft's descendants through the female line – the Ryders and the Manningham-Bullers – are still lords of the manors of Wareham, Worth and Rempstone. They tolerate, but scarcely benefit from (since oil is not the property of the landowner in Britain) the huge reserves of oil that have been pumped from under Rempstone land since the 1970s. Nearly two thousand years after nature reclaimed the industrial waste of the Iron Age, turning Rempstone into one of the wildest and least exploited parts of the English countryside, oil was discovered under Wytch Farm on Rempstone Heath. Since that time Rempstone has been the long suffering host for the largest, yet best concealed, on-shore oil field in Western Europe, from which one or two million pounds worth of high quality oil has been extracted every day. In almost any other country in the world the owners of Rempstone would have joined the ranks of the super rich. But not in Britain.

The origin of the name of Rempstone itself is disputed. John Hutchins – the great historian of Dorset – tells us that Rempstone in the fifteenth century was owned by Robert Rempston (d.1464) – but suggests that the family derived their name from the place and not the other way around. By 1664 Rempstone was in the hands of the Trenchard family of Wolfeton and ten years later George Trenchard described his 'farm commonly known by the name Rempston or Rempscombe'. A combe is, of course, Old English for 'narrow valley'. Well, the one-sided valley running from Corfe Castle to Studland in which Rempstone is situated could scarcely be called narrow. It is, indeed, hardly a valley. There is a range of hills, Nine Barrow Down, on one side and then heath and forest on the other, sloping gently down for a mile or two to Poole Harbour. This is hardly a 'combe'.

The Rose family who bought the land from the Trenchards in 1691 clearly called it 'Rempstone' when they sold it to John Calcraft in 1757 and 'Rempstone' and 'Rempstone Hall' have been on the maps and in the deeds ever since. Eilert Ekwall argues that Rempstone may derive from the Old English 'Hrempi's tun' where tun means 'homestead' or 'village', although nobody knows who Hrempi was. Alternatively, Ekwall suggests it might derive from 'Hrimpan' meaning 'wrinkled'. Far more likely, however, is that Rempstone comes from the Old English 'Hring-stan' or 'stone ring'. For centuries the most outstanding feature of the place must have been its old Stone Circle, initially as a revered religious site and, far later, to the Saxons, as a place of dread and superstition. Rempstone Hall and the Stone Circle are only some three hundred yards apart. Historians and etymologists such as Hutchins and Ekwall would not necessarily have known this.

What, then, about the sex? Well, it starts with the mystery of John Calcraft's birth, apparently in Lincolnshire on 14 August 1726. His mother was Christian Bursbie, and John was her first child. Shortly before the birth – the dates are ambiguous – she was married to an attorney, the Town Clerk of Grantham, who was also called John Calcraft. This attorney was a political animal and was in the pay of two local grandees – the Duke of Rutland and the up and coming Henry Fox (1705–1774) *[see Plate 2]*, the future Lord Holland, the owner of Holland House and Holland Park in London. Fox was twenty-one at the time of Calcraft's birth and had already made a name for himself as a libertine. In order to avoid scandal he had to go abroad at about this time, eventually returning and entering Parliament in 1735. Fox went on to become one of the cleverest and richest of politicians, first as Secretary for War in a war-like age, and then as Paymaster General (in those days a far more important and lucrative post than it is today). As a young man his interest in women was well known and, if libido is inherited, then he inherited his prowess from his father, Sir Stephen Fox, the statesman friend of Charles II, who married his twenty-six year old second wife at the age of seventy-six and had four children by her, the second being Henry, born when his father was entering his eightieth year.

Henry Fox always described the much younger Calcraft as his 'near relation' and honest attempts have been made to explain this relationship along legitimate lines. But it remains more than likely that our John Calcraft of Rempstone was Fox's child by Christian Bursbie whom the town clerk of Grantham had married, either quite innocently or under lucrative persuasion, when she had been made pregnant by a very wealthy young Henry Fox. As soon as Calcraft was old enough, however, Fox took him under his wing, invited him to London and began to give him a series of extremely well paid jobs. Contemporaries in the know had little doubt in their own minds as to what the real relationship was and political commentators and caricaturists made this perfectly clear at the time. We also know that Fox and Calcraft together cruised through Soho chatting up the ladies. This is how they picked up the most sexually attractive actress of the age – Georgiana Bellamy *[see Plate 3]*, who subsequently became John's live-in mistress (and maybe also Fox's) and by whom John apparently had two children. Poor Georgiana (or George Anne as she was often called) was very good at falling pregnant and this not only held back her stage career considerably, as theatre managers could never count upon her being sufficiently unencumbered to perform, but it also made John and probably also herself, uncertain as to who, exactly, were the fathers of her children. When Calcraft eventually cast her off – exasperated more by her remarkable extravagance than by her infidelities – she wrote a long and bitter attack upon Calcraft that is quoted from at length later in this book. Calcraft became one of a score of shareholders of the most famous theatre in the land, the Theatre Royal, Drury Lane, and obviously enjoyed the company of pretty actresses such as Georgiana. She has been described as 'one of the divine creatures of the time' but also as 'madly vain, arrogant and extravagant'.

Calcraft subsequently turned to the very young actress and singer, Elizabeth Bride, who moved in with him and became the co-founder of the Calcraft dynasty. David Garrick *[see Plate 4]* was the leading actor of the period and, whether it was a clash with John Calcraft over business matters or whether it was a dispute over a lady such as Elizabeth or Georgiana (she played Juliet to his Romeo), we do not know. Whatever the reason, Garrick challenged Calcraft to a duel. Later he thought better of it. They shook hands and became, from that time onwards, the best of friends.

Garrick was the father of modern theatre and his innovations cost a lot of money. Calcraft was one of only a score of shareholders in Garrick's Theatre Royal, Drury Lane, and possibly the richest. Both men were entrepreneurs. What role Calcraft played in the development of modern theatre can now only be guessed at.

John, Georgiana and Elizabeth probably all visited Rempstone although they never lived there for very long. Although John had bought the house in 1757, mainly for electoral purposes, he only retained part of it for his own use on visits to the boroughs of Wareham and Poole. He and his mistresses were accustomed to far grander premises in London and in Kent (Ingress Abbey and Leeds Abbey). His flat at Rempstone was, said John, merely a 'little hole'. But it was useful. He let the remainder of the premises to a 'widow Swyer and her son' (surely not another mistress?) and later to one of his Dorset agents, John Bishop, and his family.

John Calcraft was a highly successful man. As the county's leading military contractor and banker during the Seven Years War he had made a fortune, and he could claim no small part of the credit for Britain's victories. Calcraft's efficiency in provisioning its armies in Canada and India was one reason why Britain won superiority over France, providing the basis for future empire. The Seven Years' War – Calcraft's war – was Britain's outstanding military and political triumph. But Calcraft was also, secretly, hiding behind the mysterious pseudonym of Junius – a disguise in which he attacked some of the policies of the government and of the king himself. He stood for freedom of speech and support for the American colonists. When John died in 1772 he was at the height of his powers and poised for greater things. He was only forty-six and already one of the richest men in England. He had estates in Lincolnshire, Buckinghamshire, Somerset, Kent and Dorset, was William Pitt's right hand man and was expecting a title. By Elizabeth Bride he left four children, as well as two more doubtful ones by Georgiana. He had certainly been a 'free liver' but not a vicious one. His behaviour was not entirely unusual for a young London blade of the period. After his death it turned out that the reason he had married neither Georgiana nor Elizabeth was that he had been secretly married all along, and from about the age of eighteen, to a Lincolnshire lass called Bridget. Presumably, as it was almost impossible to secure a divorce in those days, he had been paying her to be quiet for a quarter of a century. But once he was dead she was able to surface, back home in Grantham, and claim a large part of his huge estates – which she did successfully, thus forcing the Calcraft dynasty eventually to leave Kent and move full time to Rempstone. By the time of John's death in 1772 the Rempstone, Worth and Wareham estates must have been bringing in quite a bit of rent. In addition to house and farm rentals, there was income from the fishing at Wareham and from the quarrymen carrying stone across the heath. There were also increasing sales of ball clay to the up and coming Josiah Wedgwood.

John Calcraft the Younger (1765-1831) *[see Plates 8, 9]*, John and Elizabeth's eldest boy, certainly did visit Rempstone more often although, as a Cabinet Minister and Privy Councillor, he had to spend much of his life in London. He seems to have been a sad and serious man, indeed, a melancholic one, ending his life in mysterious circumstances, probably murdered, in 1831, after playing a remarkably important role in passing the revolutionary Great Reform Bill – he rebelled against his own Cabinet by voting *for* Parliamentary reform in a reading of the Bill that only passed by one vote. By doing so he incurred the wrath of the Duke of Wellington and his Tory colleagues (John Calcraft was a Whig in a Tory cabinet), and died as the first ever MP for the County of Dorset. But we know little about his sex life. He seems to have been a loyal husband and the father of seven surviving children. When married, the Calcrafts certainly kept their wives busy.

In the 1790s Rempstone Hall had been enlarged considerably and it was enlarged again in the 1830s just as the next Calcraft squire, John Hales Calcraft MP (1796–1880) *[see Plates 13, 14, 15]*, moved in after his marriage to the outstandingly beautiful Lady Caroline Montagu *[see Plates 19, 21]*. This is when the trouble started. After the cheerful sexual abandon of the founder of the dynasty the pendulum now swung the other way with a vengeance. Sex became a matter for very strict control and censure. John Hales and Caroline were not just reacting against the scandal of grandfather John and his actresses, and the fact that the Calcrafts were descended illegitimately. There were at least two further reasons for the era of grim puritanical repression that now ensued at Rempstone, eventually lasting for seventy years. The first is that both Caroline and John Hales Calcraft were exceptionally sexually attractive people and both had discovered this on their grand tours abroad in the years following the defeat of Napoleon at Waterloo in 1815. The young John Hales was several times compared to Lord Byron, and to the latter's disadvantage. Calcraft was very dark and very handsome and, in Paris in his early twenties, he had attracted the attention of Napoleon's notoriously sex-mad sister Pauline *[see Plate 16]*. We know little of their affair but Pauline was not one to hang about. She got straight to the point in such matters. All we are told is that John became one of her 'favourites' and that she gave him many gifts, including some of her exiled brother's lace ruffles and a lot of his books. In the grand French tradition, Pauline Bonaparte was sixteen years older than John Hales Calcraft: he was her English milord toyboy. She must have given him a very good time indeed and taught him a great deal about sex.

Where did John Hales Calcraft get his extraordinary good looks? His father had Elizabeth Bride's fair hair and blue eyes. But John Hales was as dark as a Spanish Don. So, presumably, it was from his mother Elizabeth, the daughter of Sir Thomas Pym Hales (a close relation of the remarkable Dr Stephen Hales who invented not only the method of measuring blood pressure still used today, but also air-conditioning) that he obtained his black curls and brown eyes. They were to continue in the family until the end of the Calcraft dynasty.

So, in 1828 John Hales Calcraft married Lady Caroline Montagu, the daughter of the fifth Duke of Manchester. She was twenty-three and he was a worldly thirty-two. She, too, had been abroad and, in Italy had been feted as a great beauty. That must have meant that the Italian males went mad about her. Whether or not she was actually seduced, or even raped, we do not know. All we are told is that she created a stir by suddenly refusing to attend a grand gala held in her honour. After that, so it seems, she became very serious, extremely religious and not at all a lady to be flirted with. She even turned down an offer of marriage from the heir to a European throne. It is not hard to imagine what might have happened. It was surely something sexual. A hot blooded Italian male had gone just a bit too far. Or, maybe, Caroline had fallen and been shocked to discover that she enjoyed it. Whatever the exact details, we shall never know, but after the age of twenty-one Caroline never permitted a portrait of herself to be painted, and mirrors were prohibited. She would resist vanity. She saw her beauty as a source of evil and temptation. One sketch of Caroline exists, done when she was twenty-three, and there are two photographs of her in her sitting room at Rempstone, taken when she was over eighty. The only other depiction of her during the intervening decades is a watercolour of her back view!

Why had Caroline reacted so primly to a sexual adventure in Italy? It is not hard to see. Her mother, Lady Susan Gordon [see Plates 17, 18], a daughter of the last Duke of Gordon, who had married the Duke of Manchester, had created a huge scandal in London by eloping with her footman, Hussey, in the early years of the century. Whereas it frequently happened that grand ladies had lovers and that occasionally these might have included a servant or two, it was almost unheard of for a lady actually to elope with one. This was clearly more than sex, it was a love match. The Duke, her husband, although politically enlightened, had given her full cause by publicly flaunting his mistresses. Lady Susan never came back to him and, according to rumour, remained happily domiciled in rural obscurity with her footman. This rocked the British sense of propriety at the time. Susan had broken all the rules of a snobbish society, abandoning both her husband and her children, including the little Lady Caroline. In consequence, Caroline had spent much of her childhood being brought up by her grandmother, the racy dowager Duchess of Gordon, and her aunt, the Duchess of Richmond (of Waterloo Ball fame), surrounded by an aura of scandal about her mother. As she grew a little older she would have realised that love – or sex – had been the source of all this misery for her. It is hardly surprising that she grew up determined to renounce such devilish lusts. She might, if it had been an earlier age, have taken the veil and disappeared into a nunnery but, instead, she sought and found refuge in a safe marriage and a dull life, well away from the glamours of her youth, in the depths of Dorset. Virtuously, she channelled her affections into matrimonial duty, bearing her handsome husband seven children.

However, Lady Caroline was not going to allow any further sexual scandals in her family and she imposed, by the force of her formidable character, a strict puritanical regime upon her offspring. Her three beautiful daughters, who survived into adulthood, all became extremely religious but eventually married. Her three sons, on the other hand, managed to resist her evangelical religion but all remained single. Only one, Sir Henry Calcraft [see Plate 25], was ever rumoured to be gay. How the other two reacted to their mother's trenchant views on lust remains rather a mystery. All were handsome like their father. All were eligible and wealthy enough to attract or buy sex wherever they sought it. William [see Plate 28], the youngest, comes across as an obedient mother's boy. As the last Calcraft squire of Rempstone, he was said to be a quiet man. Maybe he was that old fashioned creature – a true Victorian bachelor and lifelong virgin, but that is doubtful. John Hales Montagu Calcraft (1831–1868) [see Plate 23], however, his eldest brother, was far more outgoing and worldly. If his mother was going to be hostile to the women he found attractive then, too bad, he would not marry them. He was a Member of Parliament and a Naval Captain who had fought in the Crimea. His life away from Rempstone offered him more than enough opportunities for sex.

So was Rempstone in the nineteenth century a scene of entirely stifled sexuality? Did Lady Caroline's puritanical principles succeed in extinguishing all lustful tendencies in her husband and her children? Jane Panton, writing in 1909, heavily insinuates the opposite. But what exactly happened we do not know. Strangely, the only evidence is from the supernatural and, if one can suspend any disbelief for a while, that evidence is fascinating.

The final chapter of this book deals in greater detail with what has happened at Rempstone Hall after the end of the named Calcraft dynasty. One part of it concerns the amazing findings of some of the country's leading occultists and mediums after they visited Rempstone in 1996. James Calcraft Dudley Ryder [see Plate 54], one of Lady Caroline's great great grandchildren, the then squire, had been struck by how few women living at Rempstone had been happy since Lady Caroline's time. Why was this? A friend suggested a psychic cause, and so James Ryder agreed to invite some London experts for their opinion. James and his daughter Lara Manningham-Buller [see Plate 55], accompanied them as they quietly toured the house. The occultists found that Rempstone Hall was exceptionally well haunted and by three principal ghosts: first and foremost was that of Lady Caroline herself, disturbed and disgusted by the sexual antics of the twentieth century, and disapproving of the women who had dared to marry her descendants and to live there. Next, were the eroticised ghosts of sexually aroused Victorian servant girls in the dark attic rooms that were once the servants' quarters. There were many women who worked at Rempstone in the nineteenth century, and obeyed their masters' orders. We know from the census of 1861, for example, the names of many possible secret sexual partners for the young Calcraft boys – Eliza Deens (aged 36, Nurse), Jane Lane (aged 31, Maid), Eliza Gover (aged 21, Under Maid), Selina Walker (aged 21, Ladies' Maid), Emily Morley (aged 21, Nursing Maid), Eliza Vincent (aged 19, Laundry Maid), Anne Volter (aged 30, Cook), Maisie Tompin (aged 39, Ladies' Maid), Mary Chenton (aged 16, Scullery Maid) and Marion Carter (aged 23) [see Plate 27].

What an extraordinary community it was at Rempstone. Three repressed and handsome young men, not to mention their father, all under the same roof with ten subordinate young women! Of course things happened. And they were not always to the displeasure of the women servants themselves although, according to the mediums, one at least of these was exploited and abused. There were also some young women who lived in cottages in the grounds. In 1871 Anne Barnes was twenty-one and Emma Dibben, the laundress's daughter, was nineteen. There was, surely, no shortage of temptation. Nor of opportunity!

Large houses in the country were self-contained communities. They grew their own food, had their own rules and ran their own economies. They have been studied more by dramatists than by sociologists. Yet they are worth thinking about. In the days before telephones or cars they were often quite isolated and so could develop their own idiosyncratic cultures. Differences existed between one country house and another: one could be a happy community while the next, perhaps five miles away, was miserable. To an extent they were microcosms of the greater world outside – like slices of the wider social order. In a hierarchical age they, too, would be hierarchical, with the head of the house, kinglike in his authority, with unfettered powers to hire and fire and to rule over the private lives of his dependents and servants. In an average country house, everybody knew their place and their roles. The mistress of the house was expected to be the controller of all that went on indoors, while the lord of the house dealt with all that went on outside, including relations with the neighbours and the world at large. Usually, the man had control of the finances.

Each country house community was like a little state. The ideal, established in the eighteenth century, was that these states should be enlightened and humane dictatorships. There was no democracy or equality, and little freedom. But there should be justice. In as much as the servants elected to be servants, no socialists or egalitarians were to be expected among their ranks. If they did not like being part of a hierarchy then they could leave. Nobody stopped them.

As in any society, there were rituals and ceremonies. During the nineteenth century, servants would often be required to attend daily prayers led by the squire or his wife. There were occasional big events – such as

Christmas and Easter and balls to celebrate a wedding or a baptism. All the servants' work was ritualised: tables had to be laid correctly, meals served correctly, fires made correctly, mantelpieces dusted correctly, and letters delivered on salvers correctly. Visitors would come in from the outside world and stay for days at a time. That would be an opportunity for the lord and lady to show off the culture of their little state – its beautiful possessions, its orderliness and the decorum of its staff.

The divisions between upstairs and downstairs, between the family and the servants, were very marked. This was part of the social class game that everybody played. But both teams, the family and the servants, had their own hierarchies. Among the family, age was more of a factor than was gender. Certainly, males and females were expected to have different roles, but their prestige or standing was much the same. Adults, however, ruled the children entirely. Indeed, adults and children were almost like two different species and, in many upper class families, there was little real intimacy between the generations. Becoming an adult was a long and difficult process but was, on the whole, rewarded by a gradual increase in privileges. Little attempt was made to *understand* children, only to educate and discipline them. The emphasis was upon correctness rather than psychology. Children lived in nurseries where they often saw more of their nursemaids than they did of their parents. This was a time in their lives when the social gulf between the classes was at its most narrow, but as they grew older it would widen. The servants, too, were regarded almost as a distinct species from whom the adult above-stairs world kept itself aloof. Certain topics were not to be discussed before the children or the servants. Even as late as the 1950s, Vee and Jack Ryder would sometimes attempt to preserve such secrecy by using broken French when children or servants were present – 'pas devant les servants'.

Among the servants the most powerful figures were the butler and the housekeeper. Under them came the cook and the ladies maids, and then the rest. The scullery maids seem to have been regarded as the lowest rung on the ladder. But the ladders could be climbed. As a career, being in service offered plenty of opportunities for promotion and career development. It also offered security and structure and entertainment. The servants not only had their own relationships to deal with but life above stairs was also a constant fascination. It was like today's soap operas. In the evening servants could get together to quietly gossip (so as not to incur the butler's disapproval) about the aberrations, power struggles and romances of their employers. Families could be large and visitors frequent. There might be ten or twenty servants below stairs and a dozen toffs above. Occasionally, the barriers between the two social groups were partially broken, usually by sexual relations between the men upstairs and the female servants below. These were, strictly speaking, taboo, but taboos just increased the excitement, and so, no doubt, did the dominant and subordinate nature of such relationships, however politically incorrect that might seem today. Liaisons had to be secret. Rarely did they ever develop into romance.

In grand families there were some figures who moved in the grey area between the two classes. Lawyers, doctors and clergy used the front door unlike bailiffs, merchants or visiting servants, but the professional classes were not always invited to aristocratic social events in the Victorian era. Governesses and tutors were somewhere in the middle; often the children of gentry or professional people themselves, they were, nevertheless, employed. Usually, they would eat meals with the family, but sometimes on their own in their separate accommodation near the family schoolroom. Naval and military officers were acceptable in the drawing room but other ranks definitely were not. Bishops, of course, were entirely acceptable but a curate might feel ill at ease on a grand occasion. Indeed, curates were often the butt of jokes which reflected their social insecurities. Etiquette was terribly important and if you did not know it, you were in serious trouble.

A certain amount of conscious or unconscious rivalry took place between country houses. Having a large number of servants was one way of showing off to the neighbours. In consequence, there was often not enough for the servants to do. To fill the time, various unconscious time-wasting devices seem to have been developed. Everything was done the hard way. Shortcuts in working practices were abhorred: things had to be done 'properly' and in the traditional manner. Clothes and servants' uniforms were often elaborate, awkward to work in and time-consuming to put on, with myriad buttons, laces and loops. Etiquette decreed that they frequently had to be changed: there were morning clothes, outdoor clothes, walking clothes, raincoats, sunhats, solar topies, dinner jackets, smoking jackets and night attire. For the servants there were aprons, ribbons, lace caps, liveries and bonnets. All had to be laid out, ironed, mended and put on, usually with assistance. Stays had to be tightened, corsets squeezed into, hats brushed, cufflinks and studs put in, spats and gloves whitened. There were house-shoes to clean, and walking-shoes, dancing-pumps, slippers and riding boots. It was all an elaborate charade: a huge regime of occupational therapy for the unemployed upper classes and their minions.

The same applied to gardening. Five Victorian gardeners were employed to look after a garden where one does it today. It was not just a matter of machinery but of ritual. Everything in the country house communities was done according to custom. There was a reassuring regularity about life in those times. Eccentrics, of course, especially among the family, were to be expected. Every family had its dotty members as well as its black sheep. Severe mental illness was usually dismissed as 'nerves', 'shyness' or as a 'peculiar sense of humour'. Total psychosis was put down to in-breeding or being 'highly strung'. All this was considered to be part of the warp and weft – the raisins in the bread and butter pudding.

Socially, of course, the Victorian Calcrafts' lives must have been immensely dull. Restricted by the conventions of the day there were few with whom they could properly consort. To reduce their opportunities still further, some of the correct class were disapproved of for other reasons, or simply disliked. For example, the earlier Calcrafts regarded the Bankes family as odd and difficult. There was a scandal, too, in the mid nineteenth century, attaching to the exiled and homosexual William Bankes. As for the Drax family of Charborough Park – they were seen as traditional political enemies. At many an election the Whig or Liberal Calcrafts fought the Tory Draxes with a considerable intensity. The Calcrafts were not a really old Dorset family like the Williams of Herringstone, the Pitts of Kingston Maurward, the Framptons, the Clavels, the Ashley Coopers (Earls of Shaftesbury), or the Digby's of Sherborne, but there were certainly some more recent arrivals than them: the Portmans of Bryanston, for example, and the Scotts of Encombe.

Finally, and most unusually, among Rempstone's ghosts there is the conjured spirit of a man in armour in the dining room where there had been, so the mediums said, black magic and talk of war. But even this ghost has a sexual link, perhaps unknown to the mediums, and that is of a very exceptional nature. A conjured spirit is one that has been raised by magic. Did the mediums realise that in 1910, at the invitation of Lady Caroline's grandson, the bearded and rather mysterious Captain Guy Montagu Marston RN [see Plate 33], no less a magician than Aleister Crowley [see Plate 38] himself had stayed at Rempstone on at least one occasion? Crowley – the so-called Wickedest Man in the World – was obsessed with sex magic and performed it at Rempstone with Leila, one of his Scarlet Women, as they raised the spirit of the great god Mars (Mars, apparently, warned them of a war to come in 1914). They also performed secret ceremonies in the old Stone Circle in the woods where, perhaps, similar rites had been conducted three thousand years before. Both Marston and Crowley were reacting against the strictures of their highly religious and puritanical mothers.

The sexual rituals performed at Rempstone depended, in theory, upon the intensity of the pleasures experienced. Crowley believed that by harnessing such sexual energies he could unlock occult worlds. For these purposes he had to have women as participants who could experience intense and repeated orgasms. He considered the female orgasm to be an essential part of the technique. Whether or not all this depended upon Leila, or whether local girls were also employed, we do not know. The risks in terms of scandal would have been immense, in the latter case, and so this seems to be unlikely. Sex was, and remained, an overtly taboo subject until at least the 1960s. We know, however, that exotic drugs such as opium, and even mescaline, were employed in these Rempstone rituals a hundred years ago.

Whatever did the ghost of Lady Caroline think of these profanities? The great sexual repression of Rempstone's Victorian era had finally erupted like a volcano into the depraved and crazed outpourings of sexual occultism.

In the 1930s Rempstone Hall became the scene for the far more innocent sexual frolics of the tennis party and cocktails era. In the 1940s Rempstone was occupied by soldiers and would have seen some bawdy goings-on. From the 1950s onwards the house seemed to pulse with sexuality. Some houses have this quality. At Rempstone it seems to come from its very stones as if, over three centuries, they have absorbed and intensified the highly pressurised loves, lusts and repressions of the Calcraft dynasty.

A dynasty is a dynasty – a completed story. Like most such dynasties the Calcrafts rose upon the efforts and material success of their founder, grew to some eminence, married into the aristocracy and then gently subsided into dignified obscurity, dying out at the dawn of the twentieth century. The story lasts only a hundred and seventy years. This book is chiefly about those years.

2

JOHN CALCRAFT
(1726-1772)
AND ELIZABETH BRIDE

According to the family trees inscribed carefully in two or three large family Bibles at Rempstone, John Calcraft was born on 14 August 1726, the son of Christian Bursbie and John Calcraft of Grantham (born 1695). His grandfather, an attorney, was of the same name, being baptised in 1661. Perhaps all this is true. Contemporary reports and his obituaries, however, insinuate otherwise. They imply that John Calcraft of Rempstone's real father was the wealthy young playboy, Henry Fox, who eventually became the famous Whig politician and father also of Charles James Fox.

The contemporary allegation that John Calcraft and Henry Fox looked alike is supported by their Rempstone portraits: both appear round featured, intelligent and benign *[see Plates 1, 2]*. Gifts of portraits were themselves sometimes indications of close kinship, but it is believed Fox did not like this particular picture and so it may have had little significance as a gift. It was the last portrait painted by Hogarth, who considered it to be his best.

Henry Fox himself was born in 1705 when his father was aged seventy-nine and his mother only twenty-eight. His mother was Christian Hopes, daughter of the rector of Haceby and Aswarby in Lincolnshire where John Calcraft bought some property in later years. Henry's twin sister (who died in 1708) was also named Christian. The repetition of this name, and the associations with Lincolnshire, do add circumstantial support to the theory that Fox and Calcraft might have been related maternally; both men had a sister and a mother with the name of Christian.

Whatever the truth, it is certain that by the time he was only eighteen, Calcraft was already doing well and was in a very responsible position as a Deputy-Paymaster to the military forces in Scotland which were engaged in suppressing the Jacobite uprising of 1745. His letter-book of this period survives and gives a record of his business transactions. These mainly involved collecting money in the north of England, concentrating it at Newcastle, and then taking it, under armed escort, to Edinburgh. The letters are all written in a careful and beautifully legible handwriting that is almost certainly Calcraft's own. Over the years this writing develops into a strong but always meticulous style, and the prose is concise and dry.

The 1745 letters, although superficial in content, give some flavour of the times. In February Calcraft writes to Fox:

Sir
I have the honour to acquaint you that we have here several accounts of the

19

Rebels retreating from Stirling at 7 o'clock on Saturday night that they have crossed the Firth in a great hurry and before they left Stirling nailed up their cannon there, where they have also left most of their baggage. Just as their rear was marching their magazine of powder which was in the Church of St Miniams was blown up.

Our army was encamped at Falkirk on Saturday night. I am with the greatest respect, Sir, your J.C.

The weather is still cold when he writes to Fox in March:

Sir
I have the honour to acquaint you that with great difficulty I am got so far on my journey but the snow is so excessive deep in some places that the roads are scarce passable and I am afraid it will occasion the water's being so much out as to obstruct my performing my journey in the time I proposed.

Mr Mortice is with me and making all possible haste the badness of the roads will allow. I am, Sir, your J. C.
*P.S. We had a **continual** snow for the last three days and was yesterday and Monday **belly deep** in several places.*

He writes to a friend, Anthony Sawyer, in June:

I've the pleasure to acquaint you I arrived safe here on Sunday but met with an overthrow in the way down a precipice five yards steep and thank God was only a little hurt in the neck with it.

In a P.S. he adds:

We've very bad sport and scarce any horses to run or company to see them.

On 1 July he writes hurriedly to Fox:

Sir,
I've taken the liberty of troubling Your Honour with this to acquaint you we are this day told by two Officers just come from Scotland that Secretary Murray was taken on Friday about 20 miles from Edinburgh and the next day carried before Lord Justice Clarke who committed him to Edinburgh Castle where he now is, and 'tis said he endeavoured to make his escape on the road but was prevented.

We've various reports where and how he was taken, some that it was at his own house by 4 of Kingston's horse who were discharged, others that it were at an alehouse where he was dressed like a farmer both which are mentioned in some private letters.

I hope this intelligence will come so early as to make it worth your Honour's acceptance and beg leave to assure you and with great respect, Sir, your J.C.

In mid August Calcraft pays a quick visit to Grantham, then returns to Newcastle. Correspondence then starts with a new character, John Hesse, who appears to be an old friend of Calcraft. They are having trouble with a debtor called Steele. Calcraft writes to Hesse on 26 August 1746:

> I received the favour of your last post with Mr Steele's enclosed and have always found him what you properly style him a shuffling impertinent cox-comb.

At the end of this letter Calcraft adds:

> I've just now been to see your horses watered which look very well and I make my servant look after them with my own, your little brown horse got the skin knocked off his fetlock joint by a fall at Colsterworth as your soldier told me but I've applied what is proper to heal it and it will be well in a day or two. I beg my compliments to all friends and am very sincerely, dear sir, your etc. J.C.

Calcraft frequently refers to the health of the horses, and expresses an interest in their medical treatment. In a letter of 16 September, it seems that Calcraft is anticipating his return to London and is toying with the idea of sharing accommodation with his friend Hesse. It is one of the least formal of Calcraft's letters which has survived:

> I'm quite ashamed to give you so great and frequent trouble but as I have no other friend at present in town can't tell how to prevent it and I assure you I will always gratefully acknowledge your favours and if ever I'm so happy as to have it in my power will very readily serve you in any respect; I've enclosed sent you a bill for £6.19.0 which you'll be so good as to receive and pay your cash to one Mr J. Dawtry a tailor in Stanhope Street, Leicester Fields, for the use of Mr John Lamb and send me his receipt in full of all accounts from Lamb.
>
> I hope Mr Johnson arrived safe in town with your horses both well but your soldier left the balls behind him which are now here. I had your horses shod before I got the last letter from you, I would have you defer taking our apart-ment a little longer as I expect I shall continue most of the winter here but I should be glad to know where you lodge as I shall next week have some fine moor game and propose sending you a pot which I hope will be worthy of your acceptance. I beg my compliments to Wheeler and all friends and am dear sir, your etc. J.C.

Three days later he reports to Hesse that:

> I propose going on Tuesday about 10 miles off to a place called Morpeth and staying till Friday if nothing happen to prevent me and as there are to be horse

races and assemblies hope to spend that time agreeably...

Although only aged nineteen, Calcraft was already entrusted with considerable duties. Not only did he regularly command and escort consignments of money from Newcastle, over wild and even hostile countryside, to Edinburgh, through snows he described to Fox as being 'belly deep', but the sums involved were enormous. On occasions, treasure as much as £30 000 in silver bullion was placed in his care. By today's values that amounts to several millions.

Calcraft seems to have efficiently performed his duties in the North and to have been rewarded by being made a Clerk at the War Office towards the end of 1746, shortly after Fox was appointed Secretary at War. By 1749 Fox had started to secure Army agencies for Calcraft and continued to recommend him as 'my near relative' for several years. Agents were employed mainly in the sale of commissions, but were also involved in the supplying of provisions and munitions for regiments.

Fox, himself, comes across extraordinarily well in some of his letters copied by Calcraft, and as a remarkably humane and pacific man for a Secretary at War. For instance, quite a few of his letters urge clemency in the case of court-martials and one appears to rebuke an officer for high-handed punitive action against a soldier. He seems concerned that justice should be done in such affairs and several times writes to Sir Dudley Ryder, the Attorney General (e.g. 14 August 1747 and 21 June 1749) asking for legal advice to back up, in the first instance, pardons for deserters and, in the latter, to reprimand General Anstruther for some wrongdoings against subordinates and civilians. He several times says he hopes for peace and when it comes, he welcomes it. Once or twice he puts in a good word for military widows and their families and he gets quite cross with General Churchill and Colonel Bockland for not providing proper medical care to soldiers injured by the 'fall of a Stage at Fort George'.

He writes on 17 July 1752 that Bockland should repair the 'Hospital hutt, building new hutts, or providing the hurt soldiers with everything that it may be in his power to procure, H.R.H. orders me to send this by express, to require you (Churchill) to send the surgeon of the Fort if in Scotland (if in England I will send him) immediately to his post, and to order surgeons from other Regiments, or from Edinburgh if necessary, to repair to Fort George and give their assistance and let no medicines be wanting but to provide and order whatever may tend to the relief of the men, with as much expedition as it is possible. Whatever the expense may be, it will be made good out of the contingencies.' Fox shows himself to be quite suspicious of Highlanders and Jacobites, however, but with some reason at that time. He is also a trifle sarcastic about old Lord Lovat, who was prosecuted for treason as a rebel by Dudley Ryder. In a letter to General Napier of 17 March 1746–7 Fox writes:

Lord Lovat begins his defence tomorrow and has desired Macleod at the House of Commons as a witness which I believe that said does not much like; Lovat on Friday being asked if he had anything to say to Sir Everard Faulkener who had just been examined against him answered 'Nothing, but that I am Sir Everard's honourable servant and wish him much enjoyment of his young wife.' A Clerk stands by to repeat what Lovat says and repeated this most audibly which they say sounded very ridiculously.

Lovat was duly convicted and was the last man in England to be beheaded. Fox wrote to Napier again, on 10 April:

I saw old Lovat die yesterday. He was calm, unaffected and intrepid. He said he died for his country, quoted Latin Dulce est pro patria mori, and Nescio qua Natale Solum etc., which was odd, insisted much on his and his family's strict and steady adherence to their principles. He never swerved from them from his cradle, he said; which for a man who lived a Presbyterian, fought for the King in 1715, and was dying a Papist for rebellion in 1747, seemed a most extraordinary assertion.

Fox, whimsically, adds a final sentence to his letter:

I hear old Lt. Col. Buchan is drowned at the bath. He walked or tumbled into the river, it is thought, whilst he was deep in reflection, perhaps on a game of chess.

Henry Fox, Lord Ilchester and Calcraft went shooting in August 1750 at Maddington, Calcraft being referred to by Fox as 'Jack, alias Lord William, alias Sportly, alias Vermin, alias Beau Calcraft, alias Squire Calcraft of the Grange...' Fox notes 'Mr Calcraft as bad, that is as insipid, a companion a' shooting as he is clever in all other things.' In October 1752 they went again to join Fox's brother, Lord Ilchester, but Calcraft does not seem to enjoy the sport: 'Mr Calcraft, always tender, but grown more than ever sensible to cold, went home by noon', Fox notes. Maybe Calcraft did not see much point in killing animals for fun.

In March 1753 Fox promoted Calcraft to Deputy Commissary General at 23 shillings a day. The last of Henry Fox's letters copied into the book by Calcraft is dated 27 August 1755 and thereafter the book is blank pages, suggesting that at that time Calcraft was finally promoted to a level (at the age of twenty-nine) at which his copying duties were over. The reason why he had continued with them so long may be that Calcraft was really acting as Fox's private secretary and the letters of the last few years appear in a book marked 'Private Letter Book H.F.' – so these may have been rather special letters with which he was being entrusted. Amusingly, Calcraft signs the very last one, absent-mindedly no doubt, with his own initials 'J C.' and then over-writes them firmly with the intended 'H.F.'. This final letter concerns the death of Calcraft's friend General Braddock, and his absent-mindedness could be attributed to the shock of bereavement, or to the agreeable discovery that Braddock had left him most of his silver in his will.

General Edward Braddock had been put in charge of the British army in America in 1754, and ordered to drive out the French. Before leaving England he made out a will in favour of John Calcraft, his young agent. Georgiana Bellamy had been a mistress of Braddock and, according to some reports, was actually married to him. Shortly after Braddock arrived in America his forces were ambushed by the French near Fort Duquesne and, despite the valiant efforts of Ensign George Washington, Braddock was killed. Calcraft duly inherited his table silver, which remains with his descendants.

Fox and Calcraft were, of course, on social terms with most of the leading military figures of the day. Calcraft's copy of the Army List reveals contact with famous names from the Duke of Cumberland to General Eyre Coote in India and General James Wolfe in Canada. But their lives were particularly entwined with the now rather forgotten John, Marquis of Granby (1721–1770) [see Plate 7] after whom many pubs are, however, still named. At the time, Granby was a great national hero, after dashing cavalry victories at Warburg in 1760, and at Minden in 1759 where he had led a charge upon the enemy without putting on his wig – hence the expression – 'charging bare-headed.' In 1766 he became Commander in Chief.

Granby, like Fox and Calcraft, hailed from Lincolnshire. The three men drank and wenched and gambled together and enjoyed the hospitality of Calcraft's two successive actress mistresses, Georgiana (or George Anne) Bellamy and Elizabeth Bride. Granby was always in debt and was constantly borrowing from his private bankers, Fox and Calcraft. Sometimes he fell out with his old mates but they always seemed to patch things up, and the jolly hero would come round to dinner again with Honest Jack Calcraft and his glamorous Georgiana or petite Elizabeth. To pay off his debts, on one occasion, he presented Calcraft with his 'bare-headed' portrait by Reynolds – it hangs at Rempstone still. In 1769, however, they finally fell out over the question of John Wilkes. Wilkes, another young rake, was the same age as Calcraft and, together, they stood for very much the same causes: religious toleration, freedom of speech and support for the American colonists. It may have been Calcraft who duped poor old Granby, who was not very astute as a politician, into supporting Wilkes in a vote in Parliament. When Granby realised what he had done in supporting this rebel, he changed his mind. This provoked the first Junius letters, as Calcraft used this disguise to tease his old friend in 1769. Poor Granby was forced to resign and died shortly afterwards.

By 1753 Calcraft was already living with Georgiana Bellamy, and may have just moved from Brewer Street to his larger establishment in Parliament

Street. As a quasi-banker and contractor for the forces he was amassing for himself a considerable fortune. It was said at the time that Calcraft had secured a 'revenue superior to any nobleman's estate in the kingdom'. He made large purchases of land, acquiring Rempstone in 1757 and the manor of Wareham in 1767 from Thomas Erle Drax. In the same year, he purchased all the Wareham lands previously held by George Pitt, John Pitt and John Bankes.

Fox had, during the 1750s, gained the reputation of being the most affluent and corrupt of politicians. It was a particularly corrupt period of Whig administration under the Duke of Newcastle, and Fox was considered to be the epitome of the age; furthermore, Calcraft was the old rascal's right-hand man. Horace Walpole records:

In his earlier life Mr Fox wasted his fortune in gaming: it had been replaced by some family circumstances, but was small, and he continued profuse. Becoming a most fond father, and his constitution admonishing him, he took up an attention to enrich himself precipitately. His favour with the Duke, and his office of secretary at war, gave him unbounded influence over recommendations in the army. This interest he exerted by placing Calcraft in every lucrative light, and constituting him agent for regiments. Seniority or services promoted men slowly, unless they were disposed to employ Mr Calcraft; and very hard conditions were imposed on many, even of obliging them to break through promises and overlook old friendships, in order to nominate the favourite agent. This traffic, so unlimited and so lucrative, would have mouldered to nothing, if Mr Fox had gone into opposition.

In 1763, however, Calcraft deserted Fox's cause and attached himself to William Pitt, the first Lord Chatham *[see Plate 6]*. It is not clear what occasioned this breech but in a letter to Lord Shelburne, dated 15 March, Calcraft refers to the selfishness of Fox and Bute who think only of themselves 'without considering what becomes of those who supported them'. Bellamy thinks it was caused by Fox appointing Digby and not Calcraft as his Secretary. Whatever the reasons for the break, it was a sad wrench for Fox. Pitt, however, was a distant cousin of the Pitts of Wareham, Encombe and Kingston Maurward, all of them being descended from an old Blandford family. So, for some years, Calcraft had already had a Dorset connection with the family. Friendly letters from Henry Bankes to John Bond in April 1772 indicate how the local Dorset gentry were aligned politically: it was Bankes and Bond versus Pitt and Calcraft.

From 1766 till 1768 Calcraft was MP for Calne in Wiltshire, and from 1768 till his death in 1772 he was returned for Rochester, allegedly throwing himself into the struggle for the 'liberty of the subject and parliamentary reform'. By buying up boroughs he hoped to be able to persuade voters to return the men of his choice to Parliament. It is not certain that he was successful in the case of Wareham for the members returned during the last few years of Calcraft's life (Burton, Keen, de Grey and Palk) are not known to be Calcraft men. Indeed, a surviving letter written from Rempstone in 1767 to a Mr Dunning, indicates that Calcraft's candidate was a member of the well-known and debauched family of Vansittart (three of them being members of the Hell Fire Club at about this time) and none of that name was ever elected for any local borough.

> *Rempston Hall, Sunday Night 20th Sept. 1767.*
>
> *Dear Sir,*
> *The Candidates Appearance is more and more called for, and indeed the only request now made. I must therefore beg the favour of Mr Vansittart's Attendance and will introduce him to our Friends at Wareham Tuesday; Tomorrow I cannot, being engaged to attend my Bror to Woodbury Hill Fair to meet many of his Out Burgesses; And 'tis so near Mr Drax's Out Votes, I hope to see many of them also. I have provided Mr Vansittart a Bed at the George in Corfe, where I hope he will lie Tomorrow Night (My little Hole not affording a Spare one) that we may Enter Wareham together on Tuesday Morning very early. Should Mr Vansittart chose to Dine in the Island he will find a Dinner here between three and four tho' I am out; or should he like to come by Woodbury Hill he'l hear of me there any time before five in the Evening by enquiring at Mr Filliter's Booth who is Steward of the Fair. On all Accounts the Utmost Secrecy is necessary of the Interiors of the transactions and will I doubt not be observed. One very particular Satisfaction it affords me which is that of testifying myself.*
>
> *Faithfully & Sincerely Yours*
> *Jn° Calcraft*

> *If Mr V. does not come by Woodbury, I will wait upon him on my return, here or at Corfe as he shall chance to be. Pray rem^r me kindly to Parker.*

This letter contains many fascinating references – Rempstone is described as 'my little Hole', and presumably the 'George in Corfe' is now the Greyhound (the Calcraft crest). Mr Filliter was a prominent figure in local politics and the rivalry with the Drax family is already under way. The delightful phrase about the 'Utmost Secrecy is necessary of the Interiors of the transactions' is typical of the politics of the period, and also of Calcraft.

Calcraft did succeed in getting his profligate younger brother Colonel Thomas Calcraft elected for Poole in 1762 and again in 1768. After the latter election there was a big row and the younger Calcraft was accused of bribing the Corporation to return him. This sort of row seems to have happened quite often at the time.

The Junius Mystery
Only one speech of John Calcraft's is recorded. It occurs during the well-known debate on the 'Liberty of the Press' initiated by Sergeant Glynn on

December 6th 1770. This arose out of the arrest and conviction for libel of a publisher named John Almon for selling copies of the infamous 'Letter to the King' by the exceedingly popular satirical pamphleteer Junius. Glynn, Edmund Burke and Pitt (Lord Chatham) questioned the legality of the conviction and called for an enquiry into Chief Justice Mansfield's action. They were supported by two members whose names are familiar – 'Mr Dunning' and 'Mr Calcraft'. While Calcraft's speech lacks the lightning and thunder of Burke's (or of the young Charles James Fox who, strangely, opposed the motion) it nevertheless sounds well:

> *The fabric raised by the abettors of the motion, is too firm and solid to be blown away by the breath of sophistry. Being founded on a rock it will laugh at all the quirks and quiddities of the long robe. Shall we allow the spirit and letter of our laws, which say, that no subject shall be fined to his undoing, to be thus flagrantly violated? If we do, we have forgot the ends of our institution, the redress of wrongs, and the protection of the people.*

The motion in fact failed and it was only some twenty years later that Fox, in his more radical middle years, allied with Pitt to reverse the effects of Mansfield's ruling.

Junius was the pseudonym used by the mysterious author of sixty-nine notorious letters published between 1769 and 1772. These attacked the government of the day, and even the king himself. Their author's anonymity was essential to avoid arrest and for over two hundred years Junius' identity has remained an enigma. The historical significance of Junius is that his letters were a blow struck for democracy and the freedom of speech. At the time, they were a political sensation and admired for their wit, insolence and inside information. They mark the beginnings of the importance of the press in modern politics.

The identity of Junius is still uncertain but it is generally considered that the author who hid behind this pseudonym was the young Irish scholar and adventurer Philip Francis *[see Plate 5]* who had been a clerk at the War Office from 1756. His father had written plays in which George Anne Bellamy had performed; these being failures, Philip Francis (Senior) had been forced to take up alternative work and George Anne had prevailed upon Henry Fox to appoint him a tutor to his son, Charles James. Calcraft was well acquainted with the Francis family and, indeed, in his article on Francis in the *Dictionary of National Biography*, Sir L. Stephen writes:

> *His great patron was Calcraft. Francis says that he 'concurred heartily' with Calcraft's schemes, which offered his only 'hope of advancement'. Calcraft had been in close connection both with Chatham and Chatham's brothers in law, Lord Temple and George Grenville... Calcraft's plan was to discredit the rump of Chatham's administration, to reconcile Chatham to the Grenville party... Junius was undoubtedly the close (even if unknown) ally of the clique*

to which Calcraft and Francis belonged.

William Hunt in *The History of England*, vol. X. p. 99, writes that:

> *Junius is now generally believed to have been Philip Francis, then a clerk at the war office and later a member of the East India Council and a knight, though, if he was the author, he probably received help from some one of higher social position, possibly from Temple.*

Was it Lord Temple, or does John Calcraft better fit the bill? Surely Junius was a pseudonym to conceal not one author but a partnership – Francis employed to supply the polished style and satirical brutality, while the less eloquent Calcraft was the real political driving force.

The letters of Junius were written in some profusion from 1769 onwards, rather suddenly ceasing shortly before Calcraft's death in 1772. This fact alone compels attention, since the usual contenders for the sole authorship, Lord Temple and Philip Francis, lived on in good health for several years. In his will Calcraft writes – 'I give unto my much respected friend Philip Francis of Duke Street Westminster ESq' the Sum of One thousand Pounds' and adds, that in the event of Francis not leaving sufficient provision for his Widow, that she should have an annuity of £200. According to the *Dictionary of National Biography*, Calcraft had wanted Francis to become MP for Wareham.

In a letter of Oct 5th 1771, Junius swipes (gently for Junius) at Calcraft:

> *Even the silent vote of Mr Calcraft is worth reckoning in a division. What, though he riots in the plunder of the army, and has only determined to be a patriot when he could not be a peer? Let us profit by the assistance of such men while they are with us, and place them, if it be possible, in the post of danger, to prevent desertion.*

W. P. Courtney considers this attack to be a deliberate 'blind' to disguise the identity of Junius – Francis being known to be one of Calcraft's friends. But how would Calcraft, Francis' chief patron, have tolerated such behaviour, unless the disguise was meant to conceal him as well?

In presenting his case for Temple being the author of Junius, W.S. Smith repeatedly draws attention to parallels between what Calcraft is writing in his letters to Pitt and what Junius is simultaneously sending to be published. But he fails to draw the obvious conclusion, namely that Calcraft is Junius, or at least a major part of him. Smith also notes 'A continual interchange of very intimate correspondence and communication was kept up during the years 1769, 1770 and 1771 between Mr Calcraft, Lord and Lady Chatham and Lord Temple... and it will appear that in many instances the information conveyed in this correspondence coincided with that used by Junius... The letters from Calcraft in the Chatham Correspondence are very numerous.'

Smith also cites as evidence some eccentric spellings shared by Junius and Temple; but Calcraft also shares at least two of these – 'cloath(ing)' and 'dutchess'.

In 1763 Calcraft had started writing to Pitt in an effort to draw him into an alliance with Bute against the Grenville administration. When Wilkes was arrested, Calcraft was among a small group of men holding Government or military office who supported him. The others in this group were General Conway, Colonel Barré and Lord Shelburne. George III felt personally affronted by their action. Grenville notes in his diary for Nov 30th 1763 that 'The King consented to remove Colonel Barré from his employment, and Mr Calcraft from his, but said he could dismiss nobody except General Conway was to be of the number, reckoning the offence in him who was in his Bedchamber greater than the others'. On 2 December, Grenville writes – 'Mr Calcraft was dismissed from the office of Deputy Muster Master yesterday. The King waits to determine upon Colonel Barré 'till Mr Conway has seen Mr Grenville'.

It was from this time onwards that Calcraft began to become ever more friendly with Pitt (Chatham) and, later in the decade, became instrumental in effecting the alliance between him and Lord Temple. By 1770 Calcraft appears to have been Pitt's main political intimate.

There are several pieces of evidence that Philip Francis had at least one small house in Wareham. On 24 November 1766 'Philip Francis of the War Office' rented a property apparently at the intersection of Roper's and Tinker's (or Sithe) Lanes and, on 25 November 1766 Francis rented a property in Roper's Lane for £40 per annum from William Cribb. These deeds were witnessed by James Brown and John Bishop (Calcraft's agent). On a map of Wareham of 1770, the surname Francis also appears on a property off Bonnett's Lane in Wareham.

The only evidence against Calcraft being Junius is a letter in the Osborn Collection at Yale, which is alleged to be from Junius to Calcraft, with a supposed date of March 1771. Its provenance is unknown and it could easily be in Calcraft's own handwriting.

Professor John Cannon, probably the leading expert on Junius, has found himself very much in agreement with the opinion that Francis actually wrote the letters but that Calcraft was, at least, in the know. He mentions (Private Correspondence, 7 January 1976) that there are fragments of letters from Calcraft to the publisher Almon which include a reference, in Cannon's words, to 'a letter to come out shortly'.

It seems almost beyond doubt that Junius was indeed Calcraft. Calcraft employed an able scribe, his old friend Philip Francis, to do the actual writing while he was the source of all the inside information and the political direction. Calcraft himself was not particularly good with words; he was a 'numbers man', so he needed a professional writer like Francis. The evidence is strong: not only did Francis live in Calcraft's Wareham, where Calcraft hoped Francis would one day be MP, but he was also the only beneficiary (other than relatives, executors and household servants) in Calcraft's will. The political direction of Junius – against the King and in support of Pitt, the American settlers and freedom of speech – was Calcraft's. Furthermore, the letters of Junius abruptly ceased when Calcraft unexpectedly died in 1772. Calcraft had the money, the motivation and the cleverness to be Junius. Finally, according to Namier, Calcraft had been in the habit of using disguises; for years he had employed pseudonyms for gathering intelligence.

Ian McIntyre has recently written that, by the year 1772, 'the question of what malign intelligence lurked behind the pseudonym of Junius had exercised political and Court circles for almost three years... personal abuse was no novelty in English political controversy, but the unbridled savagery with which Junius laid about him was unequalled.'

At this juncture the publisher, Woodfall, who had been found guilty of 'only printing and publishing', hinted to Garrick that Junius would write no more letters and Garrick, unwisely, had leaked this news to the Court. Almost immediately he received a sinister threat from Junius – 'Keep to your pantomimes... Meddle no more, thou busy informer! – it is in my power to make you curse the hour in which you dared to interfere with Junius.' The rattled Garrick gamely replied to Woodfall that 'I am with great regard for Junius' talents but without the least for his threatenings.' The swashbuckling malignity of Junius was surely provided by the anti-establishment 'chip on the shoulder' Francis and not by his dying patron, Calcraft.

Shortly before he died Calcraft had been the subject of several political cartoons and scurrilous attacks, probably prompted by Bellamy or Fox. One, dated October 1769, in the *Town and Country Magazine*, refers to him as the Amorous Agent or 'Crafterio'. It calls Calcraft one of the 'state vultures' who play with public money while lavishing it upon their mistresses and building their 'Asiatic fortunes'. It refers to the army agents:

Some of whom have amassed immense riches, squeezed out of the pittance of the poor soldiers and the still poorer half-pay officers. Among the foremost of these is Crafterio, a man of obscure birth who, obtaining the place of a petty clerk in a public office, found means to ingratiate himself into the favour of Volpone (Fox), who at the head of that department, and by his parasitic assiduity was at length appointed to the agency of three-fourths of the army. It is, indeed, said that Volpone shared in the spoils of this military plunderer, and thereby added many thousands to his ill-gotten pelf. Be this as it may, Crafterio, though he has lived with all the pomp and luxury of nobility, has realized an incredible fortune.

He had scarce attained this lucrative employment, before he looked about for a lady to solace him, in his hours of relaxation from business. Miss Bellamy was then in her prime, a first-rate actress upon Covent Garden stage, admired and adulated as well for her personal charms as her mental accomplishments. Sir George M-g-y Metham had, by perseverance and stratagem, at length prevailed upon her to make him, as he expressed it, the happiest of men. She had already borne this gentleman a son, who is still living; when Crafterio, deeply smitten with her charms in the part of Juliet, resolved to exhaust all the powers of rhetoric and gold, finesse and art, to obtain this lady.

Although a lampoon, the piece gives us quite a pleasant sketch of Calcraft's appearance: 'It must be acknowledged that Crafterio was a tall handsome man, with a ruddy complexion, an easy address, and a facility of speech that greatly recommended him.' The piece goes on to describe the relationship between Bellamy and Calcraft and its demise:

An altercation that took place at this time between Sir George and Miss Bellamy, concerning some infidelities she had discovered on his side, was a powerful auxiliary in Crafterio's favour.

A connection soon took place between them, which appeared to be founded on the most lasting basis; and a beautiful girl, a pledge of their mutual affection, seemed to rivet the alliance still stronger. Miss Bellamy placed so entire a confidence in Crafterio's generosity and esteem, that though she might easily have obtained a handsome settlement, she never once urged it to him; which omission she has, however, had much reason since to lament.

After an alliance of several years between Crafterio and Mrs Bellamy, in which envy and malice were silenced by her discretion and irreproachable conduct, the term of his expiring passion approached. Miss Bride, a young actress upon the Drury Lane stage, kindled a new flame, which nothing but fruition could extinguish.

When Mrs Bellamy found herself abandoned by Crafterio, she also found herself in very distressful circumstances; involved in many debts she was unaprized of, and which he absolutely refused acquitting, though created during her living with him.

In this situation it was expedient to leave the capital; and she repaired to Edinburgh, where she performed at that theatre, and where she formed a connection with Mr Diggs, a near relation to l-D-r.- Success, however, did not crown the enterprize of the theatrical adventurers in that part of the world; and she judged it expedient to return to the capital, where she now gives universal satisfaction, as a very accomplished actress, upon the Covent Garden stage. A most agreeable alliance has taken place between her and that excellent comedian Mr W-d, who finds infinite satisfaction in her amusing and sensible conversation.

We then get our only description of Elizabeth Bride, the co-founder of the Calcraft dynasty:

Miss Bride was at the time she captivated Crafterio, about eighteen; she had made some little progress upon the stage, in low comedy, at a small salary. Her person was slender, and rather under the middle stature, with fair hair, blue expressive eyes, and a fine complexion. Upon the whole, she might, without the least partiality, be styled a very agreeable girl; and considering the lowness of her extraction, she had sentiments and personal accomplishments, that were astonishing, and to our hero irresistible.

At her first entering upon the stage, her father moved in the humble sphere of a bill-sticker and a scene-shifter at the Playhouse: he was, nevertheless, reckoned an honest man; and was very unwilling that his daughter, in whom he took great delight, should ever swerve from the strictest path of virtue. We wish we could say as much in praise of Mrs Bride; for it has been currently propagated, that her daughter, who had imbibed just notions of virtue and delicacy from her father, repelled every overture made by Crafterio; till her mother prevailed upon her to accept his very advantageous offers, she at the same time participating of them by an annuity of three hundred a year, which she obtained for life.

Mrs Bride was, however, far from being reconciled to this measure by the splendour of the guilt; and it affected his peace of mind so much, that, in a fit of phrenzy, he destroyed himself.

Miss Bride, having quitted the stage, now shone forth with all the pomp and brilliance of a duchess; her jewels, her equipage, her liveries could not be surpassed, and were scarce equalled by any woman of fashion in town.

She has now been united to him for near five years, in which time she has borne him three children; and the Scandalous Chronicle has been so indulgent to her as not even to insinuate, that she has favoured any other admirer with a testimonial of her affection.

Crafterio's children will, probably, all be very handsomely provided for; and particularly the young lady, daughter to Mrs Bride, as some overtures have already been made, for marrying her with a fortune of a hundred thousand pounds; and it is even said the Marquis of Granby proposed his hand to her upon those terms; but finding her father intended to deduct one half of her fortune, which the Marquis was in arrears to him, it has occasioned a demur with respect to this alliance.

The piece ends with an all-out attack on Calcraft's political career:

The late political conduct of Crafterio has greatly astonished the world. From being the creature of the court; a stickler for every m-l measure; the sycophant of the premier, and the advocate for all Volpone's conduct; he has joined the three brothers [the Pitts], and is promoting a petition of grievances. This is variously accounted for; some say he has taken umbrage that his brother has not met with more speedy promotion in the army; others are of opinion that, conscious of the injustice of his former conduct, he is willing to obtain some popularity, and avoid in time being set up as a mark of the public's just resentment: but the most probable solution of these paradoxical measures is, that Volpone and he having quarrelled about the adjusting of their accounts, and being thrown out of his lucrative employments, he has availed himself of the present general discontent against the paymaster, to gain some applause by acting diametrically opposite to his pursuits and interest.

Whilst this conduct displays Crafterio's ingratitude, it at the same time blazons Volpone's m-l influence; as he has not only obtained the Duke of Grafton's remerciments to Crafterio, but so completely destroyed all his hopes of being a future placeman, that he has rendered him a desperate opponent.

The acquisition of such a character as Crafterio, is doubtless an honour to any party; for though his oratory never before displayed his amazing latent talents, it is now believed from this specimen that he will be able to make a figure next sessions in the House of Commons, and vociferate aye or nay as emphatically, and with as much judgement, as Sir Francis Wronghead himself.

We shall now leave him to prepare himself for presenting the B-k-re petition, and collecting his ideas for an unexpected speech in the House upon the necessity of compelling public defaulters, and all state leeches, to disgorge the national treasures they have illegally obtained.

John Calcraft clearly had a penchant for pretty actresses and, in the Calcraft papers at the County Record Office in Dorchester, there is a contemporary handwritten eighteenth century play-part – that of the character Maria Barnwell in a play entitled 'George Barnwell'. Unfortunately there is no indication as to which of Calcraft's actress-friends this part belonged. It is not likely to have been Georgiana (or George Anne) Bellamy since the part does not seem to be important enough for such an accomplished performer. Perhaps it belonged to Elizabeth Bride with whom Calcraft lived from about 1764 till his death in 1772.

The Oxford historian, Sir Lewis Namier, took an interest in the Calcraft family and published his findings in 1964. He, too, suggests that John (Crafterio) may have been Fox's son, and lists all the lucrative jobs that Fox gave to him: clerkships at the Pay Office and War Office, the Paymastership of Widows' Pensions and so on. Fox employed Calcraft in connection with the rebuilding of the Horse Guards, gave him contracts for supplying coal to Gibraltar and, from 1748, presented Calcraft with army agencies until, by 1762, he was agent to fifty-seven regiments – about half the army. 'Seniority or services promoted men slowly', we recall Horace Walpole's words, 'unless they were disposed to employ Mr Calcraft'.

As an agent he arranged the supply of regimental clothing, dealt with the Board of Ordnance and handled the regiments' finances (George Anne Bellamy claims that each agency was worth between £300 and £500 per year). Calcraft then expanded his business to become a private banker to the military. Of his 57 colonels in 1762, 17 were Members of Parliament, and Calcraft also managed their constituency affairs while they were absent, and looked after their wives, children and mistresses. Naturally, this gave him increasing political influence. He was, says Namier, 'the parliamentary whip of an army group.' He controlled army contracts and commissions and ran his own network of intelligence, often using cover-names. In 1761 he acquired £160 000 of Government stock to which he added £63 800 over the next two years. In addition, he was buying land in half a dozen counties. He also held large amounts of East India stock.

Although Rempstone was purchased in 1757, he failed to gain a political foothold in Corfe Castle. Namier comments on 'his drive and ruthless energy, his unflagging perseverance and robust self-confidence... he had the makings of a modern dictator or financial buccaneer.' In 1760 he bought Lord Bessborough's estate at Ingress in Kent where he began to live. Fox's and Calcraft's political opponent, the Duke of Newcastle, wrote – 'that devilish Fox and Calcraft get in everywhere', and the king complained of Calcraft's influence with the Duchess of Rutland. From 1760, Calcraft became increasingly close to Lord Shelburne and began to criticise Fox's selfishness. When he finally broke with Fox, the old man sadly wrote – 'I loved him; I did not expect this, and I have not yet left off thinking of it.' Horace Walpole condemned Calcraft's ingratitude to Fox – 'this mushroom, overdunged, rose against him.' When Fox finally dismissed Calcraft the latter was variously estimated to be worth between £300 000 and £600 000 (multiply this by several hundred times to estimate the current values). In 1763 Pitt and Temple 'went to visit Mr Calcraft in Parliament Street' and from thenceforth Calcraft became the link between Shelburne and Pitt, and a key figure in supporting Wilkes. In consequence, as we have noted, the King dismissed him from his office as Deputy Commissary of Musters.

Immediately, he set about entering Parliament, first trying for a seat in Rochester or Grantham, scrambling to buy houses (and hence votes) – 'if you don't buy 'em Calcraft will get 'em' wrote one panic-stricken opponent. In 1766 Calcraft was elected for Calne, with Shelburne's assistance. Under Pitt's administration, Calcraft voted for the government but made no recorded speeches, going into opposition with Pitt when returned for Rochester in 1768. He helped with the reconciliation between Pitt and Temple and threw himself into a conspiracy to return Pitt to power. In 1772 he became ill, planned to recuperate in Naples with his friend Philip Francis, but died at Ingress on 23 August.

Towards the end, John Calcraft, buying nothing but the best, employed both Sir William Chambers and Robert Adam to make additions to Ingress Abbey, and paid Capability Brown £2000 to extend the gardens at Leeds Abbey. Within thirty years of his death, sadly, both properties had been sold and demolished.

As the struggle grew between the modernists under Pitt and the reactionaries under the control of an increasingly autocratic king, Calcraft might have been one of the few with sufficient steel to make a difference. However, both Pitt and the king had begun to suffer from mental instability and England was to suffer in consequence.

Elizabeth Bride

In her malicious memoirs (see Chapter 3) George Anne Bellamy states that she herself had two children by Calcraft: Caroline Elizabeth Calcraft (born about 1752) and Henry Fox Calcraft (born about 1755). Bellamy had kept house for Calcraft from about 1752 till 1761. But it seems possible that Calcraft was never certain of his paternity of these two unfortunates.

Calcraft's will (1771) is more certain of his four children by Elizabeth Bride – Katherine (born in Parliament Street, 1764), Granby (born at Ingress Abbey, 1766), Richard (born in Sackville Street, 1770) and a new-born son William (born at Ingress Abbey, 1771). Although his son, John Calcraft (born, apparently, 16 October 1765 at Ingress) received most of his estate, he is not explicitly referred to as being by Elizabeth Bride. Nevertheless, he leaves all these children, including John, to her guardianship, so this seems highly likely.

The will does also mention 'my son Henry Calcraft' and 'my daughter Elizabeth Calcraft' and these are both bequeathed £5000 each which is less than the other children who all receive £10 000 each. Henry and Elizabeth are also left further monies, but only if the other children should all die. (A family tree of circa 1870, possibly in the handwriting of John Hales Calcraft, indicates that Henry Fox Calcraft became a General and had a daughter Emily, and that Elizabeth Caroline Calcraft became a Mrs Watson, had a son Colonel Lewis Watson who married Maria Birch, and they had a son with the initials H.G. and two daughters, one of whom became a Mrs Myddleton).

Elizabeth Bride herself received £3000 at Calcraft's death and a further annuity of £1000 for life. Furthermore, Calcraft stipulated she could live at 'my Mansion house at Ingress' during John's guardianship, with £500 a year for the upkeep of the house. She is also allowed to live at either Ingress Abbey or Leeds Abbey 'during her life (if she so long continues single)' – and it is apparently she who is recorded in one Bible flyleaf as giving birth to three further children, Charles Lefebvre at Leeds Abbey (1775), George Lefebvre (1778) and Calcraft Lefebvre (1779-1780) at Clay Hill in Kent. The family tree of circa 1870 suggests that Elizabeth Bride actually married a Lefebvre after Calcraft's death. A Charles Lefebvre is recorded as having been returned as MP for Wareham in 1784 and, in 1786, he vacated his seat when John Calcraft the Younger 'was elected in his room'. It seems likely therefore that the elder Charles Lefebvre (variously spelled) was a political colleague of John Calcraft who, after the latter's death, married his mistress and kept warm the Parliamentary seat at Wareham until such time as John Calcraft the Younger, at the age of twenty-one, was able to fill it. Of the three younger Lefebures one, Calcraft Lefebure, died in infancy. The fate of the other two is touchingly recorded in their memorial stones among those of their Calcraft relatives in Wareham Church. These indicate that both brothers, Charles and George, died at the age of thirty-five, fighting Napoleon in the Peninsular Wars alongside their half-brothers Thomas Granby Calcraft and William Calcraft. The latter also died at the age of 35 years, fighting the French. All three died at the same age and on the twenty-second day of a month:

To Major CHARLES LEFEBURE, of the Royal Engineers, who was killed at Fort Matagorda, on the 22nd day of April, 1810, aged 35 years.

To Captain GEORGE LEFEBURE, of the Royal Horse Artillery, who died at Madrid on the 22nd day of October, 1812, aged 35 years.

That the bravery, skill, and zeal with which these gallant men served their country may not be entirely unrecorded, these monuments are raised by their affectionate brother.

To WILLIAM CALCRAFT; esq., late Major in the 7th Light Dragoons, who died at Santa Martha, in Spain, on the 22nd day of August, 1809, aged 35 years.

In his will, John Calcraft does not forget some of his other relatives and friends. His younger brother Colonel Thomas Calcraft MP, and his only sister Christian Lucas, are particularly mentioned, his brother receiving his Lincolnshire estates 'in the parishes of Grantham, Gonnorby and Stubton', and his sister those in 'Ancaster, Sudbrooke and West Willoughby and Howell' – with the proviso in default of the issue of Thomas or Christian, that these estates should pass back 'to my own right heirs for ever'. Furthermore, he directs that 'my old Servant George Sharpe shall have the care of the gardens and grounds at Ingress at his present wages and that Katherine Smith one of the Nursery maids to my said Children shall be continued in or supported by and at the charge of my Family during her life'.

John's main beneficiary, of course, is his son John who receives the considerable residues of all his 'Manors, Messuages, Farms, Lands, Tenements, Hereditaments and real Estates' in Kent, Dorset, Somerset, Buckinghamshire, Essex, 'and in the several Parishes and Places of Greatwell Wilsford Londonthorp Rauceby Barrowby Hulbert Caythorp Holbeach Whapload Gosberton Quadring Donnington and Birker in the said County of Lincoln'.

Calcraft had bought Rempstone from the Rose family of Dorchester. Before then Rempstone had been in the hands of the Framptons of Buckland, the Trenchards of Wolverton and, in the sixteenth century, of the Uvedales of Sherborne and the Millers of Corfe. The manor of Wareham was bought in 1768. Subsequently, Calcraft proceeded gradually to purchase the chief part of the town. Sometime after making his will in August, 1771, he purchased 'of Mr Duke and Mr Dyke the Manor of Worth Matravers' and this is mentioned in a Codicil dated 21 March, 1772, together with other lands in Purbeck and the 'perpetual Advowson of the Rectory of Swanythe otherwise Sandwythe and Vicarage of Worth in the said Island'.

A further Codicil dated 14 April, 1772, refers to some delays in completing the purchase of some lands in Wareham, following an agreement made in 1768 with John and George Pitt Esquires. These Pitts had been MP's for Wareham. At about the same time that they were selling property to John Calcraft they also sold land to the Scott family. As we have seen, while Calcraft was buying their property he was busy conspiring with their illustrious cousin,

William Pitt, to gain control of the Government. The Pitts and Calcrafts seem to have remained on friendly terms for the rest of the century, the Pitts assisting the younger John with raising his Volunteers, and providing a godfather to a Calcraft child.

Calcraft had bought most of Wareham after its great fire in 1762. Purchases continued for decades after his death not only from the Draxes and Pitts but also from other families including the Fox-Strangways and the Bankes. By the time of his death, however, the extents of the Rempstone, Worth and Wareham estates were almost complete. In the north were the Poole Harbour islands: Green Island, in Saxon times called St Helen's, where there had once been a chapel and, where, in the twenty-first century, BBC television's 'Time Team' were to find so much evidence of late Iron Age industrial activity; Furzey Island; then Round Island and Long Island lying off the peninsula of Vitower (also called Fitzworth). Ower, to the east of Vitower, was formerly a manor and a hamlet, given by King Athelstan to the Abbey of Milton. In the Domesday Book it is recorded as Ora (in Latin – 'shore') – a reflection of its importance two thousand years ago as a major shipping-off point for the stone, pottery, iron and shale goods produced in the area. Jetties from Ower Quay and Green Island almost met each other in Roman times. The main quay for stone moved to Swanage in 1710. Further east is the failed mediaeval new town of Newton and, further still, the long peninsula of Goathorn from where the clay was shipped until the early twentieth century and from where oil is now pumped. A mile or two inland lie the farms of Wytch, Churchills Green, Claywell, Flashetts, Greenland, Foxground and Bushey (that once belonged to the Okedons of Crichel), and so to Rempstone itself and the farms along the northern edge of the chalk downs – Kingswood, Rollington and Brenscombe; the latter previously the property of the Dukes of Somerset and thence, via the Strangways, to the Earls of Ilchester. Over the hills, on their sunny southern slopes, lie Challow (once the property of John Moreton of Corfe), Harmans Cross, Woolgarston and Dunshay Manor, up to the quarries at Langton and Worth, to include Weston, West Man and East Man, and down to the rocky cliffs at Winspit and the sea.

Lying separately, six miles away, were the Wareham properties which included just about the whole of the previous Pitt and Drax estates there. After Drax sold the manor and borough of Wareham to Calcraft in 1768 it was thenceforth, marginally, a Calcraft borough with approximately 500 voters and two MPs. Rempstone also owned parts of Stoborough.

When Calcraft died on 23rd August 1772, he had only just passed his forty-sixth birthday. He had not lived long enough to gain the title of the Earl of Ormonde – an achievement he was anticipating at the time of his death. If he had lived another twenty or thirty years, it is impossible to say where his meteoric career would have taken him. From a modest middle-class origin he had risen to become a notoriously rich man and his influence in politics was beginning to grow. Even by eighteenth century standards his reputation was dubious, darkened inevitably by the corruption of Henry Fox in whose shadow he had flourished. But other men had outgrown the scandal of their earlier years and there is little reliable evidence to suggest that Calcraft was particularly vicious in his personal affairs. Like Charles James Fox, his probable half brother, he was a 'bon viveur' who loved wine and women. But, like Fox, he also had a serious side. In his portrait which hangs at Rempstone he appears slightly chubby and benign, intelligent, and quite lacking in the pomposity or extravagence of dress that might be expected of such a worldly and successful nouveau riche.

The Ayliffe Affair

It appears that Calcraft's early cognomen Honest Jack was not meant to be sarcastic. If it was meant seriously, then it suggests he had an excellent reputation among the hearty military men with whom he dealt. Colourful private life or not, he was considered to be an honest man with money. There is no record of any major political or financial scandal in which he was exposed. Bellamy, however, mentions the affair of John Ayliffe who was, apparently, a tenant and agent of Henry Fox who forged the latter's signature to his own advantage, was exposed by Calcraft and consequently was hanged on 19 November 1759; even Bellamy can only vaguely inculpate Calcraft in this affair. There is a detailed account of the case in the *London Magazine* (Nov. 1759, p.623) as follows:

> *Monday, 19.*
> *John Ayliffe, Esq; was carried in a cart from Newgate, and about 20 minutes after 11, executed at Tyburn. He was about 36 years of age, born near Blandford, in Dorsetshire, of a very good family. He has left a widow, and one son, about 11 years old. He behaved at the gallows with great composure and decency, and desired, just before he was turned off, to be indulged with a few minutes for his private devotions, which was granted him. After the execution, his body was carried off in a hearse by the undertakers, to be interred in the country. Mr Sherrif Vaillant attended the execution, and has declared that, if his health permits, he will attend every one that shall happen during the continuance of his office.*

The Ayliffe affair was quite a big scandal in its day and it closely involved Pitt and Fox as well as Calcraft. The Ayliffes had been considerable landowners in Wiltshire and Dorset since the sixteenth century. At Dorchester, there is a letter of 3 September 1757 from John Ayliffe to Dr Bower at Holt. In it, Ayliffe, who says he lives at Blandford, offers to buy Knaveswell Farm from Bower. This is the same year that Calcraft bought Rempstone Farm, but it is unclear whether Ayliffe is really an agent for Calcraft or whether he is in direct competition with him. Both men are agents of Fox, apparently aiming at the same political objective, namely the acquisition of rotten boroughs such as Corfe and Wareham. Ayliffe was, in some respects, an eighteenth-century estate agent.

It is hard to piece together the Ayliffe-Calcraft relationship. George Anne Bellamy claims that Ayliffe (although two or three years older than Calcraft) was indeed Calcraft's agent and bought for him the estates in Dorset (including Rempstone perhaps); but she claims that when Calcraft found that Ayliffe had forged Fox's signature to secure a loan, it was Calcraft who hurried south from London and caught Ayliffe in Salisbury, persuading the unfortunate man hastily to repay some £11 000 owing to Calcraft, in the vain hope of mercy. Bellamy's account is as follows:

Mr Fox being upon a visit to his brother, Lord Ilchester, Mr Calcraft called at Holland-house, according to his usual custom, to enquire, before he wrote to his patron whether there were any letters for him, or any other business to inform him of. One day as he called, he found Fanning, whom Mr Fox had now made his steward, in conversation with a man who had the appearance of a farmer. Just as Mr Calcraft entered, he heard Fanning say, 'I am sure it is not my master's hand. But here comes a gentleman who can inform you better than I can.' Saying this he delivered into Mr Calcraft's hand a lease. When Mr Calcraft had looked over it he declared that the signature was not Mr Fox's.

But my good gentleman (Calcraft) no sooner discovered by this accident what Ayliffe had been at, than ever anxious for his own interest, he immediately set out in pursuit of him. He found him at Salisbury; where, under the pretext of the forgery, he had him taken by proper persons into custody. This had the desired effect. In the first emotions of his terror, he refunded the whole of the eleven thousand pounds. Mr Calcraft had him then immediately secured by Justice Fielding's [i.e. the novelist Henry Fielding] men, who had come in pursuit of him, in consequence of an application from the farmer. They clapped a pair of handcuffs on him, and brought him to town. When he was committed, an express was sent off to Mr Fox, who still continued at Lord Ilchester's, to inform him of the transaction.

It seems that Ayliffe scuppered his chances of gaining Fox's support in the following way:

The unhappy man, solicitous for life, sent his wife to me, after his conviction, to intreat that I would use my interest in his favour with his injured master, and request of him, that he would apply to his Majesty to extend his mercy towards him. At the same time he wrote to Mr Fox, who was now in town, and whom I perceived to be greatly shocked at the affair. In his letter, he requested that gentleman's forgiveness; and acknowledging himself the most ungrateful of men, should be employed in endeavouring to deserve the mercy, and to atone for the enormities he had been guilty of.

But the very same hour, he wrote to Mr Pitt, who was then minister, to inform him, that if he would reduce him from his approaching fate, he would discover such iniquitous practices of his late employer (i.e. Fox), as should fully repay the saving him. Mr Pitt, with a liberality of sentiment which does honour to his memory, sent the wretch's letter immediately to Mr Fox. That gentleman received it as he was preparing to go to court on purpose to solicit the prisoner's pardon. But this discovery of his baseness now rendered it impossible; as such an application would have carried with it a declaration of his being in the villain's power, and that he was apprehensive of his putting his threats into execution. No intercession was of course made for him, and he suffered the due reward of his crime.

Bellamy is anxious, she claims, to reveal the true story and not the one put about to discredit Fox. The detailed contemporary account in the *London Magazine* does not, however, put any blame on Fox or Calcraft. It tells how Ayliffe had been the steward of a Mrs Horner who had died leaving property to Henry Fox, together with a request to benefit Ayliffe. This, Fox had done by leasing to him for £35 per year the estate of Russley Park, Bishopstone, Wiltshire; this deed was witnessed by James Hobson and John Fannen (presumably Fanning).

On 13 April 1759 Ayliffe (described now as Fox's 'steward'), hard up for cash, borrowed £1700 from a William Clewer on the security of a secret mortgage of Russley Park. For reasons that are hard to follow, Ayliffe felt obliged to counterfeit his lease with Fox, showing a document to Clewer which purported to bear Fox's signature and indicating that he leased Russley for £5 and not the actual £35 a year. Ayliffe thus forged the signatures of Fox and the two witnesses Hobson and Fannen. This was discovered when Clewer's agent (Mr Green) visited Fox – 'and the rent being mentioned by Mr Green, in the conversation, to be £5 per year, Mr Fox said immediately, "No, Sir, you are mistaken; it is £35" – Mr Green then produced the lease.'

It all seems to have been a most unpleasant business.

Political scandal also came very close to John Calcraft when his younger brother Colonel Thomas Calcraft, who had been first returned in 1761, was again elected MP for Poole in November 1768 and was charged, by his defeated rival, of corruptly securing his election by offering to Poole Corporation a bribe of £1500. But the scandal-mongers fail to produce concrete evidence against John himself; all we can read are general allegations of his political ingratitude towards Fox when he went over to Pitt's party, and of failing to pay all of his mistresses' considerable debts.

One should also bear in mind the prevailing conventions of the age: pocket-boroughs, patronage and jobbery. Two examples, near to home but neither apparently involving Calcraft, may actually serve to put him in rather a good light by illustrating the prevalence of such corrupt practices. Among Calcraft's papers (supplied to him by his Dorset agent J.H. Bishop) are quite a few relating to a scandal occurring some years before he appeared on the Dorset scene; these refer to allegations made against Henry Bankes that, in 1733, he unconstitutionally assumed the title of Mayor of Corfe Castle in order to have his brother John Bankes elected MP for that borough. (The two

MP's for Corfe Castle were for many years representatives of the Bond and Bankes families.). The other example is recorded in a copy of a letter sent by one John Tomlyn in 1765 to a Mr Chalk, butcher, of Queenborough, Kent, clearly threatening him with loss of custom if he votes for Calcraft.

As we have seen, Calcraft acted as a private banker, lending money to aristocratic clients such as Lord Granby. Another client was the Marquis of Thomand, Lord Inchiquin. Surviving documents suggest that repayment of these debts continued from 1758 till at least 1810. For all these reasons, caution must be exercised before jumping to the conclusion that John Calcraft was either a totally Honest Jack or a completely wicked Crafterio; for the few remaining accounts of him are written by those who may, like Fox and Bellamy, have had heavy axes to grind.

Conclusions

Calcraft, Lord of the Manors of Rempstone, Worth and Wareham, was buried at St Mary's, Wareham, where the monument to his memory in the North chancel reads:

TO JOHN CALCRAFT, esq. MP for Rochester, who departed this life at Ingress, in the County of Kent, on the 23rd day of August, 1772, and is buried in this Church. As an Affectionate tribute to his memory, this Stone is placed to record the Gratitude of his family who owe everything to his Exertions.

This memorial makes it quite clear that John Calcraft is buried at St Mary's. In a codicil of his will dated 2 April, 1772, he desires 'to be buried at Wareham and a Vault made where Jno Card and I fixed'. The John Card here referred to was probably that 'John Card, Gent., one of the capital burgesses of this borough' whose memorial inscription is placed only a few yards from Calcraft's. Card was six times Mayor of Wareham and died in his 89th year in 1822.

Calcraft left behind him an illegitimate family by Elizabeth Bride, who bore his name and arms. In November of 1770 Calcraft had secured a charter from the Heralds Office confirming his own coat of arms (which it was claimed had been used by his ancestors) and granting this, together with a crest, to his natural children. The Arms are 'Per fesse argent and ermine, three lions passant guardant in pale sable', and for the Crest 'on a wreath of the colours, a greyhound courant sable collared argent, on the body a cross-crosslet or'. The four children (John, Granby, Richard and Katherine or 'Kitty') being natural, must show a difference in these arms in that the lions must be within 'a bordure wavy azure' and the greyhound must bear 'a pallet wavy or'. This is recorded as being 'usual, according to the custom and law of arms, for natural children, acknowledged as such to bear the arms of their reputed fathers, with proper differences'.

The three lions passant had been used as a coat of arms by the Calcrafts since at least 1720. The lions are on their wax seals and on the back of some Rempstone hall-chairs of the period; chairs that were clearly used for target practice, as several have eighteenth-century damage from pistol bullets, suggestive, no doubt, of some jolly partying – 'Gad, Sir, I will shoot your lions!' Bang! But these lack the greyhound crest. This appears, however, on John's table silver of the 1760s onwards, and on his funerary hatchment of 1772 that hung in Wareham Church. The mystery is whether the Calcraft crest, depicting a greyhound, gave its name to the Greyhound pub in Corfe and Wareham. To add to the mystery, the Greyhound in Corfe has a stone on its facade engraved with the initials 'J C' and the date '1733' – some years before Calcraft bought Rempstone in 1757. Maybe it was the other way around. Frustrated in his efforts to buy up Corfe from the Bankes estate, Calcraft may have taken the crest of a greyhound in order to give the impression that he was in control of Corfe as well as Wareham and Worth. It is sad to note that in the arms-patent no mention is made of the other two children named in the will, Henry and Elizabeth, but John had done everything that could be done in a short life, to establish a dynasty with Elizabeth Bride.

If John had lived longer the world would have heard of him. The huge success of the Seven Years' War would have given him the chance to extend his commercial contacts in India and North America. He also had business interests in Ireland, Gibraltar and Jamaica. Calcraft was an interesting mixture, politically. He was close to highly establishment figures like Granby, but he also supported rebels like Wilkes. Although he was an integral part of the national war effort, he stuck his neck out by attacking the King's policy on America. He seemed particularly concerned, like Wilkes, about the freedom of the press. Fox had made Calcraft his main liaison with the military leaders and had appointed him the agent for as many regiments as he could. Furthermore, he made Calcraft Deputy Commissary-General of Musters, thus putting Calcraft partly in control of the army's logistics and strategic organisation. Later, as we have seen, Calcraft had developed a role as a banker and as chief contractor to the army. It was said that Calcraft had 'the best head for intrigue' in the whole party (ie Pitt's) and, if his undoubted political skills had helped Pitt to hold power more continuously, then Britain's history could have been different. His desertion of Fox for Pitt is a black mark against Calcraft. Maybe, however, he had grown tired of Fox's cynicism and his mercenary approach to politics. Calcraft was trying to build a new Pitt power base from which to create a satisfactory government. If he had succeeded, and lived, Calcraft would have taken a prominent position in that administration. We are told that he had thrown himself into 'the cause of liberty of the subject and parliamentary reform'. Calcraft's strong sympathies for the American settlers might have prevailed, and the war of American Independence been avoided. Today, America and Britain might still be one. Calcraft's championship of the freedom of the press might have accelerated the decline in the king's disastrous influence in politics and promoted a more open style of government. Above all, Calcraft's experience of running a war efficiently could have improved the British handling of the Napoleonic threat at the end of the century. All this, of course, is mere speculation. But Calcraft was no mean fellow.

3

JOHN CALCRAFT
AND GEORGE ANNE BELLAMY

George Anne (or Georgiana) Bellamy was the natural child of Lord Tyrawley. The date of her birth is uncertain and the years 1727, 1731 and 1733 have all been suggested. Lord Tyrawley paid for her to be educated in a convent in France. Returning to London she met Pope, Chesterfield and Sheridan and, in 1742, she first appeared on stage at Covent Garden. In 1750, at Drury Lane, she played Juliet to Garrick's Romeo in the famous 'War of the Romeos' against the simultaneous competing performances of Mrs Cibber and Spranger Barry at Covent Garden. Garrick and Cibber were the better performers but Barry and Bellamy had the looks. One naughty lady theatre-goer remarked that if she had been Juliet to Garrick he would have 'come up' to her, but to Barry she would have 'gone down'. Something similar may well have been said about the older Mrs Cibber and the sexy young Bellamy. Eventually Cibber and Barry gave up and came icognito to watch the final performance by the victors, Garrick and Bellamy.

Bellamy's private life was stormy. She had many male admirers although Calcraft lasted the longest, from circa 1752 till 1761. After their separation she 'married' an actor, West Digges (who turned out to have another wife already). Extravagence and debt were recurrent themes in her life. She is described as being 'small in stature, fair, with blue eyes and very beautiful'.

Her autobiography, *An Apology for the Life of George Anne Bellamy*, is believed to have been arranged and edited by the author Alexander Bicknell. It was published in 1785, in five volumes, and is, sometimes brilliant and sometimes trivial, an account of the actress' public and private life. Running through the whole tale is a stream of venom, a recurrent and obsessional hatred for the lover who finally rejected her – John Calcraft. Her motive is revenge – one to which she practically admits. George Anne never misses a chance of denigrating Calcraft, of mocking his limited education, his self-importance, and above all else his alleged meanness with money. Nevertheless, the power of her contempt for him, still burning strongly nearly twenty years after their separation and thirteen years after his death, strongly suggests that at one time she loved him and, even at the time of writing, he is still the main theme in her story. Like many a true actress, George Anne comes across as vivacious, proud, self-dramatising and unruly – she tries to keep the spotlight firmly on herself, but always in the shadows is the persistent, calculating Calcraft, a quiet counterpoint to her own pyrotechnical displays, the villain to her tragic heroine.

George Anne must have been a woman of intelligence and ability. As she writes, she comes alive across the years. Perhaps, in the eighteenth century, personalities bloomed more fully, less inhibited by education and cultivated self-awareness. So, with George Anne, her histrionic scenes and dramatic swoons are elaborate and unbridled.

George Anne begins her tale by describing her mother, who was also an actress:

> *As soon as Mrs Godfrey received my grandmother's permission, she placed my mother at a boarding-school in Queen's Square, where her own daughter was educated; and here she remained till she arrived at the age of fourteen, when she unfortunately attracted the notice of Lord Tyrawley. This nobleman, who was in the bloom of life, and as celebrated for his gallantry as for his wit, courage and other accomplishments, meeting accidentally with my mother, whilst she was upon a visit, was struck by her beauty, and was determined if possible to gain possession of it. And as my mother on her part was equally captivated with his assiduous addresses, and found her vanity gratified by receiving the devoirs of a person of his consequence; it is no wonder that, young and inexperienced as she was, his Lordship at length succeeded in his designs. Her heart soon yielding to the soft impulse, there needed not many intreaties to induce her to elope from school. She accordingiy seized the first favourable opportunity, and leaving the protection of her kind patroness, sought for happiness in the arms of her lover.*

They set up together in Lord Tyrawley's apartments in Somerset House. But the gallant Lord soon took off to his native Ireland and then to Portugal as ambassador, where he formed a liaison with one Donna Anna. Angry and resentful, the rejected schoolgirl hastily married an Englishman, Captain Bellamy, whom she met in Lisbon and, writes George Anne, 'I was born on St George's Day, 1733, some months too soon for Captain Bellamy to claim any degree of consanguinity with me.' The Bellamys parted and George Anne was taken care of by fosterparents at Lord Tyrawley's expense, in due course following in her mother's footsteps by taking to the stage. She had also followed her mother's example by being abducted by a nobleman at an early age (in her mother's case by Lord Byron and an un-named 'ignoble Earl' who whisked her off in a coach to 'a lonely place at the top of North Audley Street, fronting the fields' and thence to a house in Carnaby-market).

While still very young, George Anne took up with one of her admirers, Sir George Metham, and lived with him in York, giving him a son called George, after some carefully recorded assistance from a 'man-midwife'.

Her first meeting with Calcraft was in her house in Frith Street, Soho, probably in 1750. She had extravagantly hired a coach and six horses for a visit to Tunbridge Wells and on her return found herself 'without a shilling in my pocket'. While she was desperately sending out messages in order to try to borrow the money needed to discharge her debt, two gentlemen passed by.

Upon observing the equipage, the elder of the two, addressing the other, wondered whose it was. To which my boy pertly replyed, 'My mistress's.' 'Ah!' returned the same gentleman, 'I should be glad to know who is to pay for it'. They then went on. Poor Peter, who could not brook any indignity offered to his mistress, immediately came to inform me of the event; which so much affected him, that the tears stood in his eyes.

Seeing the lad so much hurt, I called him a fool and asked him why he did not tell the rude man that it belonged to him, if he had no objection. The messenger not being returned, the coach still stood at the door, and Peter had resumed his station, when the same gentlemen repassed. Upon which, Peter hearing the remark repeated, addressed the elder of them as I had hinted he should have done before. To this the gentleman said he could not have the least objection; and without any ceremony, they walked up stairs, to the no small surprise of Peter and myself.

Who should the gentlemen be, but Mr Fox and his commissaire Mr Calcraft. I own I was much startled when they entered, having never seen Mr Fox but once before... Mr Fox introduced himself by saying, that he hoped the whimsicalness, in the first place, and the irresistible temptation, in the second, would plead as an apology for his intrusion. His attendant entered with an awkward blush of inferiority, which would have passed unnoticed by me, had it not been remarked by the servant who was in the room. The messenger now returning with money from Mr Brudenell, the horses were discharged. Just at this time General Wall and Comte Hafling, passing by, and seeing the house lighted up, they honoured me with a call. Some conversation upon general topics now passed.

When Mr Fox withdrew, he requested that I would permit him the pleasure of calling upon me; as he was in town, and much alone, from Lady Caroline's being obliged, through ill-health, often to sleep in the country. I was not at this period acquainted with the virtues of that great man, or I should have embraced the offer with infinite readiness. I therefore, out of respect to his lady, cooly replied, that I should be happy in the honour of seeing him, whenever he had leisure. Thus ended a visit, produced by levity, and concluded with cold civility.

Nevertheless Fox had, on this occasion, left behind him a bank-bill for fifty pounds which, although George Anne assures her readers that she had every intention of returning, she was eventually persuaded to keep by her old friend General Wall.

According to her own account, George Anne saw little more of Calcraft until he attended George Metham's birthday party sometime later, possibly in 1753. George Anne had prepared an elaborate feast, so elaborate indeed, that its extravagence outraged the honoured host:

When the desert was placed on the table, it was extolled in the highest terms.
It was indeed more sumptous than it could be supposed Mr Metham's fortune
would afford; and the ordering of it seemed to reflect no great honour on my
prudence.

When George Anne made a joke to the effect that she hoped someone would
bale her out of debtor's prison should she ever go there, Metham 'arose,
more like an inhabitant of Moor-fields, than the master of the feast, and
declared I might rot there before he would release me'. After a dead silence,
Calcraft turned to Metham and remarked chivalrously 'I hope, Sir, you will
not be angry with those that will'.

George Anne claims that Metham's outburst was due to 'mistaken jealousy' concerning her entirely innocent relationship with the attractive Lord
Downe. Whatever the reason, it seems that George Anne had tired of
Metham and used the opportunity offered by this public insult to begin to
sever her relationship with him.

She goes on to tell the story of how Calcraft later proposed to George
Metham and Colonel Sandford that they take a trip to Oxford, and that on
the way they received a message recalling Calcraft to town, apparently on
urgent business. On his return, however, Calcraft joined George Anne as she
watched a play at Covent Garden, then accompanied her to her house for
supper and a 'tête-â-tête'. This presumably was the beginning of Calcraft's
affair with her.

The following night George Anne was accosted by a drunken Irishman
and Calcraft gallantly came to her rescue, knocking the stranger down. The
next day Calcraft 'paid the stranger an early visit in the morning, and insisted on his either asking my pardon, or exchanging a shot with him'. The
stranger, preferring the former, they all met at Metham's house where the
apologies were delivered. But no sooner had the poor Irishman departed,
when:

Instead of thanking Mr Calcraft for having rescued me from the insults of an
intoxicated brute; with all the hauteur of an eastern monarch, Mr Metham
asked him what right he had to inlist himself as my champion.... when I came
to myself, I heard that a challenge had been the consequence, and that
General Burton and Colonel Heywood were to be the seconds; but what was
the result of their meeting, I never heard...

George Anne gives a description of Calcraft at the time of their first acquaintance. Her mixed feelings for him show through quite clearly:

It will be necessary to give some description of a person who will constitute so
conspicuous a part in the dramatis personae of my work. He was at that time
called honest Jack Calcraft. Whether his conduct since intitles him to this
invaluable epithet, I shall leave to your discernment. He was tall, rather

inclined to the en bon point, of a florid complexion, blue eyes, auburn hair; and, taken altogether, he had a manly handsome face, and a well made person; but from a slouch he had by some means or other contracted, or perhaps from not having learned to dance, as Coupee says, he had a certain vulgarity in his figure, that was rather disgusting. Indeed, but few men appeared to advantage, when Mr Metham was present, as his form was eminently attracting, and his deportment truly elegant. Mr Calcraft did not attempt to impose himself on his acquaintance, either as a man of letters or a wit. He had sense enough to know that such a deception would prove too manifest to pass without discovery.

His father was the town clerk of Grantham. He had given his son a country school education, that is, he could read indifferently; but to make amends for this he was an adept in figures, and was perfectly acquainted with keeping a ledger. This qualification, joined to unremitted assiduity, enabled him, from being a clerk with a salary of only forty pounds a year, to acquire a princely fortune.

This is quite an unfair description, for John's Letter Book of 1745 shows that, even at the age of eighteen, he was writing moderately well-composed letters in a most meticulous handwriting, albeit without punctuation.

After all the talk of duels, George Anne went into hiding with an elderly couple, Mr and Mrs Gansel, leaving both Metham and Calcraft convinced she had eloped either with the other, or with the intriguing Lord Downe. In due course, Calcraft tracked her down and presented her, so she says, with a contract promising marriage at some future date.

My confusion at so unexpected a proposal deprived me of the power of speech. Upon which Mr Gansel went on to inform me that Mr Calcraft, in whose praise he launched out, had it not in his power to marry me immediately, as his dependence on Mr Fox prevented him from doing so. But that the paper he held in his hand was the copy of a contract of marriage, in which Mr Calcraft had engaged, under the forfeiture of fifty thousand pounds, to make me his wife within the term of six or seven years; in which time, from every appearance, there was no doubt of his acquiring such an independency as would enable him to avow his situation. But at present he could not suffer the ceremony to be performed, as his patron had enjoined him upon pain of his displeasure, and the loss of his support, not to enter into a serious engagement with a woman in public life. That as these were the sentiments of the man to whom he was indebted for his present affluence, and on whom his future prospects depended, he thought he was bound in gratitude to obey his injunction on this head. Therefore, though he loved me to distraction, he had too great a regard to his honour, which he had pledged to his patron, to purchase even me at the expense of it.

George Anne consented to Calcraft's offer, signed the contract in January

1752 or 1753, and eventually went to live with him in his house in Brewer Street, becoming his housekeeper (on a budget of one hundred guineas a quarter), mistress and emanuensis, helping him, so she claims, with his business affairs. Writing thirty years later she denies any feeling for him and professes only indifference:

> *Mr Calcraft and myself may be justly said, to be joined, not matched. For, with a soul of fire like mine, and thoughts which out stripped the wind; to be happily united to a being, who was only sensible of the effects of passion, but totally unacquainted with the delicate sensations of an exalted affection, was a consumation not to be hoped for.*

For Georgiana the word 'passion' is equivalent to our use of the words 'sex' or 'lust'. Her 'great attention to the business of Mr Calcraft's proffession' was nevetheless shortly to be interrupted by the birth of her daughter Caroline Elizabeth. According to Hartman, this was in February 1754, the day after she played in the final performance of Dr Philip Francis' play 'Constantine'. 'This event seemed of more consequence to Calcraft, than if he had been made master of the world' writes Bellamy. 'He imagined the Marmoset to be already the wry likeness of himself; and was in hopes that this pledge would insure to him my affection in future. Lady Caroline Fox, Lady Tyrawley, and Mr Fox, stood sponsers in person. This circumstance put the certainty of my being married out of all doubt; as it was not to be supposed that I should have been so highly honoured had it been dubious.'

George Anne maintains that, on recovering from her lying-in, Calcraft bestowed on her 'an estate of one hundred and twenty pounds a year, at Grantham, which he had just come into possession of by the death of his grandmother, upon me for life, and afterwards upon my little girl Caroline Elizabeth.' She says this deed was executed in the year 1752.

> *He at the same time gave me his will; in which he left me the interest of eleven thousand pounds in the funds, which he had accumulated whilst he was paymaster and contracter to the king's troops, during the rebellion in Scotland. A place he had been promoted to by the interest of Mr Winnington, Mr Fox's intimate friend.*

This latter comment is certainly inaccurate. Calcraft's letter books clearly indicate that the help that Calcraft received came from Fox himself and not from Winnington. It appears that Fox was a regular visitor at Brewer Street 'and generally honoured us with his company at dinner' and George Anne speaks very highly of him, in order, perhaps, to make Calcraft appear more ungrateful and villainous by comparison.

> *Mr Fox's private character was truly amiable. He was one of the tenderest husbands; too indulgent a father; the best of masters; and the warmest and*

most attached of friends. He was blest with penetration, wit, learning, and every social virtue. But notwithstanding he possessed all these valuable endowments, he could not escape the shafts of calumny, nor the stings of ingratitude, from those serpents he fostered in his bosom.

This was clearly a swipe at Calcraft. George Anne goes on to tell a famous story about Fox and his son Charles James:

I cannot here help taking notice of an instance, among many, of this worthy man's fondness for his son who justly makes so conspicuous a figure in the political annals of the present times. The wall at the bottom of the lawn before Holland House being to be taken down, and iron pallisades put up in its room, that the passengers on the road might have a better view of that fine antique building, it was necessary to make use of gunpowder to precipitate the work. Mr Fox had promised master Charles that he should be present when the explosion took place. But finding the workmen had completed the fall of the wall without giving him notice, he ordered it to be rebuilt. And when it was thoroughly cemented, had it blown up again, in order to keep his word with his son. He at the same time recommended it to those about him, never, upon any account, to be guilty of a breach of promise to children, as by doing so they instilled into them an indifference with regard to the observance of their own promises, when they arrived at years of maturity.

George Anne gives an interesting portrayal of the two great rivals Fox and Pitt ('one of the best actors I ever saw, I will not even except Garrick') and she praises Fox's professional abilities:

Mr Fox continued at this time Secretary at War, in which employment, neither any of his predecessors nor successors have been held in greater estimation. He honoured me with his company often. And as I considered Mr Calcraft's interest as my own, I made it my business to get acquainted with as many of the military as I could. In this I succeeded so well, that we had generally several officers of the first rank at our table.

George Anne is anxious to emphasise that the expensive wining and dining was all in the line of business. Besides Fox, there were other regular guests at the table such as Sir John Mordaunt, General Campbell ('the late Duke of Argyll'), General Braddock, Colonel Honeywood, Lord Kildare, General Hervey and the Marquis of Granby. She comments: 'We had company to dinner and supper every day, which consequently was productive of an expence three times as large as what Mr Calcraft allowed me'.

George Anne also claims that she became ever more closely involved in Fox and Calcraft paper-work. 'Mr Calcraft's business was so much increased, that he could not copy all the private letters. Therefore, as I wrote remarkably quick, and could be confided in, I was chosen amanuensis to the

Secretary at War and his Comis'. Later, she says she not only copied Fox's letters for him but constantly attended House of Commons debates – 'my retentive faculties being almost as extraordinary as his own'. In typically melodramatic style she portrays her own exertions on Calcraft's behalf:

> Mr Calcraft's agencies increased daily. And my company and business kept pace with that increase. I was so much interested in promoting his emoluments, that I did it at the hazard of my life. Hearing one night, at a late hour, of a promotion that was about to take place, I arose from my bed, to which I was confined by illness, dressed, and went to a masqued ball at the Haymarket, where I heard the two gentlemen I wanted to apply to were, on purpose to remind them of their promises. These were Colonel Lascelles, and General Honeywood. They recollected having given me a promise, and I succeeded in my application. But the fatigue I went through to do this occasioned my being confined to my bed for a fortnight.

Such increases in business made it necessary for Calcraft to take a larger house to accommodate 'his additional clerks and servants'. George Anne took a holiday in France while her gentleman sought new premises and, she alleges, carried on an affair with 'a lady of easy virtue, ycleped Lucy Cooper'. She writes:

> Upon my return to England, I was set down at our hotel in Parliament street; for so it really was in comparison to the house in Brewer street. I was very happy to find things comme ils faut; in consequence of which my maid was to return to her former situation, and be termed my woman, Mrs Clifford. Mr Calcraft had now fourteen or fifteen clerks, which made the whole of our servants to amount to upwards of thirty. He had engaged a most reputable maitre d'hotel named Guince, who had lived with Mr Pelham till his death. Having made so considerable an addition to our stile of living, Mr Calcraft agreed to allow two thousand five hundred pounds a year for the table; which, with the produce of the farm, presents, &c. was fully sufficient to maintain, in this point, the magnificence we were entered into. For though the quantity of the provisions was thus increased, the quality was by no means the same.

Calcraft soon purchased what was probably his first country seat, Hollwood Hill, four miles from Bromley, Kent and, despite her complaints, George Anne sounds happy there. 'General Campbell sent me a gardener, and supplied me with many shrubs and exoticks from Combebank... in the garden I built a hot-house, a succession-house, a green-house, and an ice-house'. The following year, 'Mr Calcraft took an adjacent farm, which was sufficient to maintain the house' and presented George Anne with six Alderney cows and a bull. (Hollwood was later to become the younger Pitt's favourite home).

However, it is clear that arguments about money were now spoiling any domestic happiness that either Calcraft or George Anne had enjoyed. Without doubt George Anne was recklessly extravagent. She even admits as much herself, although trying to make her prodigality a virtue by calling it generosity. Long before she met Calcraft she was having problems with her debts, as is made plain when she describes a reunion with her father years before:

> I had the happiness to effect a reconciliation with Lord Tyrawley. And it was fortunate for me that I did so, as his bounty was very needful to me at this time. For notwithstanding my salary, which was a handsome one; the emoluments of my benefit, which were great; and the generosity of Mr Metham, which was unlimited; I frequently found myself without a guinea. A circumstance far from pleasing to a disposition like mine; to a heart susceptible of no gratification equal to that of relieving the necessities of others. Of all the pleasures this world can bestow, that of giving is certainly the most exquisite and satisfactory. I claim, however, no merit for the little assistance I have been enabled to bestow on others. It was an impulse of nature that I could not resist. It was an impulse of nature that I wished not to resist.

Later, it seems that her lavishness was possibly part of the reason that she had separated from Sir George Metham. This was also to be the case with Calcraft, a man who lacked the inherited wealth of some of her other admirers and whose own fortune was being earned through hard-work, honest or not. Despite this, he seems to have endured her demands for a number of years. She describes one such scene, in a way which is supposed to show Calcraft's meanness but reflects rather more her own extravagance:

> Mr Calcraft, having detained me, he concluded with saying, that if I would once convince him that I knew the value of money, he would give me a thousand pounds for every hundred I then required. Tired with this pecuniary conversation, which always was the most unpleasing to me of any, and now holding him in sovereign contempt, I replied, that I left it to plodders like him, who were possessed of no other knowledge, to set a value upon such trash. Upon this, he pulled out his purse, and laying down three hundred and odd pounds, which, with the thousand and fifty before received, just made up the amount of the bills owing, he walked down to his desk; there to bless the mammon, by which he hoped, at some future period, to purchase himself a title, or at least to become, through it, a Leader of the House of Commons.

Some of her debts have a delicious quality. She was applied to by a Mr Woodfield, 'to pay a considerable sum for some red champaign, which, by Mr Calcraft's desire, I had ordered from him to send to Lord Granby in Germany. And I had another demand from Finmore, of the Star and Garter tavern, for claret, which I had likewise indiscreetly wrote an order for Calcraft, when I resided in Parliament street.'

As her memoirs continue, George Anne's descriptions of Calcraft become increasingly unkind. She pours contempt upon his lowly origins even though these were, arguably, no lower than her own:

> *His love of money increased every day. And from accumulating, as he did, a fortune so rapidly, he assumed a consequential air, which rendered him ridiculous even to his own servants. For, endeavouring to appear the great man, his ignorance led him into vulgarity. Indeed, he possessed two qualifications necessary to the acquirement and enjoyment of a fortune, and those in an eminent degree. These were the art of keeping a ledger (which I have already celebrated), and an excellent judgment in wine. In the latter, he was a complete connoisseur. And as the interest of his patron, and his connection with me, procured him the honour of the best company at his table, he had an opportunity of displaying this valuable branch of knowledge. A propriety of demeanour upon an elevation from a low station of life to a high one, is what cannot be acquired by a little mind.*

To make matters worse for Calcraft, it was at this time, according to George Anne's testimony, that she discovered, while in conversation with Henry Fox, that he was not the reason why Calcraft had declined to marry her. Fox informed her that he had always imagined that they were in fact married. However, this discovery by Fox – if it really was such – that his principal agent was not married to the lady of his house, did not seem to spoil their working partnership, as another sarcastic little story by George Anne inadvertently reveals:

> *Mr Fox made a point of procuring for his Commis every thing within the reach of his interest, or of his power with his Majesty, which was then very great. Besides ninety regiments to which Mr Calcraft was agent, and likewise six independent companies, together with the coals and cloathing to the colonies, he had been named pay-master to the board of works, and deputy commissary of the musters. His Majesty having frequent occasion to sign his name to papers, wherein my gentleman was mentioned, he was led to enquire who his beloved John Calcraft was? This notice of his Sovereign, added to his princely income, made him conceive himself really a man of great consequence; and determined him to satisfy the royal curiosity, and commence courtier, the next birth-day.*
>
> *As my taste in dress induced the gentlemen to consult me as well as the ladies, Mr Calcraft did me the honour to ask my advice upon this important occasion. As he was a man of business, I recommended him to have a brown rateen, which at that time was much wore, with a white sattin lining, and gold buttons. This dress I thought would at once be suitable to his profession as a financier, and hide his ungenteel deportment and uncouth figure, which, by the bye, was not unlike that of a drayman. But not approving of my fancy, he determined to follow his own; which, when the*

long-expected day arrived, afforded great entertainment to my company as well as myself.

The day at length arrived, and upon it all those who had consulted me with regard to their dress, and those who upon other occasions visited me, came, in their way to court, to make their obeisance, and to shew their cloaths. Lady Rochford, being in mourning at this time for her father, which prevented her from going, her Ladyship did me the honour to spend the day with me, in order to partake, in some degree, of the pleasure of it. The bevy of belles and beaux who called upon me was no inconsiderable one. And among them, to my unspeakable surprize, who should make his appearance but my own would-be beau, bedizen'd out in a milk-white coat, apparaments of blue velvet, waistcoat and breeches of the same, and adorned with embroidered silver frogs.

The grotesque figure he cut induced the Countess of Rochford, in the first emotions of her surprise, to cry out, 'Ah, quelle figure'. The exclamation struck the gentleman so forcibly, that he hastily retired, and left us to laugh, and pass our comments upon his absurdity. I have often wondered how persons, without being able to form the least pretensions to taste in dress, will venture, by adopting their own ideas, to render themselves conspicuously ridiculous. They do not consider, that fashion is the child of adoption, and more arbitrary, whilst she reigns, than even the Grand Sultan. Whether Mr Calcraft went to court in his fine cloaths, I know not, nor ever gave myself the pains to enquire. But, at dinner, he appeared in his blue frock and, till he had drenched himself with champaign, which he drank as small beer, he seemed to be mortified at having, in the forenoon, contributed to the mirth of the company.

Over the next few years – George Anne claims to have lived with Calcraft for nine and a half – the bitter rows about money continued. She felt she had a right to demand that Calcraft paid all of their debts and threatened to leave him if he did not do so. Calcraft, she alleges, refused to do this, claiming 'that he had lost a great deal of money; that he had purchased two estates; and that he had expended considerable sums for Lord Granby. Through these united drains, he said, he was really distressed.'

The mention of Lord Granby is interesting for it is suspected that Granby became, at some time, one of George Anne's other lovers. Granby, therefore, was not only Calcraft's debtor but also, possibly, his rival. George Anne certainly admits giving Granby a fine Arab horse which necessitated Calcraft finding another one for her. She tells us that the unwise Marquis made her his cash-keeper – 'which Mr Fox humourously compared to the lame leading the blind'.

Finally, in 1760, George Anne took herself off to Ireland. Calcraft's letters to her were hardly ever answered. On 17 January 1761 he wrote to her, desperately:

My Dearest Georgianne,
Packet after packet arrives from Ireland without a letter from you: why won't
you write, and fully? I never am so well pleased as when I hear fully from
you; nor ever so uneasy as when I do not. The children are both well, and
charming ones. I have been with my brother to Poole this week, and have
secured his election, I hope, without opposition. Pray do write. You don't
know the distress your neglect occasions to
        Yours ever and ever.
        JC

When the relationship with Calcraft was finally breaking up, George Anne persuaded him to give her £4500 in exchange for some jewellery-receipts:

He then commented upon my extravagance. Told me that my late hours
affected my health, and consequently made me low spirited. Said that I
enjoyed every pleasure the world could afford. And concluded with assuring
me, that with regard to my debts, he would be satisfied I had some regard for
him, before he parted with so capital a sum.

She claims that Calcraft had the jewellery broken up and failed to pay her the surplus of what it was worth. Calcraft however, maintained that he had received a list of her debts amounting to £10 300.

At about this time, George Anne claims that a friend informed her 'that the man whom I looked upon as my husband, neither was, nor, in all probability, would ever be so; as he had been married some years before he knew me, to a young woman at Grantham, who then resided with an aunt of his, named Moore.' George Anne reacted melodramatically, and was 'struck with instant madness by such unexpected information' and 'fell down senseless,' remaining in a collapsed condition for some weeks. Her dramatic account of this subsequent illness is heavy with self-pity. She was sent to the hot-wells at Bristol 'to celebrate my Christmas':

At that season of the year, the Wells are only frequented by emaciated wretch-
es, who are sent there to receive their quietus. I had totally lost the use of my
limbs, could not lift my hand to my head, and was carried like a child, in the
servant's arms. During the journey, I was ordered not to make my stages more
than twenty miles a day. And notwithstanding it was intensely cold weath-
er, I was obliged to travel with the windows of the chaise down. As I was well
known on that road, the masters and mistresses of the inns seemed by their
looks to take a last leave of me, and to regret the loss of so good customer as
I had been to them.

She ran up considerable doctors' and nurses' bills but, as she admits, 'I should not have been in the least concerned, had I spent Calcraft's whole fortune upon the occasion.'

There seems to have been a temporary reunion with Calcraft. She had tried to go to live with her mother who was now Calcraft's tenant in his old house in Brewer Street, but Calcraft begged her to return to live with him in Parliament Street, and for a while, she did so.

She tells the story of how General Braddock, who had died in America, had left Calcraft his official government silver. The Treasury attempted to get this back from Calcraft but failed and, says George Anne, 'we were left in possession of the royal donation, and the lions, unicorns and hares, made their appearance at table.'

Despite all the spiteful things she has to say about him, Calcraft somehow emerges as long-suffering and sometimes generous, even when they were scarcely on speaking terms:

I was now never at home, except when I had parties, which prevented Mr Calcraft and me from meeting, but now and then at dinner. On New Year's Day I had always a concert and ball. This year, (probably 1762) Mr Calcraft, in consideration of my not having any theatrical engagement, sent me a hundred guineas by the house steward. I own I was greatly surprised at this unexpected fit of generosity. And, though it was very inadequate to the expenses of the day, as I had the first performers at the concert, and a great number of ladies as visitors, together with the foreign ministers, I accepted of it.

Calcraft made his last attempt at a reunion, offering to pay all her debts if she went to live in Dorset. But shortly after this, George Anne ran away to Edinburgh with an actor called West Digges, leaving her two children to be cared for by Calcraft and her aged father, Lord Tyrawley. George Anne and the elegant Digges performed a number of plays together in Edinburgh, Digges calling himself 'Mr Bellamy'. One of their most enthusiastic supporters was the Duchess of Hamilton, unaware, no doubt, of George Anne's previous friendly association with her rival, the Dowager Duchess of Douglas, over the famously contested ownership of the great Douglas estates.

Nevertheless, George Anne still continued to complain bitterly about Calcraft's reluctance to give her more money. She quotes a letter he wrote to her at this time in order to illustrate his meanness But, if it is accurate, it reveals instead that Calcraft still had deep feelings for her:

Christ Jesus God, why do you keep me in this torment. If you will not write, tell me so, and make me completely miserable. I have had a letter from my Lord, and have seen that to your maid; by which I find you are unalterable in your resolution. I hate Hollwood, and every place which reminds me how happy I have been in your company. Caroline has almost broke my heart with shewing me the sweet letters which accompanied your fairing. Everybody is made happy but me; but vexation and the gout will soon relieve you from the man you hate. I have ordered the plate, your new sedan, and books to be sent

you. I have sent you the parchment I have found, which I suppose is the counter part of your annuity; but depend upon it, I shall not think it sufficient for your support. For God's sake write to me, and be assured whilst I have breath, I am affectionately yours,
Signed,
John Calcraft.

George Anne heavily insinuates that Calcraft had taken up with another woman who used to be a friend of hers. She never names this woman but presumably she was Elizabeth Bride – 'my former friend, the person who had succeeded me in Mr Calcraft's affection, propogated innumerable falsehoods against me. It was industriously reported, that I entertained a partiality for a man I scarcely knew; and this was the cause of my leaving Mr Calcraft. So improbable a story I think could hardly gain belief.'

George Anne felt so injured by Calcraft that, in October 1767, five years after the separation, she tried to publish a vicious attack on him in the form of a public letter. In consequence, just before George Anne was about to go on stage at a performance of the 'English Merchant', Calcraft arrived at the theatre with a large party .... 'vowing vengeance at the same time against the piece and the theatre.' It seems that Calcraft had some financial stake in the production. At any rate, he had sufficient influence to have the letter suppressed. It was, however, in due course published after his death as an appendix to the *Apology of her Life* which appeared in 1785. The letter is a pathetic tract, full of spite and unimaginably libellous by today's standards:
'I am sorry to remind you, that when Lord George Sutton first introduced you to me, you was called Honest Jack Calcraft; an epithet, in my mind infinitely superior to Squire John the parliament man.' She accuses him of 'passion, avarice and luxury' and says she undertook to be his housekeeper at four hundred guineas a year, finding this sum quite inadequate for the entertaining of the 'constant company we kept, numbers of whom were personages of the highest rank.' She claims that she spent a great deal of her own money in furnishing the garden at Hollwood and in helping his brother (Thomas) and sister (Christian). George Anne reminds him of his faux pas when, in distinguished company at Clivedon, he enquired, crassly, what was a 'gladiator'. She calls him ungrateful and deceitful in his dealings with the Marquis of Granby with whom, she says, Calcraft tried to arrange a marriage with his daughter – 'a match unequal in every shape, as he was not only old enough to be her grandfather, but had your views been accomplished, he must, upon reflection, have been unhappy, from the idea of having polluted his blood with yours.' And so it goes on: accusations and insults that would be typical in any divorce court today.
She tells the tale of how Calcraft threatened to kill himself for her – 'You, however, soon retracted your tragic resolution, and put your sword into its

scabbard. What a pity! Had you gone off thus heroically, you might have escaped the imputation of being a monster of ingratitude, and consequently a pest to society.'

In a possible allusion to Rempstone – the only one she makes – George Anne records that 'you offered me your house in Dorsetshire'. An offer which, she says, she refused. Towards the end of her tirade she remarks: 'You well know that the first six years of our connection, I was totally insensible to happiness, and in a perpetual bustle to promote your interest. The last four were perfectly miserable.'

Although some of one's sympathies lie with her, even in this bitterest part of her self-defence, George Anne lets slip a story which must put her into a bad light. She frankly admits that 'though it may afford a proof of my indiscretion, I hope will not blacken my heart. Upon my having lost a considerable sum at play, I requested you to lend me four hundred pounds till my benefit... you told me that you would grant it, on condition that I would stay at home the same evening. Nay you went farther, for you desired a female intimate to inform me, that you would pay all my debts in the morning, if I would cease to be cruel.'

In other words, she extracts four hundred pounds from Calcraft to pay one of her gambling debts – an enormous sum by today's reckoning – and on the condition that she stay at home for that night. Immediately, she breaks her promise and goes out to a party. Worse still, she goes on to admit that she stayed away till the following morning and in the company of a nobleman. By any standards, such behaviour is, at least, provocative, and indicates more than mere ' indiscretion'.

One of the main items of interest in this scurrilous letter is the alleged contract of 'marriage' which united Calcraft and Bellamy:

Copy of the Contract, brought ready signed by Mr Calcraft.

Know all men by these presents, that I John Calcraft, of Brewerstreet, Golden-square, in the county of Middlesex, Esquire, am held and firmly bound unto Georgiane Bellamy, of Frith-street, Soho, Spinster, in the sum of fifty thousand pounds, of lawful money of Great Britain, to be paid to the said Georgiane Bellamy, her certain attorney, executor, administrator, or assigns, firmly by these presents, sealed with my seal, dated this 22nd day of January, 1752.

The condition of this obligation is such that whereas the above bounden John Calcraft, and the above-named Georgiane Bellamy, have mutually agreed to marry with each other, and therefore the above bound John Calcraft shall and do marry the said Georgiane Bellamy according to the rites and ceremonies of the Church of England, and shall not intermarry with any other persons whatsoever, save the said Georgiane Bellamy, or during the natural life of the said Georgiane Bellamy, then this obligation to be void, or else remain in full force.'

Signed John Calcraft

Despite all the mud she throws at him George Anne nevertheless gives some clues as to the real man. We are told several times that Calcraft suffered from 'gout in the head' – probably recurrent headache, quite possibly of the migraine type – an interesting observation since we know that Calcraft's grandson (John Hales Calcraft) and great grandson (William Montagu Calcraft) both suffered bad headaches, as also have other descendants. We even know, if we can believe George Anne, that John Calcraft's mother had a similar complaint – 'As he was subject to the gout in his head, he was always talking of dying. And, indeed, he had some reason to be apprehensive, as his mother died young of the same disorder.' George Anne tells us that he went to Bath to treat his gout and when he was ill 'He was unhappy if I did not put the bags with seeds to his eyes; which, he said, no person could do but myself.' Fox (who admitted kinship with Calcraft) also suffered from headaches as is recorded in a letter he wrote to Colonel Napier (Cumberland's adjutant) from Holland House on 1 September 1747 – 'I send you an Extract of Letters and orders sent today that there may be no mistake, a thing not unlikely in a letter from one whose head aches so extremely as does that of your Humble & Obedient Servant, Henry Fox.' At least parts of the following description of Calcraft probably hold some truth:

> As I have already observed, he had naturally a sound understanding. His mental faculties were strong. And, had they been properly cultivated, had he received the advantages of a good education, he would have been a dangerous member of society. For he was ambitious to a degree, and cared not at what expence, or risque, he carried his ambitious views into execution. In the same manner he gratified all his passions. But, upon every other occasion, he was cold even to cowardice. He was, besides, rapacious, insolent, and mean to the lowest pitch of parsimony.

But surely she had loved him no less than he had loved her.

George Anne gives us a few glimpses of other members of the new Calcraft dynasty. John's younger brother Thomas (1738–1783) she describes as 'genteel' and 'generous', but scarred by smallpox. John paid for his education at an academy in Soho Square, secured his quick promotion in the Army and his election for Poole in 1761. He sat in Parliament for the next thirteen years voting as John directed. For a time he was posted with Lord Granby in Germany and then in Ireland. He continued to rise even after John's death, eventually becoming a Lieutenant-General in 1782. George Anne is less complimentary about John's sister Christian (born 1730) whom, she says, was compromised by a Mr Medlicote. John rescued her, brought her to London, but declined to fight a duel with her seducer. He hoped she would marry Lord Granby but, eventually, she became Mrs Lucas-Calcraft.

Poor George Anne did not enjoy entirely harmonious relations with her own children. By Metham she had had a son, George, who went to America to fight the rebels. When he came home he fell out with her son by Calcraft, Henry Fox Calcraft (Harry, born in 1756) apparently over a debt. They nearly fought a duel – 'what a dreadful situation for a mother who doated [sic] upon her sons.' Her father, old Lord Tyrawley, had helped pay for Harry's education.

Eventually, Harry, too, became a General and, in turn, had to try to deal with George Anne's debts in her later life. As for her daughter, Caroline Elizabeth Calcraft, she could not 'look upon her in the light of a child'. She was, says George Anne, 'the true daughter of a Calcraft'. As to Harry's and Caroline's uncertain paternity she assured Calcraft - 'to my no small mortification, and their disgrace, they are, bone fide, your own'.

This is where George Anne's tale ends. Her exaggerations and posturings somewhat reduce the pathos of the autobiographical tragedy in which she heads the cast. Horace Walpole's opinion of her memoires was that they were 'spun out by a number of names, many falsehoods and a tolerable quantity of anachronisms'. Impossible though she must have been to live with, the depth of her anger towards Calcraft probably reveals her love for him. Calcraft, however, was looking for more than a mistress or a hostess. He needed a wife, a companion and a reliable mother for his children. He found such a person in Elizabeth Bride.

No better couplet sums up Bellamy's attitude to Calcraft than:

> *Heaven has no rage, like love to hatred turned,*
> *Nor Hell a fury, like a woman scorned.*

Ironically, this is from William Congreve's play *The Mourning Bride* which was another production in which Bellamy had starred with Garrick.

4

RT HON. JOHN CALCRAFT
(THE YOUNGER) 1765-1831
AND SOME NOTES ON THE RYDER FAMILY

John was the eldest son of John Calcraft (Crafterio the Army Agent) and Elizabeth Bride, and was born at Ingress Hall in Kent, on Wednesday 16 October 1765.

As a child he would have found himself in a moderately large family. He had one older full sister Katherine (born in Parliament Street, London, Saturday 1 September 1764) and who, as 'Kitty Calcraft', was destined to become the attractive subject of one of George Romney's most famous portraits (now in an American collection), and four full brothers: Granby (see later), Anthony (born 1767, died 1768) Richard (born 14 February 1770, eventually Secretary to the Audit Office) and William (born 5 July 1771), who fought in the Peninsular War as an officer in the Prince of Wales' Own Regiment and was, according to a handwritten note left by his nephew, John Hales Calcraft, murdered at an inn in Portugal on 22 August 1809. Why was he murdered? Who did it? Sadly, no one knows.

When John was born, his father was already a very rich and increasingly influential person. No doubt his actress mother would often entertain politicians and Army officers, many of them hangers-on and dependents of her man. Whether William Pitt himself ever visited Ingress Hall is not known, but Calcraft Senior was, by this time, a close political intimate of his. Why Ingress had been purchased is not clear; possibly its proximity to Gravesend, one of the main military embarkation ports, was a determining factor. Also it would only be three or four hours' drive by carriage from John's house, and office, in Westminster.

When he was only six, John the Younger inherited the bulk of the family's fortune when his father died in 1772. At this time, the family's affairs were in the hands of his mother, Elizabeth Bride, his uncle and aunt, Anthony and Christian Lucas (or Lucas-Calcraft as they became known), his uncle Colonel Thomas Calcraft MP and the various other executors and beneficiaries of his will such as Edward Barwell of Abingdon Buildings, Westminster, Thomas Williams of Dartford, John or James Meyrick (apparently another Army agent), Mr Justice Willis, Charles Graves of Rochester (Brewer), and Philip Francis of Duke Street, Westminster and Wareham.

It appears that about two years after John's death, Elizabeth Bride married Charles Lefebure and bore him three children – Charles (born at Leeds Abbey, Kent on 15 July 1775), George (born at Clay Hill, Kent in 1778), and Calcraft Lefebure (also born at Clay Hill in 1779, died 1780). Naming their last child after Elizabeth's old lover is, surely, further testimony of the enduring affection between the Lefebures and Calcrafts. Whether or not young John lived with his mother and stepfather at Clay Hill, or whether he stayed on at Ingress being looked after by servants such as Katherine Smith the nursery-maid, is not known. The Calcrafts and Lefebures stayed on good terms as Charles Lefebure became MP for Wareham and then handed over this seat to his stepson, John Calcraft the Younger, as soon as he was twenty-one.

John was educated at Harrow and Eton. During his minority, his electoral interests in Wareham were looked after by his uncle Anthony Lucas, Commissioner for Excise. Like his father, he was, initially, reluctant to speak in Parliament. He supported the Whigs from 1800 until 1828, but then joined Wellington's Tory administration, as we shall see.

The Dorset estates and their political affairs no doubt continued to be looked after by old Crafterio's friends and agents on the spot, such as Bishop, Filliter, Dunning and Card, all of whose families were doing well for themselves. Bishop continued living at Rempstone for several years, some Dunnings moved into Huish Manor around this time and the Filliters, too, were thriving. (In 1831 George Filliter, a Wareham solicitor, was to buy Trigon).

It must be realised that the Dorset properties of the early nineteenth century only represent a small fraction of the original fortune, and Rempstone itself has never been as grand a building as the elder John Calcraft's ambition and wealth would have allowed. To this day, the building lacks any special architectural interest. Years later Daisy Bevan (née Waldegrave) believed that:

> My great-grandfather had muddled away a great part of the huge fortune made by his father as an army agent in the reign of George II, and their family places, Leeds Abbey and Ingress Hall were sold and only Rempstone was kept.

But this was the story she got from the puritanical Lady Caroline Calcraft a hundred and thirty years ago. It is most unlikely that Lady Caroline, even if she knew, would have told young Daisy about Elizabeth Bride and the claims made by Bridget, Crafterio's long-concealed wife. We know that Bridget surfaced at his death and successfully sued for at least a third of his estate. In consequence, in December 1787, estates were sold in Lincolnshire (Holbeach, Whapload, Gosberton etc.), Buckinghamshire (Shipton Lee and Quainton), Kent (Footscray, Sidcup and Sutton at Hone), Essex (Chadwell) and Somerset (Henstridge). The Holbeach and Whapload estates, comprising eight farms and some 1800 acres, were sold for £20 000. Also sold in Lincolnshire was the manor house of Monksdale; and three other farms amounting to 850 acres were sold for £14 600. John Calcraft (then aged 22) also had to sell land at Rauceby, Quadring, Donnington, Bicker, Caythorpe, Wilsford, Londonthorp, Barrowby, Fulbeck, Ewerby and Greetwell, all in

Lincolnshire. He also sold the Manor House of Lee Grange in Buckinghamshire, together with 1300 acres and land at Chadwell, Tilbury, Orfett and Little Thurrock in Essex. In Somerset he sold Ogden Siles farm near Milborn Port with 149 acres. In total, John had been forced to sell some 6000 acres and many houses, for not less than £70 000.

Nevertheless, the young squire was returned as Member of Parliament for the family borough of Wareham from 1786 until 1790. Ten years later in 1800, he was again elected for Wareham and held the seat until his death in 1831, except for the long interlude of twelve years from 1806 till 1818 when he was Member of Parliament for the city of Rochester. Throughout his career he had been a staunch Whig, but in 1828 he joined the Tories and was made a Privy Councillor and Paymaster General by the Duke of Wellington, who may have had some regard for the Calcraft family; Sir Granby Thomas Calcraft, William Calcraft and the two young Lefebures all having been officers under his command during the Peninsular War.

In his youth, John the Younger may have followed his father's flair for high-living for it is claimed that he was a companion of Prinny, the foppish Prince of Wales, and indeed spoke in his support in the House of Commons on 31 May 1815. But in his later portrait he appears as a rather sad-faced and sensitive man with a florid complexion. In 1790 he married the dark and pretty Elizabeth, daughter of Sir Thomas Pym Hales of Bekesbourne in Kent. We know that part of his childhood must have been spent in his Kent estates but it seems likely that Rempstone quite quickly became his principal country seat, for his eldest child, Elizabeth Mary, was born there in 1791. The sponsors for this baptism are listed in a family Bible as being Granby Calcraft (the child's uncle), Lady Hales (presumably the maternal grandmother) and Mrs Lefebure (the intriguing Elizabeth Bride). Three more daughters, Fanny, Caroline and Arabella appeared during the years 1793 to 1795, all being born at Middle Town (perhaps the place of that name in Warwickshire). A John Calcraft is listed as one of the latter's sponsors and it seems this must have been, strangely, the child's own father. The last four children are all sons: John Hales (who was born at Rempstone Hall, 13 September 1796), Thomas Hales (born 1798, died 1810), Granby Hales (born and died 1799), and Granby Hales (the 2nd), born in George Street, Hanover Square in 1802.

John Calcraft the Younger, to a great extent, made respectable his father's achievements. He was probably more principled and more emotional than was Honest Jack. A report from the *Dorset County Chronicle* of 23 October 1823, describes how Calcraft received a Purbeck deputation at Rempstone which presented him with an elaborate piece of silver plate 'expressive of their gratitude to him for his exertions in accomplishing the repeal of the duties on salt'. Calcraft thanks the deputation by saying he hopes that the abolition of the salt duty will prove 'an addition to the comforts of the poor'. The presentation piece is described as depicting seashells, rocks and tritons, with an inscription. The newspaper goes on: 'We are not aware that any similar mark of public approbation has been shown before to any member of

Parliament in the West of England, and we feel confident that no individual, whether in or out of Parliament, better deserves a distinguishing token of respect than Mr CALCRAFT. We have great pleasure in stating that the subscription for the plate was supported by many of those 'who toil in the lower employments of life', but who have a sufficient interest and stake in the country to feel and rejoice in the alleviation of burdens which Mr CALCRAFT has been so strenuous in his efforts to remove.'

Such eulogies would be unthinkable today. Sadly, the magnificent piece of plate has disappeared. It seems quite remarkable that tenants in Purbeck could have afforded to pay for it. Gifts of this magnitude to an MP would be quite unacceptable today, but this event does suggest that Calcraft was genuinely loved by the local people.

Besides salt, he was also a liberator of that other necessity, alcohol. The *Dictionary of National Biography* says – 'Calcraft was one of the earliest reformers of the liquor traffic, his proposition being to 'throw open the retail trade in malt liquor'.

As a young man, John Calcraft the Younger was the person mainly responsible for forming the Corps of Yeoman Volunteers to protect the Dorset coast against French invasion. Letters show that he approached the local gentry for cooperation in this plan, receiving only lukewarm interest from John Bond and Henry Bankes. The Pitt family, however, responded with vigour and Lord Rivers and General William Pitt assisted in arranging for the supply of arms and money from the Crown. In 1794, Calcraft was advertising meetings:

> *Mr Calcraft requests the attendance of such Persons as are willing to promote a Plan for the Defence of the ISLAND of PURBECK, at the Ship Inn in Corfe Castle, on Tuesday the 6th Day of May, 1794, at 11 o'Clock in the Forenoon, Mr Calcraft having received the Lord Lieutenant's Authority for carrying some Plan for that Purpose into immediate Effect. The meeting at Swanage will be at 3 o'Clock in the afternoon, of the 6th, for such Persons as may find it more convenient to attend there.*

By 1797 Calcraft could report that his Company for the defence of Swanage numbered 150 men.

It seems that much of his early political career was enacted locally, not only in his military ventures but also in good works for the poor. On 22 May, 1795, he chaired a 'Meeting of the Committee appointed to apply the Subscription to lower the Price of Bread, for the Relief of the Necessitous Poor of this County, held at the Grand Jury Room in the County Hall, in Dorchester'. This was in the same month as the famous Speenhamland Act which decided that Berkshire labourers should have their wages subsidised by the parish, according to the cost of bread. Calcraft's decision for Dorset was slightly different in that the parish overseer was to buy the bread and retail to the poor at a subsidised low price.

Owing to war prices and low wages, the rural poor, especially in the South of England, were at this time threatened with starvation, and conditions in Dorset continued to be deplorable for many years. In 1846 the County was to be the subject of extensive scrutiny by *The Times*, whose correspondent reported that in the neighbourhood of Corfe Castle farm-labourers were being paid only 8 shillings a week, carters 9 shillings, but the clay-diggers as much as 15 shillings weekly. Nevertheless, 'the want of sufficient house accommodation is most severely felt in Corfe'. How, asks the correspondent, can a man feed, clothe and house a family on 8 shillings a week if it costs the Blandford workhouse 2s.2¹/2d to feed one pauper. The House of Commons debated the issue and one member likened the poverty of Dorset to that of Ireland.

Calcraft was clearly quick to take action where he felt it was needed. During the time that he was Squire of Rempstone, the poor- law expenditure in the County of Dorset increased 214 percent; in the same period, 1792-1831, the population of the county only increased some 40 percent. This does suggest, that, however misguidedly, Calcraft and other worthy gentry were doing their bit for the welfare of the county.

John Calcraft the Younger was, like his father, often referred to as Jack Calcraft. He seems to have frequented Brooks Club in St. James', together with his son John Hales. It is recorded that in 1804 he was a close support-er of the Prince of Wales and, at a dinner at Carlton House was given the honoured position of sitting at the end of the table in the Prince's presence.

In 1815 John's wife Elizabeth Hales died. The memorial in Wareham church reads:

TO ELIZABETH, the wife of JOHN CALCRAFT, esq. MP of Rempstone Hall, who died on the 2nd of July, 1815, aged 45 years, and is buried in this church. The best wife The Fondest and Most Careful Mother and a Friend to the Poor.

From John Calcraft's Parliamentary speeches for the years 1815 to 1820, and 1822 and 1824, he emerges as being consistently on the side of reform at a time of severe and unprecedented repression by the Tory Government of the day, which included Dudley Ryder, the Earl of Harrowby, and also Calcraft's near neighbour, Lord Eldon *[see Plate 10]*. He seems to have been an 'offi-cial' opposition spokesman for economic affairs and he argues persistently for the repeal of income tax, and the taxes on salt, liquor and leather. On 4 February 1817, for example, he upbraids the Chancellor of the Exchequer (Nicholas Vansittart) and Lord Castlereagh in the following terms:

[Mr Calcraft] *wished to know from the chancellor of the exchequer whether he meant to relinquish any tax that would come home to the pockets and feel-ings of the country at large? for he considered it absolutely necessary that some taxation should be remitted to the people. Under the existing state of affairs, the increased population of the country could not maintain themselves by their labour. Almost the whole of the labouring classes were supported out of the poor-rates of the country; and unless something should be done to relieve their distresses, let peace continue, let commerce flourish, let agriculture revive, they could not maintain themselves unless they were still assisted out of the parish rates. These rates however had now become so great, that it was almost impossible to increase them; and, therefore, he wished to ascertain, whether it was intended to apply the sinking fund to the relief of the country. He was strongly of the opinion, that it would be the most advantageous course to take a portion of that fund to supply some of the taxes that press so heavily on the labouring classes of the community. '*

Calcraft was, in fact, following the reforming policies of men like Bentham, Cobbett and Brougham who advocated reduced taxation and less State interference. On 2 July 1822, Hansard reports him supporting a move to repeal the House and Window Tax:

Mr Calcraft thanked his hon. friend for having brought forward this motion in so very able a manner. It was, he was aware, a reduction of 2 700 000 l., and would sensibly interfere with the sinking fund; but he was satisfied that the only means of relieving the distresses of the country was by a repeal of taxation... From the year 1815 nothing had come spontaneously – all had been wrung from ministers. In the army and navy little could be reduced; but in the civil and colonial departments much could yet be saved.

John Calcraft the Younger is urging a reduction in Government expenditure. He several times, after Waterloo, urged a reduction of military and naval expenditure, clashing with Peel and Palmerston on this issue. One of the most endearing and, I think, convincing of Calcraft's themes is his concern for the poor. He opposed removing the maximum limit on the price of bread (27 June 1815) and opposed tougher Corn Laws (22 January 1819). On 7 March 1817 Calcraft made a long speech on Poor Law relief, presenting two petitions to the House:

He could assure the House from his own knowledge, that the statements in them were in no wise exaggerated. They were from two parishes in Dorsetshire: one of them was from the parish of Langton Matravers, consisting of 575 inhabitants, and 419 of these inhabitants were at present receiving parochial relief. The rate amounted at least to 18s. or 19s. in the pound The other was from Swanage, where the population was larger, about 1,500, and the number of inhabited houses about 300. Of this population there was not one in seven able to support themselves. In this parish, the rate amounted to a guinea in the pound, and every occupier of land but one had given notice to abandon. Four or five in the other had also given such notice; and the land in a short time would thus all be thrown on the hands of the own-

ers. If it had not been for the persons who had come forward and subscribed largely towards the relief of the poor, at the head of whom was Lord Eldon, it would have been impossible to go on; but he was sorry to say, that the whole of the funds subscribed would be exhausted by the 22nd of the present month.

As often seemed to happen, Calcraft found himself opposed by the haughty Castlereagh who, on this occasion, points out that fifteen shillings in the pound of an agricultural labourer's wage could be paid for by the parish, in the form of poor relief, and that such a system should be 'discouraged as much as possible'. Calcraft replied that he:

...was glad that the noble lord had made the observation, as it gave him an opportunity of stating, that though it might apply to parishes purely agricultural, it could not apply to the parishes in question. The persons obtaining relief from them were nearly all engaged in the stone trade. He did admit that a great part of the wages of labour in many parts of the country were paid out of the poor rates. He was decidedly of opinion that the political state of the country had, in a great measure, increased the poor rates to what they at present were, and not the idleness of the people.

One of his most lucid speeches is that made on 3 March 1818 where he explains his economic philosophy with absolute clarity. The poor laws were the direct effect of 'enormous taxation' and the 'extravagence of the Government', and he went on:

Gentlemen would have their corn bill – they wanted to have a high price for corn, labour low, and moderate poor rates. But these three things they could not possibly have at the same time. If corn was high, labour could not be low, without there being heavy poor-rates. The labourers and their families must eat. Low labour was, no doubt, a great advantage in agriculture and manufactures; but it ought never to be so low as not to afford subsistence for the labourer and his family, in a style suitable to his condition in life. Whether his wages were 10s., 15s., or 20s. a week, he cared not, if it procured for him that degree of comfort to which he was entitled.

In other speeches, John Calcraft the Younger argues for prison-reform (29 June 1815); opposes the suspension of Habeus Corpus (28 February 1817); supports petitions for reform from Kent (1817 and 1822); opposes, along with only forty-four others (who included Romilly and the Hon. W. Waldegrave) the Seditious Meetings Bill (1817); supports, with Wilberforce, a treaty with Spain for the abolition of the slave trade (1818); opposes the Seditious Meetings Prevention Bill which followed the Peterloo 'massacre' (Dec 6th 1819) – a measure supported by Lord Harrowby (Dudley Ryder) in the Lords; gets support from Wilberforce and G. Tierney against Castlereagh's Seizure of Arms Bill (1820); succeeds in opposing the repeal of the Usury Laws (1824); and stands up for the freedom of the Press (as his father had done) against Castlereagh (1820).

Calcraft, as a Whig, usually finds himself in the minority along with reformers like Lord John Russell, Romilly, Mackintosh, Denman, Tierney, Curwen, Wilberforce and Brougham. His main opponents are Castlereagh, Vansittart, Peel and Palmerston. Sometimes he gets Canning's approbation, sometimes not. Usually, he appears as moderate, and quite witty and generous to his opponents. His style and sentiments are surprisingly modern. In a time of nation-wide economic distress he called for conciliation, not suppression. He was against the additional burdens of further taxation being laid upon the people 'in proportion to their inability to bear them'. Why should the increasingly impoverished have to pay taxes? They did not even have the right to vote!

In 1820, John Calcraft the Younger had been joined in the Commons by his son John Hales Calcraft, and although the latter shows the family reluctance to make speeches, he joins his father in voting on a motion on the State of Ireland on 11 May 1824. John's close political coterie is not known but it probably included those Whigs who sat with him for Wareham, such as Sir Samuel Romilly and Thomas (later Lord) Denman. He was also joined in the Commons, for a short while (1806-7), by his younger brother, Sir Granby Thomas Calcraft and, in the year he died, another son, Granby Hales Calcraft, joined John Hales Calcraft in Parliament. It was quite a family affair.

The Ryders

When did the Ryders and the Calcrafts become friends? As two political families they had been acquainted since the middle of the eighteenth century. The elder John Calcraft was an intimate of the elder Pitt, and Dudley Ryder (Earl of Harrowby 1762–1847), a friend of the younger Pitt and his second in his famous duel with George Tierney in 1798. Later, Ryder was briefly Pitt's Foreign Secretary, before a fall down the Foreign Office steps on to his head forced his retirement. This nearness to the Pitts may well have brought the families into quite close contact, politically and socially, before the end of the century. The Ryders' rise to political prominence had rather preceded that of the Calcrafts – and they had been more successful in terms of office. Sir Dudley Ryder (1691-1756) had, as Attorney General, prosecuted the Jacobite prisoners after the 1745 uprising, and we know that Calcraft had copied letters to him from Fox at this period. In 1754, while Calcraft was still a little-known civil servant, Ryder became Chief Justice. (Sir Dudley's earliest certain ancestor, Robert Rider of Wisbeach, had been born about 1590 and the connection with the ancient and knightly Yorkshire family of Ryder or Ryther is probable).

The eighteenth-century Ryders, unlike the Calcrafts, at least appeared respectable, almost to the point of boredom, although we know now that Nathaniel Ryder, MP for Tiverton, the first Baron Harrowby, had, in fact, two families with whom he shared his time. One can only assume that his wife knew about the mistress. Both women were well-born daughters of church-men. Dudley Ryder (Earl of Harrowby) *[see Plate 12]*, Nathaniel's son, was continuously in office from 1789 until 1827, several times refusing the prime ministership. During this period, the second Calcraft, only three years younger than Harrowby, was almost perpetually in opposition. However, Ryder was, by the standards of his day, a moderate Tory, and Calcraft was a moderate Whig. During the 1820s both moved closer to each other's point of view; but whether this was the cause or effect of their families' friendship is unclear. The Westbrook Hay estate in Hertfordshire had been held by the Rt Hon. Richard Ryder (1766–1832) who had been Home Secretary from 1809 till 1812. He had married Frederica, the daughter of Sir John Skynner, but had died without issue. John Calcraft surely must have known these Ryders also.

The late Lord Harrowby owned three letters written by John Hales Calcraft to the First Countess of Harrowby in 1826, and some letters to her from Lady Caroline Calcraft. John Hales was, of course, some twenty-four years younger than Lady Harrowby, and a most handsome young man of thirty when these letters were composed. Lord Harrowhy considered that the tone of them is 'as one might write to an elder sister'. Be that as it may, the tone is certainly warm and solicitous. It seems that young John Hales Calcraft had been seriously ill. He writes:

> *My dear Lady Harrowby*
> *I was delighted to get your kind note, but am much too spoiled and vain to be satisfied by your even coming down to the carriage door to see me, for who can say when that day may be, but seriously, I have been seriously tempted to ask you for some days past to pay me a visit, now that I am able to sit up till eight o'clock without fatigue – and as various ladies have already honoured me with their company... and as you will come (if at all) when my sisters are always out in the carriage I can meet you half way in the drawing room, which will at all events save you the pain in the side you must have had when you were good enough to mount up to my crows nest...*

Calcraft was probably writing from his London house. He was already a friend of Granville Dudley Ryder, (the Countess's second son). In October 1834 Granville (along with Lord William Montagu and the Viscountess Mandeville) would be a sponsor at the baptism of John Hales' second son William Montagu Calcraft, and on 1 December 1857, his second daughter Georgiana Emily Calcraft would marry Granville's eldest son Dudley Henry Ryder of Westbrook Hay.

In his three letters to Lady Harrowby of 1826, John Hales Calcraft twice mentions his friend Granville Ryder, who also seems to be ill: 'I am sorry you speak so frettingly of Granville. I thought him improved and he seemed to think so too.' And in another letter:

I have rather retrograded during the past week, but I think myself rather on the advance again today – I have not seen my Dr. since Sunday – you will perhaps think that better late than never applies to my seeing a new one, which I have promised to do, as my father seemed as anxious I should. I think it an unwise measure and expect harm and not good from it. I have requested it may be Dr. Black if at all as I liked Granville's account of him and I shall be glad to make his acquaintance though he shouts out about strengthening me with tonics.

Granville Ryder had married Lady Georgiana Somerset (daughter of the Duke of Beaufort) only the year before (1825). His friend John Hales Calcraft was to remain a dashing bachelor for another two years, marrying Lady Caroline Montagu (daughter of the Duke of Manchester) on 13 February 1828. John Hales Calcraft, as we will see later, had already enjoyed an affair with Princess Pauline Bonaparte in France, a woman far older than him. Was he now flirting with Lady Harrowby, his friend's mother? Did he have a taste for older women?

Anyway, the Ryders and Calcrafts were well acquainted by the 1820s. In 1857 the two families would intermarry.

The Great Reform Bill
Meanwhile, John Calcraft, John Hales Calcraft's father, had been up to some strange tricks. In 1827 Harrowby temporarily retired from politics on the death of Canning, whose moderate Tory policies he had espoused. There followed the Ultra-Tory Government of Wellington, Peel and Eldon (Scott) and, most surprisingly, John Calcraft, after a lifetime in Whig opposition, accepted a post in this Government as Paymaster General. It seems that his skills as an economist were in demand, regardless of party. Admittedly, it was a time of change when party boundaries were breaking, but on the face of it, Calcraft had gone over to the enemy – it was like Aneurin Bevan accepting to serve in Churchill's Cabinet, or Wedgewood Benn joining with Mrs Thatcher. Nevertheless, it turned out that the 'No-Surrender' ministry of Wellington sometimes gave in to the pressures for reform. To everyone's surprise, the Iron Duke capitulated to a series of demands, including Catholic emancipation, and was denounced (along with Peel) by the High Tories whose champion he had lately been. In other words, by apparently turning traitor, Calcraft had in fact got himself into a Cabinet which had, albeit reluctantly, begun to put into law the sorts of reforms which for years he had been demanding from the Whig opposition benches. It would be presumptuous to assume that Calcraft significantly influenced Wellington and Peel, and yet one must wonder a little at a man who could appear to turn his coat and who yet can be said, ultimately, to have achieved his aims. The actions of the Wellington Ministry made inevitable the great reforms that followed; on one issue, however, Wellington refused to move, and that was electoral reform – the widening of the franchise so as to include thousands of new voters.

In November, 1830, Wellington fell from power and old Lord Grey formed a Whig administration which brought in the Reform Bill. This historically scraped through by only one vote at its reading on 22 March 1831, with John Calcraft controversially voting for it. He had voted against his own cabinet! When it was blocked a month later, Parliament was dissolved and, amid scenes of almost revolutionary chaos, the ensuing election returned the Whigs with a larger majority. Calcraft carried the county of Dorset in the reform interest. A satirical cartoon published in May 1831 depicts Calcraft eating his own words – a reference to an anti-reform speech (in line with his Cabinet) that Calcraft had previously made. Locally, Portman was another pro-reform candidate while Bankes and Eldon, both Ultra Tories, were, of course, against.

What happened over the next few months is far from clear. The Second Reform Bill came before the Commons, but ten days before it passed to the Lords, Calcraft died. According to the *Dictionary of National Biography* 'Under the reproaches of the Tories with whom he had co-operated from 1828 to 1830, his mind became unhinged, and he committed suicide at Whitehall Place, London, 11 Sept 1831'. His arch opponent, Castlereagh, had done likewise in 1822.

Lady Holland noted, rather paradoxically – 'He was an amiable, useful and clever man... he has not left a more ready debater behind him, and if he had much of the appearance and some of the faults, he had all of the merits, of that race of unprincipled politicians who formed the majority of our leading publick men during the greater part of the last century. He was frank, bold, friendly, and honourable to his party, as long as he professed to belong to it, though incapable perhaps of chusing or adhering to it from any publick virtue.' Is this really fair? John Calcraft had turned against his ex-Cabinet colleagues to vote for reform. This surely was an act of principle.

Murder Most Foul

There is a sad account of the death of John Calcraft, published in the *Annual Register* of the year 1831:

In Whitehall-place, aged 65, the Right Hon. John Calcraft, knight in Parliament for the county of Dorset. He was the son and heir of John Calcraft, esq. an eminent army agent, who accumulated a great fortune, and became proprietor of large estates in Dorsetshire. He died in 1772, being then MP for Rochester. The late Mr Calcraft was first returned to Parliament in 1796 for the borough of Wareham, in which he possessed considerable property; and was rechosen in 1802. He generally voted with the opposition; but for a time attached himself more particularly to the interests of the Prince of Wales. On the formation of the Grenville Administration, Mr Calcraft was appointed Clerk of the Ordnance, 15 February 1806. In the same year he was returned to Parliament for Rochester, where he was re-elected in 1807 and 1812. In 1818 Mr Calcraft lost his election for Rochester; and from that time *until the present year he sat for the borough of Wareham. In June 1828 he accepted the office of Paymaster of the Forces, and was sworn of the Privy Council. He retired from office with the other members of the Wellington administration, with whose views he appeared to coincide until the debate on the Reform bill on the 22 of last March, when, **to the astonishment of all his acquaintance, he voted with the 301, which formed the majority of one by which that measure first passed a second reading.** On the credit of this vote, Mr Calcraft became the Reform candidate for Dorsetshire, in opposition to Mr Bankes; and, after a severe contest, he was successful. For the last three or four months of his life, he was remarkably low and dejected, and on the afternoon of the 11 of September, whilst his youngest daughter (the only member of his family in town) was absent at church, he terminated his existence by cutting his throat.*

The report concludes:

The deceased had been unwell for the last three months, during the two latter of which he had not quitted his residence, and appeared extremely low and dejected. Mr Freeman, surgeon, of Spring-gardens, and Dr Wilson Phillip had both attended the family for the last three months, and, observing the deceased to be labouring under great depression of spirits, which at length settled into deep melancholy, they had thought it their duty to caution Captain Calcraft, who did not reside in the house, but who called occasionally, that the deceased ought to be watched. Dr Phillip was asked by one of the Jury, if Mr Calcraft had ever expressed disappointment at not being elevated to the peerage; the Doctor answered that he did not believe he ever entertained any expectation of such an event. He had latterly fancied that he was continually watched by a man sitting on the top of a house. The Jury returned a verdict of – Temporary Mental Derangement.

Another newspaper report indicates that Calcraft's body, lying face down in a pool of blood with a razor in his hand, was found by his unfortunate daughter, Arabella *[see Plate 11]*, when she returned from church. She had fallen to her knees crying 'Father, father!' Could there really have been events in his life that had driven him to this horrific act? It is true that there had been a minor scandal when his son, Captain Granby Calcraft, had sued his secret wife, Emma Love, an actress, for divorce in 1830; she had eloped with Lord Harborough and been accommodated by the peer in a cottage on his estate. It is also true that John had recently lost his job as Paymaster to the Forces, but, on the other hand, he had more recently been elected as the first MP for the County of Dorset. Also depressing for him, if it was true, he had not been given the peerage he may have been expecting and longing for as a fulfilment of his father's unfulfilled ambition. Furthermore, the previous year he had witnessed the horrible death of his friend William Huskisson MP, when Huskisson had become the world's first victim of a railway accident, being run down by the engine 'Rocket' at the opening of the Liverpool to Manchester railway. The accumulation of all these sad events could have caused depression but not, most probably, the apparently paranoid delusions that he was being spied upon by a man atop a church tower or from a house. The method of suicide, too, in a man who owned several guns and therefore could have shot himself, was bizarre. Someone must be very deranged to be able to almost cut off their own head.

But there is another possible explanation for Calcraft's awful death, and that is murder. Cutting one's own throat does seem extreme, and Calcraft was neither extreme nor frenzied. He was moderate in all things. He may have been depressed, but as a sensitive man why did he not choose an easier way out? Maybe the 'delusions' that he was being spied upon by certain Tories and watched by a man with a spyglass were not delusions at all. Perhaps he was the victim of a vindictive assassination by an anti-reform fanatic or clique, or by a professional hit-man.

The inquest involved a jury who saw the corpse and inspected the house (17 Whitehall Place). The surgeon (Mr Freeman) stated: 'I found a wound across the throat, dividing the larger vessels on both sides, laying bare the vertebrae of the neck, and a considerable quantity of blood covering the body and the floor...'. One juror then asked – 'The wound in the deceased's throat is very extensive, and **I have heard respectable medical men say, it is not possible such a wound, which nearly severs the head from the body, could have been inflicted by the party themselves**' *[author's emphasis]*. The coroner and the surgeon disagreed, saying they had encountered similar cases. Nobody, however, witnessed the death and the surgeon remarked that the razor was on the table and not in Calcraft's hand. There was no suicide note. Furthermore, Arabella's absence at church was probably quite predictable to anyone who had been watching the family for some time.

The political atmosphere and context of the times need to be borne in mind. The revolutions in France (1789) and America (1776) had encouraged radical factions in Britain although the wars against Napoleon had, temporarily, suppressed such revolutionary sentiments. After Waterloo in 1815, however, agitation again increased, and the government of the day adopted draconian measures to prevent rebellion. Starvation and economic hardship afflicted many parts of the country. Many feared revolution. Military suppression of a protest meeting in Manchester in 1819 had caused the deaths of eleven peaceful demonstrators, cut down by soldiers. This so-called Peterloo Massacre became a symbol of defiance for the working classes and for those who sought reforms. In 1820 government spies successfully infiltrated a conspiracy in Cato Street to murder members of the Cabinet as they dined at the house of Dudley Ryder (the Earl of Harrowby), and five of the conspirators were subsequently executed. In 1828 a new Corn Law was passed and was followed in 1829 by the Catholic Emancipation Act. The reform of the electoral system then became the main issue. The Whigs sought reform while Wellington and most of the Tories remained firmly opposed. In 1830, agitation reached a new peak, encouraged by the success of the July Revolution in France. In England, Lord Grey and the Whigs were swept into office on a tide of reform. Many now felt that revolution was inevitable. Agricultural hardships fanned outbreaks of rural violence, especially in the south, and there were riots in the cities. Opponents of reform argued that any changes to the electoral system would be the thin end of the wedge and would prize open the floodgates of revolution. Reformers argued that, to the contrary, modest reforms would defuse the revolutionary pressures. This is the background to the First Reform Bill that was introduced in March 1831 by Lord John Russell. It was passed by the Commons, thanks to the much publicised reversion of John Calcraft back to his Whig principles, by just one vote, although later it was lost by an amendment in Committee. In April, Parliament was dissolved, and, after a vicious election, the Whigs were returned. As already reported, Calcraft was elected MP for Dorset but died just as the crucial Second Reform Bill was being introduced into the House of Commons. It was passed only ten days later.

We have seen that the *Dictionary of National Biography* notes that, shortly before his death, Calcraft suffered 'the reproaches of the Tories with whom he had cooperated from 1828 to 1830.' Who were these people who reproached him? Could one or several of them have been fanatical enough to kill, or to employ someone to kill, the man they saw as a traitor, before he could vote for the Second Reform Bill? It does not seem at all impossible. Clearly, Calcraft was a frightened man – but was his fear a manifestation of insanity (as was claimed) or was it well founded? Political assassination was not unknown at the time – a Prime Minister no less, Spencer Perceval, had been killed in 1811. Furthermore, several captured British assassins sent to murder Napoleon had had their throats cut in French prisons and their deaths recorded as suicides. Cutting throats and claiming it was suicide was, as it were, a known procedure. But it would have been rash for the Calcraft inquest to have returned a verdict of murder in September 1831, as it could have been the spark that set the country alight. It was, therefore, important that the (strangely) unnamed coroner should arrive at a less provocative verdict.

Historians have not concentrated upon the fanatical anti-reformers in, for example, the shadowy military and ex-military clique that gathered around the Duke of Wellington. When the military reactionaries did show themselves, they were ruthless, not only as regards the Peterloo Massacre but in the putting down of other reformist protest meetings and riots. In Bristol, for example, some four hundred protesters were killed and wounded by the sabres of the cavalry under Major Mackworth. Greville noted at the time – 'more punishment has been dealt out than has been generally known... one body of Dragoons pursued a rabble of colliers into the country and covered the fields with the bodies of wounded wretches.' Numbers of rioters were also cut down by troops under Lord Hill and ridden over, others were driven into burning houses out of which they never returned.

Some of the Ultra Tories, like the Duke of Newcastle, even armed their own militia with heavy artillery to suppress, as they saw it, the incipient revolution. Eldon and Bankes, Calcraft's neighbours, were both violently anti-reform and the whole county of Dorset was reckoned to be exceptionally reactionary. Calcraft, therefore, was that rare thing – a landed Dorset reformer. But he was virtually on his own. No wonder he showed signs of stress! Some of the anti-reformers were frankly lunatic: the Ultra Tory Spencer Perceval (the Younger), for example, was a religious fanatic who saw reform as the work of the devil – an attempt to topple the Lord's anointed. Among more senior politicians, too, there were extremists like the loutish Lord Wetherill, the romantic Sir Richard Vyvyan and the despotic Duke of Cumberland. Most of the Ultras within Parliament itself, however, were honourable men who would not have stomached the assassination of one of their fellows. But on the fringes of politics, and among those ex military followers of the Duke in particular, such an act would have appeared a perfectly correct way to deal with a traitor – one of their own who had gone over to the enemy. They had dealt death to similar traitors when fighting in France and in the Peninsular Wars. Some of them would have been well accustomed to the cutting of throats.

Wellington himself had praised the Peterloo Massacre and had privately expressed a longing for full civil war so that the reform movement could be totally defeated. Also, as Paymaster to the Forces, Calcraft had, very possibly, made a few military enemies. In the last few months of life Calcraft had been fearful. He had reason to be. But a fearful man, unlike a frenzied or a ferocious one, is unlikely to have had the resolution to practically cut off his own head, in cold blood, with a razor. It seems just as likely that Calcraft was a brave man who stood by his principles and was murdered by practised killers who had been watching his house for some time and knew when he would be alone there. If so, then he is, more than ever, the unrecognised hero of Parliamentary Reform.

What part, if any, the Ryders played in all this, is not entirely clear. We have proved that the two families were already well acquainted. Perhaps old Lord Harrowby had pulled a few strings to get Calcraft his job as Paymaster-General in 1828; or perhaps Harrowby had been one of the Tories who had been criticising Calcraft for voting for the Reform Bill. Possibly significantly, only three weeks after Calcraft's death, Harrowby himself came back into politics and supported a measure of parliamentary reform in a speech in the Lords. As the leader of the so-called Waverers, or moderate Tories, he helped ensure reform. Like Calcraft, he tried to mediate between the extreme factions and gained the enmity of both. It seems that both Ryder and Calcraft had, in their final years, fallen between two stools. But they had struck blows for Parliamentary reform and for democracy.

John Calcraft was buried in the chancel vault of St. James's Church, Piccadilly. His memorial tablet in the church at Wareham reads:

In memory of the Right Honourable JOHN CALCRAFT, one of His Majesty's most honourable Privy Council, and for many years Member of Parliament, having been nine times elected to represent the ancient borough of Wareham, thrice the city of Rochester, and once the county of Dorset. In the House of Commons he was diligent in his attendance, able and earnest in the performance of his duties, and zealous for the welfare of the country; during two short periods he held office under Government- in 1806 as Clerk of the Ordnance, in 1829 as Paymaster General of his Majesty's Forces – both which situations he filled with uprightness and ability. Born October 16th, 1765; died September 11th, 1831.

The juror's words return to mind: 'I have heard respectable medical men say it is not possible such a wound, which nearly severes the head from the body, could have been inflicted by the party themselves.'

One of the most glowing tributes to Calcraft was made during his lifetime, and is recorded in a newspaper report which suggests that he was genuinely respected by his Dorset constituents. It describes him as 'an ornament to the Senate, the agriculturalists' advocate, and the poor man's friend'. John Calcraft the Younger was certainly a good man and one who was sincerely dedicated to reform.

5

SIR GRANBY THOMAS CALCRAFT
1766-1820

Granby was the second son of John Calcraft (Crafterio, the Army Agent) and Elizabeth Bride. He was born at Ingress Hall in Kent, Nov. 8th 1766, the year after the birth of John Calcraft his older brother, who was to become Paymaster General.

In March 1788, aged twenty-one, Granby joined the Army as a cornet in the 15th Light Dragoons. In 1793 the French revolutionaries guillotined the King of France and declared war on England. British troops under the command of the Duke of York were landed in Flanders in support of the Dutch and Austrians, and Calcraft, promoted a lieutenant, participated in their two early victories at the battles of Famars and Valenciennes.

Calcraft must have been already a dashing and successful officer. On 24 April of the following year, when the tide had turned in favour of the French, he outstandingly distinguished himself when a force of only 160 troopers of the 15th Light Dragoons along with 112 Austrian Hussars defeated a corps of some 10 000 Frenchmen and, allegedly, saved the life of the Austrian Emperor Francis II. This was one of the few successful actions fought by the Allies at this time.

Some years later, on 7 November 1800, the Emperor rewarded the eight British officers involved by making them all knights of the military Order of Maria Theresa. On 21 April 1804, the Emperor, desperate for British help against Napoleon, further promoted Calcraft to the rank of Baron in the same order. The citation reads:

...We have therefore considered the knightly manners, virtues, sense, fidelity, bravery and other excellent qualities with which is endowed our beloved subject Granby Thomas Calcraft, knight of the Imperial and Royal Order of Maria Theresa and Lieutenant Colonel in the Royal British Cavalry of Great Britain, and more especially we have taken into consideration that in the last war with the French, in the year 1794, a French Regiment of 24 000 men advanced from Cambray and attacked our troops and the Hessian Outposts, stationed on the Selle, and dislodged them from the banks of that stream; likewise that when the heavy Cavalry, called up to support them, had lost their way, and our 2nd Squadron of the Royal British 15th Light Horse Regiment had attacked the superior force of the enemy with such fury that their Cavalry was forced back behind the Infantry, over a thousand of the enemy killed, the remainder beaten back to Cambray and three cannon seized, and that in this

action Granby Thomas Calcraft, then Captain of the aforesaid Royal British Light Horse Squadron, has especially distinguished himself by his personal bravery and wisdom, also by spurring on his men and thus rendering an essential service to our army, and that he has pledged himself to maintain unto his death this exceptionally brave, clever and upright behaviour as he from his praiseworthy qualities can, must and shall do. We, therefore, on account of the above-mentioned reasons and motives and in gracious consid-eration of these things are graciously pleased to confirm him in our highest esteem, and after serious thought, good council and proper knowledge, as also by power of our Royal and Ducal Sovereignity, to raise Granby Thomas Calcraft to the rank, position, honour and dignity of all the Barons and Baronesses of our Kingdom, Principality and Lands, as likewise all his legiti-mate heirs of both sexes and the heirs of their heirs unto succeeding genera-tions, for ever and ever, as long as any of his posterity may exist. We also join him, associate him and make him equal to the other Companies, Communities and Corporations of other members of the Holy Roman Empire, and of all the Barons of rank of our inherited Kingdom, Principality and Lands.

We honour Granby Thomas Calcraft and we raise him and all his legiti-mate heirs of both sexes to the rank of these Barons, Baronesses and Ladies.

We associate and join them to the society and community of all the very noble Barons, Baronesses and Ladies of rank of our Kingdom, Principality and Lands and we make them their equals.

We grant, desire and permit that they shall, can and may use everywhere and before everyone not only the Red Wax Seal but also the title of honour 'Sir' [in German: 'Wohlgeboren'].

It can be seen that the defeated French force in this report is claimed to be even larger than in other accounts of the action. Granby was justifiably proud of this award and took the title of 'Sir' which is only an approximate translation of the order. Even Wellington, however, used this title when addressing Calcraft.

One should not belittle this achievement of Granby Calcraft. There is no shadow of doubt but that he was a brave and skilful soldier. The decoration itself is one of the most distinguished of all European awards. In 1975 Prince Weikersheim confirmed that the Order of Maria Theresa was the Empire's highest award for gallantry 'equivalent to the Victoria Cross, but much rarer'.

The Austro-Hungarian Empire was, at the time, one of the main powers of Europe. Francis II, in descent from Charlemagne, was still Holy Roman Emperor, although in 1804 Napoleon forced him to change his title. So Calcraft can perhaps claim to have been the last, or one of the last, Barons of the Holy Roman Empire. Conceivably, the title could have been claimed by John Calcraft and his heirs when Granby died in 1820. Although the patents and seals (both badly damaged) survive, the medal and other insignia (of great monetary value) were stolen, along with other gold and silver objects, by D.C.D. 'Jack' Ryder's London butler in 1931.

Granby was wounded at the second battle of Alkmaer on 1 October 1799 and then promoted Major. In the following year he was transferred to the 3rd Dragoon Guards of which he became Lieutenant-Colonel on Christmas Day 1800 and he commanded that regiment with great distinction until 1813. For a short while he accompanied his older brother as MP for Wareham, then resigned from Parliament when his regiment was posted to fight the Napoleonic armies in Spain and Portugal in 1808. At the end of 1808 Madrid fell to Napoleon and in the following January Sir John Moore, the British commander, was killed at Corunna. In early July Napoleon had defeated Austria, but Arthur Wellesley inflicted a defeat upon Napoleon's armies at Talavera later in the month and was created Viscount Wellington; when General Fane fell ill, Colonel Calcraft assumed the command of the Heavy Brigade for this crucial battle.

During 1810 and 1811 Calcraft was continuously engaged in Wellington's campaign against Marshals Massena, Soult and Ney, some of Napoleons finest generals. Wellington's small Army was able to resist the much larger French forces partly because of the friendship of the native Spanish and Portuguese populations. Wellington was especially short of cavalry and Calcraft and the Heavy Brigade were busy in the actions around Tores Vedras, Foz d'Aronce, Campo Mayor, Albeura and Los Santos.

On 8 January 1812 Wellington besieged the garrison town of Cuidad Rodrigo and after a brilliant assault, took it on the 19 January. The Heavy Brigade, again under Calcraft's command, covered this siege, expecting at any moment the advance of a French Army under Marshall Marmont. Two letters, from Wellington to Calcraft survive, indicating some of the tension in the air. The envelope is addressed:

Colonel Sir G Calcraft K.M.T.
3d Drag. Guards
St Espiritus.

Ciudad Roderigo Jany 25th 1812 ¹/2 past one pm.

Dear Sir Granby,
I received your letters at ¹/2 past 7 last night.
I have no accounts from Salamanca of a later date than the 22D; & have none from Major Grant or Lt. Blanchley who are both forward towards the Head of the Tormes beyond Tamames, of the Enemy's advance in that Direction. I should think therefore that the troops of which you have heard cannot be so numerous as they have been reported to you to be; and that they have been sent forward solely to ascertain our movements after the fall of the Place.
I mention this because I hear that you have sent away your Baggage to

Barquilla; and I fear you will be distressed. At all events it need not have come farther than this place.

Ever Yours most faithfully
Wellington

On the previous day Wellington had written.

Ciudad Roderigo
Jany. 24th. 1812
$^1/_2$ past 3 P.M.

My Dear Sir Granby
I have just received your Report of this morning that the Enemy's Cavalry had arrived last night at Ledesma & Rollan. I should think they must be recon-noitring parties probably to ascertain the fate of this place.
    You are aware of the situation of Don Julian's & Don Carlo's Detachments on the Yeltes & the Huebra & at Tamames. Communicate with them; and if you should find the Enemy advancing in too large force for you, you will retire upon this place.
    Don Carlos has a party at Bajajo [Bogajo] and Villa Vieja to keep the Bridge at Puenta de Yecla over the Yeltes, & another at Cerralvo for the same object in respect of the Bridge at that Place. The Enemy's Detachment at Ledesma would move towards these Bridges; and you should have a steady Noncommissioned Officer with each of them to give you early Intelligence of what happens.
    You should yourself observe what happens on the Road by Sanmunoz which is the High Road from Salamanca across the Yeltes; & you should com-municate with Don Julian's Officer at Tamames.

Ever Yours most faithfully

Wellington

During the summer, after his victory at Salamanca, Wellington's army entered Madrid, Calcraft's cavalry distinguishing itself at Llera where General Slade specially mentioned Calcraft's 'conspicuous gallantry'. Later in the year, when threatened by an overwhelming French force of some hundred thousand men, Wellington was forced to retreat on Salamanca, Calcraft cov-ering the infantry.

In December 1812 Colonel Calcraft was made a knight of the Portuguese order of the Tower and Sword; another exalted award which Wellington himself had received a few months earlier. On 4 June 1813, aged forty-six, Calcraft was promoted Major-General, as Wellington's victorious army pushed the French back across the Pyrenees. In the same year he was recalled home and placed in charge of a brigade in England. He had fought throughout Wellington's Peninsular War and had seen three of his brothers (one Calcraft and two Lefebures) die alongside him. Perhaps because of his Whig politics and his alleged criticism of the jobbery in Government circles, he became relatively neglected. Rather disgruntled, he resigned his appointment in 1814, so missing the opportunity of fighting at Waterloo the following year. He felt 'an ill-used man'.

His memorial in Wareham Church reads:

Major-General Sir Granby Thomas Calcraft, Knight (of the orders of Maria Theresa and Tower and Sword) a distinguished Officer in the 15th Regt. of Light Dragoons and the 3rd Regt. of Dragoon Guards, son to the late John Calcraft of Rempstone, he departed this life at Bath, August 20th 1820, aged 53 years.

6

JOHN HALES CALCRAFT
(1796-1880)

LADY CAROLINE CALCRAFT (1804-1892)

On 5 March 1790, John Calcraft the Younger, aged 25, had married Elizabeth, third daughter of Sir Thomas Pym Hales, Bart, of Bekesbourne, Kent. They had eight children – Elizabeth Mary born 4 July 1791, Fanny Catherine born 9 January 1793, Caroline Jane born 27 January 1794, Arabella Margaretta born 31 July 1795, John Hales born 13 September 1796, Thomas Hales born 10 February 1798, Granby Hales 27 October 1799–9 November 1799 and Granby Hales (the second) born 18 January 1802. Elizabeth Hales, the wife of John Calcraft, died at Clifford Street, London, on 2 July 1815, aged 45.

It is believed that John and Elizabeth lived a good deal at Rempstone, enlarging it in their early years together. Between 1790 and 1800 John was not a Member of Parliament and much of his local activities (such as raising the Volunteers and fighting poverty in the county) took place during this decade. It seems likely, therefore, that their children spent at least their infancies in Dorset during this period while John added considerably to the house.

Hutchins reports that Granby Hales Calcraft became a Captain in the Army and died at New York in 1850, that Mary Elizabeth married Sir John Burke, Bart, of Marble Hill, Co. Galway and that Arabella Margaretta married Captain Rochfort R.N., and had three daughters. Hutchins also supplies details of the issue of Mary Elizabeth and John Burke namely six sons; Thomas born 1813; MP for Galway, Charles-Granby (born 14 November 1814 at Rempstone, Barrister-at-law, who married Emma Jane daughter of Ralph Creyke of Rawcliffe Hall, Yorkshire) James born 1816, Edward-Howe born 1817, Maurice-William-Otway born 1819, Henry born 1822 and two daughters; Elizabeth-Anne and Caroline-Jane.

John Hales Calcraft and Lady Caroline

John Hales Calcraft [see Plates 13–15], the eldest son of John Calcraft the Younger and Elizabeth, was born at Rempstone Hall, 13 September 1796 and died there in 1880. The sponsors at his baptism were Lady Hales, Richard Calcraft (his uncle) and the local squire, William Morton Pitt. John Hales Calcraft was three times Member of Parliament for Wareham from 1820–1826, from 1832–1841 and from 1857–1859. He was a Justice of the Peace (in an age in which the JP still to an extent ran the affairs of the countryside) and High Sheriff for Dorset in 1867. We know that by 1826 he was already a friend of the Ryder family, particularly of Granville Dudley Ryder whose son was to marry his daughter in later years. His politics are scarcely recorded, save that he continued the family's Whig tradition. He admired reformers and writes enthusiastically to Lady Harrowby that he looks forward to meeting William Wilberforce during one week-end in 1826.

We also know that in his early twenties, John Hales Calcraft had galivanted around Europe having an affair in Paris with Napoleon's petite sister, Pauline. At least he seems to have learned some French in the process as his library is full of French books. Finally, however, he settled down and on 13 February 1828, he married Lady Caroline Katherine Montagu (1804–1892) *[see Plates 19–22]*, the daughter of the fifth Duke of Manchester (who had been Governor of Jamaica at the time of the slavery-reforms). Lady Caroline's parents had an unhappy marriage and lived apart in later years. Caroline was brought up in England by her mother (née Lady Susan Gordon, the third daughter of the fourth Duke of Gordon – the famous Cock o' the North) *[see Plates 17, 18]* but, after her mother eloped with one of the Duke's servants, the young Caroline was looked after by her ducal Gordon uncle (see later).

John Hales Calcraft married Lady Caroline at about the time that John Calcraft, his father, joined the Tory faction and gained office. Before the latter's tragic end in 1831 three grandchildren had been born – Eliza (1829-30), Katherine (born 1830) and John Hales Montagu Calcraft (born 1831). Having married into the true aristocracy, new shoots of the Calcraft tree now sprung up amidst some heavily titled undergrowth. This can be seen in the names of the sponsors for John Hales' children entered in one of the three family Bibles. For Katherine there was the Marquis of Cholmondeley, the Duchess of Gordon (Lady Caroline's socially well-known grandmother) and Lady Georgiana Baillie (Lady Caroline's sister). For little John Hales Montagu there was the Viscount Mandeville (Lady Caroline's eldest brother), Lord Wriothesley Russell and Lady Elizabeth Steele. For Georgiana-Emily (born 1832) there was John Labouchere, Lady Georgiana Baillie and Lady William Montagu (Lady Caroline's sister-in-law). For Susan Charlotte (born 1833) there was Lord William Montagu again, the Marchioness of Cholmondeley and Lady Charlotte Sturt. Henry George (born 1836) was honoured with Lord Cholmondeley, Sir Walter Farquhar and Miss Caroline Calcraft, his aunt. Georgiana, Susan and William were all born at Rempstone; Henry in Carlton Terrace, London.

Everyone who saw John Hales speaks of his good looks, and they can be seen in the portrait painted around 1820: he was indeed dark and handsome *[see Plates 13, 14]*. His bride, too, was beautiful. Writing in 1927 in her unpublished memoirs, Daisy Bevan (née Mary Waldegrave, daughter of Susan Calcraft who had married Lord Radstock) gives some descriptions of John Hales and Lady Caroline:

> *'The latter was born in 1805 and was a daughter of the fifth Duke of Manchester, whose mother was the famous Jane, Duchess of Gordon. My*

greatgrandmother after she had borne several children to her husband, ran away with her footman, so my grand-mother was brought up by her uncle, the fourth Duke of Gordon. Her many stories of her travels with her uncle were thrilling and as she grew older she remembered the past more and more clearly. She stayed much with her aunt, the Duchess of Richmond, who gave the ball at Brussels on the eve of the battle of Waterloo, though she was too young to be present at it. 'Grandmama' as we called this grandmother, was a beautiful woman to the day of her death, and as a girl created a furore in Italy and had countless offers of marriage, one from the heir to the Belgian throne. At Naples she was elected 'Queen of Beauty' and a large 'rout' was arranged in her honour. To this party, however, she did not go, as she, through what influence I do not know, became quite serious and thenceforward withdrew from the more frivolous side of life though she never, I am glad to say, lost her sense of humour nor her quick, shrewd manner of summing people up. She was a great autocrat and had a strong will, this latter quality must have been shared at any rate by one of her sisters, about whom she was very fond of telling me the following story. An unwanted suitor of this sister was staying at Kimbolton with them, and she, very bored one day, went out early in the morning hoping to get a respite from his attentions. She had, not, however walked far when she espied him following. In front of her was a shallow river, behind the bore; without a moment's hesitation she calmly walked through the river, appearing to be unaware of it or her pursuer. This apparently did damp his ardour and he turned back without also damping his feet. I think it must have been the same sister who was rather éprise with another man staying with them, but not being sure if his calves were genuine, slowly arose from her knees during family prayers, stole across to the dubious man and planted a long pin in his calf. He did not flinch and the pin remained where she put it!

The story of Grandmama's confirmation shews the way those matters were arranged in those days. She was at lessons one day, when her elder sister, Emily, (afterwards Lady Emily Peel), who was a lady-in-waiting, came into the schoolroom and said, 'Go and put on your new muslin dress and bonnet'. When she had done this, her sister whisked her away in a coach to the Palace and only then did she discover that she was to be confirmed together with one of the Princesses.

My Grandmother's marriage was a real love match and not the brilliant one that was expected of her. She met my grandfather, John Calcraft, in Italy. He like her, was a most beautiful person up to the last, but as a young man he must have been dazzling – many people mistake his portrait for that of Byron – but I think he was undoubtedly more handsome. Before his marriage he was a close friend of Pauline Bonaparte's and she gave him a quantity of Napoleon's books; some of his lace ruffles and some locks of his hair – these I regret to find, have been stolen. However, these two beautiful young things, 'forsaking all others', settled down and lived happily together till my grandfather died. Rempstone, as it was then, must have been a curious contrast to both of them after their lively youth, spent largely on the continent. It was then simply a shooting-box, surrounded by wild, heathy country, dotted with a few ancient farms.

Even as a child, life at Rempstone struck me as romantic and it certainly was unique in it's unchanging ways – up till twenty-five years ago anyone staying there might have wondered whether the clocks had not been stopped a hundred years ago. All the grand-children used to go there frequently, sometimes with their parents and more rarely without. I personally adored being there as I was very fond of grandmama and did not find her, as so many people did, at all alarming. She was very strict about some things – manners, 'deportment' and above all, never sitting with idle hands. When she had, in the latter part of her life, to stay in her sitting-room upstairs, she spent countless hours in making picture-books for hospitals and also ravelling or shredding out little scraps of material for stuffing cushions for the poor, but even this occupation was put out of sight on Sundays.

She pronounced several words in 18th Century manner – 'balcóny' – 'yallow' and said 'ain't it?' etc. I liked it and felt I was living in a book whenever I was with her. She remains for ever my beau ideal of a beautiful old lady.'

Lady Caroline emerges as a very upright and formidable person. She was, it seems, a typical Victorian. Paradoxically, her puritanical attitude towards sex was probably instrumental in ending the Calcraft dynasty. Because of it, none of her three eligible sons married and produced a legitimate heir. Strangely, however, her three devout daughters all did so. But the Calcraft name was gone, destroyed by the sexual pruderies of the high Victorian era. It seems that Lady Caroline was content for her daughters to marry provided they did so very respectably: Katherine married a parson (Marston), and Susan a religious fanatic (Lord Radstock) of whom Caroline no doubt very much approved. Only Georgy married a secular figure, although the Ryders too had their devout envangelical connections and, besides, one of her Ryder son-in-law's grandfathers was an Earl and the other was no less than the Duke of Beaufort!

We have one short letter in Lady Caroline's hand. It invites a Miss Steward to apply for the post of temporary school-mistress, presumably for a Wareham school. It is dated 18 November 1833:

Miss Steward,
I have not succeeded in finding a temporary school mistress so that if you think that we should suit I shall be happy to engage you from the beginning of next year. Perhaps you know the place – there are between 40 and 50 names in the school book but seldom more than 36 or 38 children attend at a time. I shall be glad of an early reply and I hope that we shall both make it a subject of prayer that we may be guided aright,
Yours truly,
Caroline Calcraft

*The salary is £36 per annum, the cottage is furnished and there is a garden.
Mrs Roe used to sell vegetables.*

What lives of frightful boredom many Victorian ladies must have led in
their isolated country houses: no partying, no cars, no buses, no radios, no
television, and denied by the servants even the opportunity to perform the
ordinary chores of life.

Like many outstanding political families, the Calcrafts declined gradually
into rural obscurity. The calculating energies of Crafterio and the Whig ide-
alism of the younger John Calcraft, gave way to seventy years of kindly
squiredom and politics that were more local than national. The heads of the
family – John Hales Calcraft and his son William, stepped back from the
spotlight of London events and took up the less conspicuous life of the
country. In consequence, less is known about them.

They continued quietly to live a highly ritualised life surrounded by an
unnecessarily large number of servants. Alexander Hamilton-Fletcher, after
an analysis of the census returns for Rempstone, has concluded that in 1861
the Calcrafts had ten resident servants – a butler, two footmen, a cook, a
cooksman, two ladies' maids, an under maid, a scullery maid and a carpenter. (This total excludes non-resident daily workers, outside servants, and
several Waldegrave servants who happened to be visiting on the day of the
census). Ten years later, incidentally, Kitty Mansel is recorded as staying at
Rempstone on census day, although her home is stated to be Church
Knowle. On this occasion the total of Calcraft servants had risen to thirteen
but seems to include some who resided in cottages in the grounds: a butler,
a footman, a coachman, a cook, a ladies' maid, two housemaids, a kitchen
maid, a scullery maid, two laundresses, a carpenter and a gardener.

Until the 1920s most of the servants were housed in Lower Rempstone.
While Upper Rempstone was kept smartly painted and limewashed, Lower
Rempstone (which had been added in 1790) was screened by trees and
shrubs, its walls covered with creepers.

Sadly, like too many countrymen with not enough to do, some of the
Calcrafts now took to slaughtering game with guns and nets. The
Rempstone Game Book records a gradual increase in the numbers of animals
killed from 1817 to 1857, and primarily responsible for this constructive use
of time are John Hales' two sons, John Hales Montagu Calcraft and William
Calcraft; only young Henry was busy following a career in town. The game
book records the names to whom game was sent. Most recipients appear to
have been local, ranging from tradesmen to gentry. The Bankes, Bonds,
Clavells and Scotts are so honoured. So also are the Calcraft in-laws, the
Baillies and the Burkes. In 1817, Lord Granby gets two partridge and a hare
(an indication perhaps that the slight political quarrel about Wilkes between
the two families, of fifty years before, had left no permanent scar). In 1826
'Mr. Lefebure of 28 Chester Place, Kensington' gets four partridge. (Could
old Charles Lefebure *still* be alive?).

Some names which often appear, such as Horlick and Capel, are mysterious, others such as Clark (who first receives a gift in 1837) are destined to become familiar names in later times. Large consignments in earlier years are despatched to 'General Fox Calcraft', the last on 15 September 1830; this is George Anne Bellamy's boy Henry Fox Calcraft ('Harry') who had always wanted to go to sea, but ended up in the Army along with so many of his relatives. It is interesting to find that he was still in touch with and receiving gifts from his *younger* half-brother's estate, from which he had been disinherited.

The Calcrafts had certainly provided their share of military men: first, Colonel (later Lt-General) Thomas Calcraft, MP of the 1760s (younger brother of Crafterio), followed by his distinguished nephews Major-General Sir Granby Thomas Calcraft, and the general's elder brother the Rt. Hon. John Calcraft of Rempstone who had been Clerk of the Ordnance and had raised the Dorset Yeomanry, then the young Major William Calcraft killed at Santha Martha in 1809 and his two half-brothers Major Charles Lefebure and Captain George Lefebure who died in the same campaign and also, so it seems, these young men's other half-brother General Henry Fox Calcraft who survived long enough to receive half a dozen Rempstone partridge and a hare on the eve of the Great Reform Bill.

When the Rt Hon. John Calcraft died violently in 1831, his Dorset estates passed to his son John Hales Calcraft who lived there until 1880. Old John Hales Calcraft far outlived his eldest son John Hales Montagu Calcraft (1831–1868) *[see Plate 23]* who was the last of the Calcraft MPs in the year of his death. (The family had been represented in the House of Commons almost continuously for a hundred years since Crafterio's election for Calne in 1766 and his brother Thomas' return for Poole in 1761 and 1768.) Little is known of this nautical man. At his death he left a number of unpaid bills suggestive of the good life: from 22 March 1867 till 17 August 1868 he had bought tobacco to the value of £44 10s.10d; the Royal Hotel at Weymouth charged 50 shillings for champagne; the King's Arms at Dorchester claimed Soda and Brandy one shilling, Bed and Breakfast half-a-crown each. He seems to have been actively fishing, smoking and drinking until shortly before the end, and the only clue as to why he died so young may be the invoice of Walter Cole (chemist) Weymouth, for chilblain and neuralgic liniments costing 6 shillings and sixpence. We know that John Hales Montague Calcraft was a magistrate and Deputy Lieutenant of Dorset. He entered the Navy aged only thirteen in 1844. He served in the Crimean War and was retired from the Navy due to ill health in October 1852 with the rank of Commander. He was first elected to Parliament, as Liberal MP for Wareham, in July 1865. He was returned at the general election in 1868 and sat as MP until he died on 1 December of that year.

In the summer of 1975 the Calcraft vault at St Mary's Church, Wareham, was twice opened. Ralph Fooks the Churchwarden, the Rempstone foreman, the

Rector Mr Thorne, Jack and Vee Ryder, and sons James, Ben and Richard, his grandchildren Lara and Melanie, Audrey Ryder, and Alexander and Giles Hamilton-Fletcher were present on one or both occasions.

The vault, which no longer has its porch, is situated at the North-East corner of the Chancel and extends under the altar. Its entrance is outside the church and is sealed under cemented flagstones. On raising these a short flight of stone steps can be seen descending into a white-painted brick chamber about five yards wide and six long.

Hutchins writes that when the Calcraft vault was made in 1772, many bones had to be removed from under the altar, along with a coffin containing a body wearing gloves and a belt, perhaps that of a medieval Prior. (Some of the bones were used to fill the Stoborough causeway).

Against the far wall, that is to say more or less under the centre of the church, lie three simple brick tombs one on top of the other, each separated by a layer of flat stones. On the ground in front of these is another, the brickwork of which appears possibly to be more recent. To the visitors it all seemed strangely neat and clean. Overcome by the eeriness of the occasion, the estate foreman, at this stage, found a reason to leave the vault.

James Ryder, with some boldness, raised the stone lids of the only two accessible tombs. Under the lid of the one nearest the entrance to the vault was revealed a fine dark wooden coffin secured with great brass nails. On its lid a brass plate bore the name 'John Hales Calcraft' some of its engraved lettering still painted black. The tomb at the back and nearest the ceiling revealed a coffin named 'John Hales Montagu Calcraft'; the condition of this coffin too, although placed there in 1868, appeared good.

John Hales Calcraft at his death had been described as 'a moderate Liberal... a supporter generally of Lord Palmerston's policy... (and) in Parliament ranked as a Conservative.' He sat for Wareham from December 1832 until July 1841, and again from April 1857 until 1859 when he retired. He was High Sheriff of Dorset in 1867 and died on 13 March 1880.

Fresh Leaves and Green Pastures

Some glimpses of the last Calcrafts can be gleaned from the notorious book *Fresh Leaves and Green Pastures* published in 1909. The author, Jane Ellen Panton, was the daughter of the well-known Victorian artist W.P. Frith, who painted 'Derby Day' and other closely-observed portrayals of contemporary life. Although most real names are altered or omitted in the book, several reviews easily identified the target as being Dorset, and in August of 1909 Captain Guy Montagu Marston, R.N., (the son of Katherine Calcraft and the Rev. C.D. Marston) *[see Plates 24, 33]* began to take action for libel. This came at a sad time for the author, being the year of her father's death and a short time after one of her sons had been 'found dead on the Cornish coast with his hands manacled'. These details did not deter the outraged squirearchy, and Bond and Mansel supported Marston of Rempstone in the hounding of their quarry – 'that vulgar woman'. The surviving legal correspondence reveals an unpleasant vindictiveness and unscrupulousness on the part of some of Marston's advisers. The only libel alleged was that Marston (who is not named in the book) had, on inheriting Rempstone from his uncle William Calcraft in 1901, destroyed historically valuable documents – hardly a libel worth troubling about in comparison to what the earlier Calcrafts had to contend with at the hands of Junius, George Anne Bellamy and the *Town and Country Magazine*. Mrs Panton's actual words in the book (page 27) are:

Stores which were ruthlessly burned in the stable-yard of the mansion when the grandson came into possession, could not afford to live there, and in this manner disposed of priceless historical records, because the house was to be let furnished, and he had neither time nor wish to go through the multitudinous documents which filled every available place.

In the elaborately bound memorandum which proudly records the whole affair, Marston's solicitors Meynell and Pemberton note: 'This is the libel on Captain Marston. It is true that he did burn a number of unimportant receipted bills, letters, and circulars but before doing so he went carefully through them... what he destroyed was in fact useless rubbish'. Marston adds in the margin that he also burned 'old cheque books, accounts, bank books, newspapers, tracts, drawings that I and my brother made at school' and he crosses out the words 'and he (i.e. Marston) can swear that no document was more than 40 or 50 years old'.

With Marston at the time of the burning was his sister Katherine Marston and his agent Edward Clark. The latter's son, Harry Clark, inherited some interesting letters of the nineteenth century, which he believed may have been given to his father at this time. Certainly, there is a remarkable paucity of Calcraft family documents surviving in Dorset; all that really is available today, are books, deeds and some official papers. One might have expected a great deal more letters, political memoranda and personal items.

Marston duly obtained damages of £250, costs, published apologies and the withdrawal and pulping of all unsold copies of the book. In some bitter final letters to Marston, the publisher, James Eveleigh Nash writes:

The author and sufferer for the libel in question is an elderly broken lady, whose health has been shattered by the recent tragic death of her favourite son... Your indignation regarding the accusations made against your grandfather did not prevent you, I repeat, from taking steps to go into Court to publish to all the world, what could only have been recognised by about a dozen people, and that is where your attitude is quite unconvincing.

The one outstanding benefit of this libel action is that it has helped to identify the Dorset characters mentioned anonymously in the book. In this respect it has been useful. The book itself is a colourful collection of tittle-tattle and probably incorporates much of the best Purbeck gossip of the second half of the nineteenth century. Jane Panton is quite capable of showing kindness and admiration for those she writes about, and the solicitors' notes confirm that much of what she describes is true to life.

In two sections of the book there are descriptions of the Calcrafts: in Chapter II Panton writes that there used to be 'about seven county families which ruled the place; all more or less kind, if they had their own way; all more, not less, condescending to the townsfolk'. She rather laments the passing of the old fashioned squires and complains that most of the big houses (identified by Edward Clark as Rempstone, Tyneham, Encombe, Smedmore and Egliston) are unoccupied or let to strangers. The situation facing the local gentry sounds more adverse in 1909 than it does today. She says of the Calcraft family:

One of the families, now vanished entirely – not one member of the large family I recollect being alive at the moment – had in its time made a considerable part of the history of England; and among my many regrets for the wasted opportunities I had, had I only recognised them; is one for the manner in which I did not avail myself as I could have done of the stores of history pushed away in the desks and drawers of that house.

I have never seen a handsomer family in my life than that special one. The mother [Lady Caroline Calcraft] was tall and stately, moved in the most beautiful manner, and spoke in a low, musical voice; and she was one of the most militant and fervent old-fashioned Protestants I have ever met. The house [Rempstone] was about six miles from a very small station, and lay in a hollow behind some hills covered with beautiful plantations sacred to pheasants and game of all sorts and kinds, and the house itself faced a little-used road. But despite this fact, a second road was sacred to the house itself, and on this no one was supposed to drive, unless one had business at the Squire's. The upper road was public only. Now there are gates added to the lower road to keep folks away. In the old times these were not necessary; we knew our place and kept it, and would no more have driven on the lower road than we would have flown.

In the lawyer's brochure Marston writes, opposite the description of Lady Caroline: 'She was exceedingly religious; the Bible was always by her side.'

The Squire himself [John Hales Calcraft] was one of the most magnificent old men that I have ever seen, and I should think had given his wife cause for anxiety in the days of old; and indeed at the present time one can recognise his brilliant eyes and magnificent hair and build in many a person round who has never heard his name; and the daughters and sons of the house were one and all good to look at. The three sons [John Hales Montagu Calcraft, William Montagu Calcraft and Henry George Calcraft] never married; all the daughters did, however [Katherine married the Rev. Charles Marston,

Susan Charlotte married Lord Radstock and Georgiana Emily married Dudley Henry Ryder]; *and one can only wonder how they found husbands, for they never seemed to leave home, or to have many people there, though no doubt the sons brought home friends who were kept out of the sight of the townsfolk. Yet how this was managed I do not know, as every one who went to the house must have come to the station and been driven the whole six miles in the great landau, which, painted to imitate basket-work, was one of the carriages we never failed to see on the weekly market-days.*

Opposite the phrase 'and the daughters and sons of the house were one and all good to look at', Marston writes: 'this passage also is true – see photographs'. Panton goes on:

When I was first married that stately carriage turned up our lane and brought the owner to call; and as I was out a message was left bidding me to return the call on a certain day. Not being accustomed to such ways, I swore and declared I would do nothing of the kind, but I was persuaded to go, and found the stately lady at her stateliest in one of the most arid drawing-rooms I have ever been in. The room was large and well proportioned, and possessed six windows, each window being provided with a skimpy pair of red rep curtains; the furniture was in holland covers bound with red braid, no doubt concealing beauties I for one never saw; the carpet was green, with large red roses all over it. There were a few ornaments about, a clock, and some engravings of portraits of the family and other local celebrities; but there was not a book, not a flower, not a plant, and her ladyship sat very upright by the fire, sparkling in its steel grate; tatting, her foot in a species of stirrup, and her pale long fingers twisting the thread as she endeavoured to find some common ground on which we could meet.

The lawyers here comment: 'the coldness of Lady Caroline's reception of a vulgar woman like Mrs Panton has rankled in the latter's mind and is the cause of the libel'.

I think I must have appeared to her somewhat as a savage appears to the discoverer of a strange island, for I naturally had not one single thing in common with her, nor had she with me. She tried local topics, of which I knew nothing, gardening, of which I was then profoundly ignorant, and finally fell back upon religion, which I suppose she imagined was all alike and not to be argued about, as she was much surprised that I knew Colenso and had read 'Essays and Reviews'. This brought us on a little, but when she remarked quite calmly that she could not understand how any one could read the 'unedifying talk of an intoxicated old man', by which she meant the 'Pickwick Papers', we sheered off Dickens, and, having received a tract and an invitation to a prayer-meeting in the near future, we parted, and never met again. Though I constantly saw the men of the family, more especially about election times, and was as constantly asked by them why I never appeared at any of the aforesaid religious ceremonies, at which, by the way, they were most con-spicuously absent.

By the piece about Lady Caroline's disapproval of Charles Dickens, Marston comments: 'This is not unlikely to have been the case.' Edward Clark con-firms that the sons were not religious but that Lady Caroline and her daugh-ters were so; to which Marston adds – 'to a very marked degree'. Clearly, he had suffered from it. Panton continues:

For years and years I saw her driving through the streets in the carriage, grad-ually getting older and older. Her husband died, then her children, until she was left alone with one elderly son; and when she too passed away she was placed in her stupendous coffin by two of the undertaker's men; such poor common folk that she would not have dreamed they could ever have been admitted to her bedchamber to clean it out, let alone to touch her sacred remains. I think if she knew aught of the fact, and realised that she was placed in her last bed by such humble, gnarled hands, she would then have understood what the bitterness of death could be, and recognised that nothing is as humbling as is one's status, after one has left the body to any one who likes to do the last offices for it. Even now I cannot understand why such sac-rilege was allowed.

The lawyers here expostulate – 'this is probably a gross libel' and Marston adds '"sacrilege" seems a grossly libellous word.' He admits he was in the house when she died but notes that he left 'almost as soon as the death was announced.'

Her ladyship died in the room to which she came as a bride nearly seventy years before the day of her death, which occurred when she was ninety-one, and the room was as it was in those days, now over a hundred years ago, for she has been dead nearly twenty years. The bed was an enormous four-post erection, which stood out in the centre of the great room, and was made of beautifully carved oak, and at the head thereof were carved the initials and dates of the different couples who had slept therein, and had gone to their last rest from beneath its sheltering canopy. It was so extremely high from the ground that a set of three steps was used to climb into it, and it was furnished with two separate sets of curtains, one for the summer, of the most marvel-lous Indian chintz, and the other of a dull grey moreen, a stiff fabric never seen now, but which apparently never wore out, for I could put my hand at the moment on portions of this same material that was old when I was born, and which seems as strong and good now as the day on which it was made. The carpet was a good old Brussels, with a large square cut out under the bed, because it was considered healthy in those days for the house-maid to go over it with a damp cloth every morning when she 'did' the room; and I daresay

*the fact that the great bed was made of feathers caused this operation to be nec-
essary. Anyhow, it was done, and the space was hidden from sight by a deep
flounce which went all round the bed, which in its turn served as a regular
dusttrap, or would have done, had not dust been conspicuous by its absence in
that clean country place. It always saddens me to see a similar bed-chamber,
and this one remains even now as it must have been well over a hundred years
ago. In fact, the bed itself is a very great deal older, for I think it was bought
for the first member of the family who built the house, and, leaving his great
business in London, retired to end his days far from town, hoping to found a
race of stalwart men and women that should continue until the world ended.
But it is curious to note how these vast families have died out in the male line,
and how names that should have gone on from father to son have entirely disappeared; and I for one should not blame that daughter's son who went back
to the old cognomen and once more revived the traditions which must always
cling to the very name. It would be a revelation to many nowadays could they
see the enormous wardrobe, the stupendous chest of drawers, and the hideous
washing-stands to be found in such a house; and which point to the fact that
the daintier Chippendale and Sheraton furniture was removed for the last bride
who ever came to the Hall, and replaced by that which still remains precisely
where it was then put. The wardrobe is eight feet long and of solid mahogany,
and all the shelves and linings are of cedar-wood, while the washing-stands are
quite awful, with low backs and furnished with a double set of ware, apparently to hint that dressing-rooms were not needed, and that husband and wife
could never be absent from each other at any moment of the night or day.
Bathrooms, of course were never dreamed of, but these have been placed in the
house now, as without them it would not let at all. Yet, as no young bride has
come to the Hall, the furniture has never been replaced or altered, as it has only
been let to bachelors for the shooting. Because even in these days of motors few
women would consent to live in such an out-of-the-way spot, the arid drawing-
room is still arid, and what life is in the place is centred in the great untidy
hall, the library and dining-room, and the gaunt bed-chambers, with their vast
beds and their out-of-date carpets and gear. I often wonder where the big landau has gone, or if it is mouldering in the coach-house. I have never heard of
its being sold; if it were I trust it has long since been broken up for firewood. I
should not like to think of that stately vehicle filled to over-flowing by Bank
Holiday people at half a crown an hour; rather let it stand idle, falling gently
to pieces in its old home, standing where it stood when it returned from the
funeral of the last son of the house [William], who ought to have married and
continued the family history, but who never did, no one could think why. No
stories hung to his name as they did to those of his forebears; he was a gentle,
melancholy, unambitious man, much loved, much looked up to; but greatly
concerned with his health, which need not have troubled him had he gone out
into the world more and lived more away from the solitary place where he was
born, and lived, if living it could be called, and where he died, not very long
after his very old mother passed peacefully away.*

Marston's lawyer, Pemberton, comments beside the portrayal of John Hales Calcraft: 'this is a true description of Mr J.H. Calcraft the grandfather of Captain Marston but the statement as to his causing his wife jealousy and being the father of numerous bastards is a gross libel'. The description of William Calcraft is also said to be 'very good' and Marston underlines the phrase 'much looked up to' and comments – 'this is particularly true. He was High Sheriff for the County in 1898 and took an active part in all local affairs'. Panton mentions a landau. In fact John Calcraft's town coach of about 1820 survived at Rempstone until 1950 when it was sold, ending up in the collection of Lord Oranmore and Browne in Ireland.

Jane Panton first visited Wareham in 1858, according to her own testimony, and at this time she would have been a girl aged ten. In 1869 she married James Panton of Wareham and lived there for many years while her husband (according to her publisher) was one of the Calcrafts' political agents. The Pantons had probably been on good terms with the Calcrafts for years and they are recorded in the Game Book as being sent presents of hare and partridge.

The Calcrafts, having been Whigs (with a few short-lived deviations towards the Tory party, such as Crafterio's flirtation with Pitt in the late 1760's, and his son's short sojourn in Wellington's Cabinet), became in due course members of Gladstone's Liberal party, which developed out of the Whigs in the 1860s. The Calcrafts' Tory opposition at Wareham was usually a member of the Drax family and, in particular, John Sawbridge (1800–1887), who married a Drax and took his wife's surname. This Drax was MP for Wareham for almost forty years from 1841, except for two short Calcraft interruptions (John Hales 1857–59 and John Hales Montagu 1865–68). Jane Panton's earliest memory is probably of John Hales' electoral defeat in 1859. On the next occasion it was Drax's turn to lose. But old Drax won the next two elections in 1868 and 1874, losing in 1880 for the last time.

Elections and nominations in those days were great sporting occasions, with a good deal of violence accompanying them. Wareham politics were particularly fierce since Drax was a bold and bloody-minded reactionary and Dorset had been an area of terrible poverty in the 'hungry forties'. Furthermore, as we have seen, Purbeck had sustained in his later years the 'Geordie' John Scott, Lord Eldon (1751–1838) *[see Plate 10]*, one of the leaders of the arch-conservative faction that had opposed the Reform Bills. As an oppressive Lord Chancellor he had been one of the most unpopular men in the country: the relationship between him and the reforming John Calcraft, who turned against even the moderate Tories to vote for the Bill in 1831, can only be imagined. Encombe and Rempstone represented the two opposite political poles of the squirearchy and it is comforting to think that the Calcrafts stood for progress and humanity in the local struggle. Not only did John Drax represent a far right-wing position politically he was also controversial in his personal life. Indeed Jane Panton describes Drax as the 'Wicked Squire'. She says of him:

...a man who might have come straight out of a penny dreadful, and whose existence would, I should think, be quite impossible in these days, for surely some journalist would have slain him with his pen, and pilloried his doings in many a paragraph. He was an old man when I knew him forty years ago, but he looked as evil as any Mephistopheles could look, and his language was as revolting as his manners and customs. He had inherited large estates from his wife, who soon died, leaving him two daughters, to whom the property was to go should they marry. This would not, naturally, have suited his book at all, and they were kept in strict seclusion, but somehow the younger managed to make acquaintance with a neighbour's son; they eloped out of the library window and married. The Squire had to give up her share of the property, and he kept the elder sister closer and closer, until she became a melancholy wreck, and took to winding all the clocks, to mark the passing of the sorrowful hours, so that they should never be an instant different from each other. Then she never went out except to church, where she sat in the square pew that she would never allow to be cleared out of the chancel (she was lay rector) – or improved in any way. Indeed, her interest in the church once took the embarrassing form of cleaning and repainting it in such a manner that it resembled a music-hall more than a grave place of worship, and all were thankful when the decorations faded and were replaced at her death by others more in keeping with the sacred building. I always wondered how much truth there was in the stories told of this especial man. I have heard, when he owned the hounds, that his servants hunted in white satin breeches; that money and wine flowed like water; that he breakfasted at dinner-time and dined in the middle of the night; that the many lodges round the estate each held a fair and frail friend, and at the end a broken heart; that he scourged the lads with his hunting-whip whom he found picking the snowdrops in February in the Park, and that finally he built himself a mausoleum, which he kept warmed because he did not want the place to be damp when his time came to be placed there. Finally he had a grand rehearsal of his funeral one wet day when he had nothing much to do, and was found by his agent swearing profusely, because the tall gamekeepers entrusted to carry the coffin could not keep step, and so would shake his corpse uncomfortably when it was placed therein. About all these items I can say nothing personally, except about the denizens of the lodges; some of those at least owed their fall to the 'wicked Squire', while I quite well recollect the hurry the village mothers were in to get their girls away from home and into decent service before the Squire realised they were pretty and grown up, less they too should find themselves an object for his attention and be found a place under the housekeeper at the Hall. What a cruel tyrant he was, too, to the wretched tenant-farmers. But more of that in another chapter, as I saw specimens of that side of his character myself. As I also heard samples of his language; once when he fell over a croquet-hoop on the lawn, when he was endeavouring to get a promise of a vote out of a man who had never voted for him, and never would. The last time was when

the poll was declared after an election that saw his back turned on the town, for his name was at the bottom. So he solemnly cursed the place and people, and, ordering his carriage, told his coachman at the top of his voice to drive him to a locality, where, if it exist, he is at the moment no doubt paying some of his many, many debts. 'I will die with MP on my coffin', he used to swear, but when he died the letters were not there, and the borough he had bullied and coerced for years had ceased to return a representative to Parliament, and had been merged into one of the four quarters of the county.

Opposite these powerful statements Edward Clark, so quick to deny the veracity of any slight criticisms made of Calcraft or Marston, makes approving comments. Beside the Mephistopheles paragraph he writes – 'This is perfectly true', elsewhere stating – 'Depicted here is the late Mr Drax who lived at Charborough Park, Wareham, and was the owner of a considerable landed property. The description of him is pretty correct. I knew him personally... the description of Mr Drax and the anecdotes recorded about him on this and the next page are correct in detail'. The story about Drax ordering his coachman to drive him to hell is endorsed by Guy Marston with the following words – 'Lady Caroline Calcraft has told Capt. Marston this story many times'.

Let Mrs Panton describe the Calcraft and Drax saga in her own colourful way:

Before the days of the ballot canvassing was a much easier matter than it is now. At the time of the first election I recollect the interests of both parties were so equally divided that the votes of the 'heath-croppers' and a few independent men in the town were enough to turn the election. The 'heath-croppers' were generally favourable to the man who came first and invested in whatever they may have made up their minds to sell. The others could neither be moved nor bribed; though they could be and were made most uncomfortable for some few months after the election by the man for whom they did not vote, and for whom they never had the smallest idea of voting, were they canvassed and cultivated never so wisely. The Liberal side was naturally the unpopular side, though one of the Squires [Calcraft], being of the old Whig persuasion, called himself Liberal, and endeavoured to act up to the name. He, of course, could not be ostracised by his peers, but his followers were; and I always admired the men who stuck up for the cause they believed to be right. Not only did they sometimes drop out of the shooting parties that made the autumn and winter months a joy to them, but their women-folk were not wanted at the big houses. A man who had his own shooting and a certain number of staunch friends of his own class did not care; but the women did. I think it speaks well for both sexes that the men never wavered in their allegiance to the Liberal party. They did suffer for conscience' sake in a way that sounds puerile enough, but that made an enormous amount of difference to the social life of the ladies of their families at any rate.

The race then was to have the heath-croppers' vote, and many wiles were resorted to, to get these men to commit themselves to one of the two parties, in some way that would ensure a victory. I recollect quite well at the first election my uncle [one of Calcraft's agents] *adding up the votes night after night, the dubious votes even at the end of the canvassing being enough to turn the election; and he was somewhat comforted by hearing that the other side had marked as doubtful the very same votes that he had marked too. When we reached the red house the market square* [in Wareham] *was simply packed and crammed with folks of all sorts and sizes. We were just opposite the hustings, which in those days were put up outside the old Town Hall, and were in front of the place where criminals were detained until they could be dealt with by the magistrates. As this was immediately under the clock-tower, being 'put under the clock' was a delicate way of breaking the news of his fate to the family of the offender against the laws. Here the stocks were always kept, but I do not remember their ever being used in my day to punish the unhappy prisoners, though I am inclined to believe that there are worse ways of dealing with orchard thieves, wife-beaters, and other disagreeable criminals than this mild detention before the mocking eyes of their friends and relations!*

In those bygone days the nomination day was generally the most exciting, if the most useless one, of the two days set apart to determine the winner of the fray. As a poll was invariably demanded by the candidate who was not satisfied with the show of hands (which said show was always a farce), the nomination day was a mere waste of time, although it was an entertaining spectacle for those who looked on behind the safe shelter of a good plate-glass window. As I remarked before, we always arrived early on the scene, but even then the market square was a seething mass of riotous humanity, while prominent amongst the crowd were two enormous men, one armed with a great stake, the other clad in a venerable Militia uniform, which I suppose he imagined gave him a certain amount of authority and importance.

Presently the candidates themselves hove in sight. The Squire from the north [Drax] *rode in at the head of his vassals. The labourers were accommodated in waggons decked with blue ribands, and the great horses were wreathed also in the Tory colours. The farmers as a rule rode splendid animals, for they were one and all ardent huntsmen, while yet more horses were bestridden by the Squire's neighbours and even the clergy did not disdain a place in his train. The Squire from the south* [Calcraft] *had a vast following in his turn, but it as a rule consisted of a large and dangerous crowd of pitmen from the neighbouring clay-works, who were one and all spoiling for a fight. The appearance of the candidates and their supporters on the hustings was the sign for the most appalling noise to be started. In vain the candidates, their proposers and seconders, endeavoured to make themselves heard; if there were a moment's cessation of the groans and cheers the two men mentioned before howled out a continuous chant of 'Our Squire for iver; throw t'other in the river'.*

Plate 1
John Calcraft MP, (1726–1772), the founder of the dynasty. Known to his friends as Honest Jack and his enemies as 'Crafterio', he was a close political confidant of first, Henry Fox and then of William Pitt.

He bought Rempstone in 1757 and died one of the richest men in the country. He had, it has been said, 'the makings of a modern dictator'.

Plate 2
Henry Fox, Lord Holland (1705–1774), by Hogarth. Fox is believed to have been John Calcraft's father. They worked closely together.

Plate 3
Georgiana Bellamy, actress. She starred with Garrick and lived nearly ten years with John Calcraft.

Plate 4
David Garrick, the father of modern theatre, who became Calcraft's friend after calling off their duel.

Plate 5
Sir Philip Francis (1740–1818), Calcraft's friend and Junius co-conspirator.

Plate 6
William Pitt, the Elder. John Calcraft became his right-hand man.

Plate 7
The Marquis of Granby, national hero and friend of John Calcraft, painted by Reynolds circa 1760.

Plate 8
John Calcraft the Younger (1765–1831), son of John Calcraft and the actress Elizabeth Bride, painted by Richard Cosway, circa 1785.

Plate 9
Rt Hon John Calcraft MP the Younger as Paymaster General in 1830 – the year before his throat was cut.

Plate 10
John Scott, the Ultra-Tory first Lord Eldon, who bought Encombe in 1807. His policies were entirely opposed to those of Calcraft, his neighbouring landowner.

Plate 11
Arabella Calcraft, circa 1825, who found her father with his throat cut.

Plate 12
Dudley Ryder, Earl of Harrowby (1762–1847), refused to be Prime Minister, but helped to secure the Great Reform Act after his friend Calcraft's macabre death in 1831.

Above left: **Plate 13**
John Hales Calcraft MP; crayon by K.W. Wilkin, 1823.

Above: **Plate 14**
John Hales Calcraft MP (1796–1880), the son of John Calcraft the Younger. He was considered more handsome than Lord Byron. He married Lady Caroline Montagu in 1828.

Left: **Plate 15**
John Hales Calcraft MP in old age; print c.1870.

Right: **Plate 16**
Princess Pauline Bonaparte, who had an
affair with John Hales Calcraft in Paris
in the early 1820s.

Below: **Plate 17**
The daughters of the 4th Duke of
Gordon painted in 1783 by W. Smith.
Three of them married dukes. Lady
Caroline Calcraft's mother, Susan, in the
centre of the back row, married the 5th
Duke of Manchester.

Right: **Plate 18**
Susan, Duchess of Manchester, holds
her daughter, the future Lady Caroline
Calcraft. Susan eloped with a footman.

Plate 19
Lady Caroline Montagu (1804–1892) aged 23. She married John Hales Calcraft in 1828.

Plate 20
The back view of Lady Caroline Calcraft painted about 1840. She refused to sit for any other portraits until old age.

Above: **Plate 21**
Lady Caroline in old age in her upstairs sitting room.

Right: **Plate 22**
Lady Caroline at Rempstone in her eighties. There has had to be an exorcism of her ghost.

Plate 23
The handsome John Hales Montagu Calcraft MP (1831–1868), Lady Caroline's eldest son, died unmarried.

Plate 24
The beautiful Katherine Calcraft, Lady Caroline Calcraft's eldest child (1830–1879), painted by Weigall, about 1855. She was the mother of Guy Montagu Marston.

Plate 25
Sir Henry Calcraft (1836–1896), Lady Caroline's youngest son, later Permanent Secretary at the Board of Trade, died unmarried. Portrait by Weigall.

Plate 26
Some of the Rempstone servants, c.1880.

Plate 27
Combined Ryders and Calcrafts at Rempstone, c.1880.

Plate 28
William Calcraft (1834–1901), John Hales Calcraft and Lady Caroline's second son, the last Calcraft Squire of Rempstone, died unmarried. Photographed in 1898.

Left: **Plate 29**
Watercolour of Daisy Waldegrave and her friend Bex Wilberforce, with Rempstone in the background, c.1880.

Below: **Plate 30**
Dudley Henry Ryder and his sons by his wife Georgy (née Calcraft), circa 1900. Lady Isobel Douglas Hamilton married Cyril (third from left, seated).

Plate 31
Georgiana-Emily ('Georgy') Calcraft (1832–1915), John Hales and Lady Caroline's second daughter, who married Dudley Henry Ryder in 1857.

Plate 32
Douglas, 13th Duke of Hamilton, pictured at Studland c.1900. His sister, Isobel, was Jack Ryder's mother.

Plate 47
Vee Cook dressed for presentation at Court, 1922. She married Jack Ryder in 1938.

Plate 48
Vee Ryder with Simon, at Rempstone, 1939.

Plate 49
Vee Ryder with the combined Ryder and Hamilton-Fletcher children at Rempstone in January 1942, just before the Army took over the house.

Plate 50
Prince George Chavchavadze, Vee's lifelong friend. A great raconteur.

Plate 51
Jack Ryder and two granddaughters, Tamsin and Polly Winser, in the Drawing Room at Rempstone in 1962.

Plate 52
Major D.C.D. 'Jack' Ryder J.P., circa 1975. Quite a stickler for discipline and self-discipline.

Plate 53
Jack Ryder, with granddaughter Emily, dressed for a wedding in 1981.

Plate 54
James Calcraft Dudley Ryder, Squire of Rempstone 2005.

Plate 55
John Hales and Lady Caroline Calcraft's thrice great granddaughter, Lara Manningham-Buller (née Ryder) with her son, Ludovic, who now live at Rempstone.

Plate 56
Rempstone Hall, from the south, as it is today with Lower Rempstone (in the centre), built in 1790, fully exposed to view. Upper Rempstone (on the left) was originally a sixteenth and seventeenth century building.

Marston here comments: 'Calcraft for ever, Drax in the river'.

But as a rule it was utterly impossible to hear a word of either speech. Finally some of the clay-pit rout thrust dolls on long sticks into the face of the northern Squire [Drax], meaning to draw attention by these means to his well known amatory adventures, while a couple of other dissentients cast loaves of bread in his face. His sayings about dear food and his dealings with his farmers were well known; and as one of his favourite remedies for the supposed lack of prosperity among the landowners and farmers was a tax on wheat; and a return to Protection was his panacea for all ills, these sentiments had naturally made him more than usually unpopular, with the lower classes at any rate. In those bygone days the poor recollected too well what Protection meant, to be deluded into voting for a man who advocated returning to the bad old times once more. Not that the very poor had a vote; all the same they could and did make a most tremendous noise, which increased every moment. Presently the crusty half of a loaf flew straight against the window of the Town Hall, which it smashed, and a most fearful row ensued. The farmers, armed with their heavy hunting-crops, rushed from the hustings and struck out right and left. The clay-pit men retaliated; but they were not in full force, and they were soon rapidly getting the worst of it. Indeed, the two big men were being thrust out of the town, when a batch of about thirty of their friends was seen rushing in over the bridge, waving huge palings which they had seized as they came along, and breathing fire and slaughter; and all bid fair to murder each other, when fortunately the gigantic police inspector and his constables turned out. The clay-pit men were rather more than 'half-seas over'; the stout inspector and his men went behind them; and while the inspector clasped their arms behind their backs one by one, the constables disarmed them; and prominent men on the pink and blue sides respectively intervened and persuaded the belligerents to cease warfare until the day of the poll at all events.

It was entirely due to the fact that the clay-pit men had announced that if the pinks wished it, the blues should never enter the town that blood was not really shed in quarts. Early in the morning they had refused to work as usual and were arming for the fray, when news came into the town of what they intended to do. One of the pinks went off on his pony and met them coming in; by judicious cajolement and promises of free beer he distributed the men over an area of about four or five miles on the southern side, and kept them well occupied. They had become almost quiet, when women tore out from the town screaming that the blues were murdering their comrades. Then nothing would hold them, and if the blues had not departed at once there is no doubt that most serious riots would have taken place. As it was the pinks contented themselves by smashing every pane of glass in the blue hotel [Red Lion]: which, by the irony of fate, belonged to the most prominent Liberal in the town [Calcraft]: and by smacking the heads of any blues left in the place who had sufficient hardihood to show themselves in the public streets.

When the day of the poll came the excitement grew every moment. In those days the state of the poll was shown from hour to hour by numbers on boards hung on the hustings, and the agents flew about from place to place counting up votes, and looking up absentees and bringing them in, to write their names down, or put their marks under the eagle eye of the returning officer.

Our colour being pink, my aunt had decked us all out in oleanders that she had grown and carefully cultivated for the occasion. But her efforts at decoration were eclipsed by one frantic adherent to the cause, who promenaded the town clad in a full costume of pink. Pink shiny cotton stuff formed the many-flounced crinoletted dress; pink feathers waved in the pink hat; and the waving of a pink parasol led the cheers when the pink Squire [Calcraft] headed the poll, and retired meekly into temporary obscurity when the blue man [Drax] went ahead and our hopes fell to freezing-point.

The poll closed then at four o'clock, and at three we reluctantly discovered that every known vote was recorded save and except the doubtful seven, who had not been seen or heard of. Messengers both blue and pink were despatched hot-foot, and the blue man was beginning to look most disagreeably triumphant. The clay-pit men went for the farmers, and the farmers and even the gentry joined in the fray; even my beloved 'Idstone' of the Field *flew to the rescue of a small blue farmer, and used his fists to such excellent effect that he rescued the man at once, and left the clay-pit man amazed at such a display of 'muscular Christianity'. Still the time went on, and the seven voters were still absent. The moments crept by. If they turned up and voted pink the Liberal was in by a bare majority of five; if blue, the state of the poll would still be in the northern Squire's favour. But just before the time a carriage came galloping into the market square, and out the seven tumbled; and as all to a man voted pink our candidate was in; and the fearful noise that ensued will never be forgotten by any one who ever heard it. It turned out that the blue agent, having been driven to despair by the vacillation of the seven, had inveigled them out to an island in the estuary known as Horse Island, where horses were taken to be out at grass. He knew that, deprived of this unknown quantity, the election was safe as far as his side was concerned; and after inspecting a horse or two that these men had for sale, he had made for the boat and left them on the island cursing. They were safe there until the tide turned at least, and by then the election would be over and won. Unfortunately the noise the prisoners made was heard by some fishermen in the harbour; they came to their rescue, and the men were brought off in time to punish the agent by voting as they never intended to do, until he played them this dastardly trick.*

The declaration of the poll was followed by another free fight, until some one persuaded the Squire and his escort to depart. And lucky for them they went. The last man had scarcely vanished before the whole of the clay-pit men rushed into the town, breathing fire and slaughter. At last nightfall brought peace; the last of the belligerents were interned 'under the clock', and all were frankly delighted that the day was over.

The next election was somewhat remarkable by reason of the fact that some of the more particular members of the County had revolted against the yoke of the northern Squire [Drax], and had provided themselves with a candidate of their own [Montagu Guest]. One or two of the landowners put up weird structures in the meadows to give their servants votes who were outside the borough; but the northern Squire put up two to their one on the other side of the town, and still hoped to win. That he did not was owing to the fact that the Tory vote was split. But I do not recollect much about that election, and I do not think I was there on the day, though I saw a good many of the election squibs, and was mightily amused by most of them.

The Tory headquarters was a pub owned by the Calcrafts (the Red Lion), while the Calcraft supporters met in an inn owned by a Tory (the Black Bear). Jane Panton describes dining on election night with J.H.M. Calcraft and Georgy and Dudley Ryder, in 1865. They were all expecting defeat:

I wended my weary way home to look after my dinner, to which the candidate, his sister and brother-in-law and other folks were coming. Now our candidate, though a Liberal, [J.H.M. Calcraft] was the grandson of a duke, and his relations were likewise gorgeous folk, and I had that dinner very much on my mind. I went upstairs, and, meeting the governess, I remarked, 'I believe we have failed after all our trouble.' 'I always thought you would,' she replied with a sniff, and passed on with her charges into the schoolroom.

My table looked beautiful, and my good little cook assured me my dinner was quite all right, and I proceeded into the drawing-room in fair spirits. We were half-way through a most successful feast, and only half-way, when suddenly the most appalling turmoil that was ever heard burst on our astonished ears. The ballotboxes had been brought in from the outlying stations with unexampled speed; the votes had been counted; we were ahead by, I think, twenty-four votes; and all the town, Conservative as well as Liberal, appeared to have emptied itself into our house and garden. One man stood on a chair waving a napkin round his head; another helped himself to a glass of wine, of which he stood sorely in need; while yet a third fell prone into an armchair, and had to be fanned and given brandy before he recovered his normal state of health.

By the way, that election saw the last appearance of the Tory Squire [Drax] in the place. He came out on the porch of the inn to make his farewell speech after the declaration of the poll, but when he was received with derisive yells and screams by the victorious party he turned green with rage; paused for a minute to obtain silence, and then solemnly and completely cursed the town and the inhabitants thereof in the most appalling manner possible. Then he called for his coachman and told him to put in his horses and drive him straight to the warmest locality known. The man looked amazed, and faltered out that he did not know the way; but the Squire, with another loud oath, swore he would soon show him, and banged into the carriage, and the last thing seen of him was the fist he was indignantly shaking at every house and person he passed. He never stood again for the borough; education, the ballot, the advance of knowledge, all were against him; and the Conservatives knew that they must bring forward some one quite different, or the borough would remain a Liberal stronghold for the rest of its days.

It does seem that the Wareham elections were exceptionally violent and corrupt, even by the standards of the day. As late as 1857 Drax, the unsuccessful Tory candidate, petitioned against the election of John Hales Calcraft. A Select Committee of the House of Commons supported the election of Calcraft but found that bribery of voters had taken place on both sides. The Committee named Calcraft's man William Joseph Pike as the main villain of the piece, but acquitted Calcraft of any knowledge of the bribery. The coercion and bribery used by Pike took the form of securing votes for Calcraft by promises to reduce rents or to write off rental arrears or by threats of loss of employment. Drax's agents, John Meadon and William Best, used more direct methods: for example, they paid William Bridle, a natural Calcraft voter, five pounds to be in Portsmouth on the day of the election.

Jane Panton's now unobtainable book *Fresh Leaves and Green Pastures* is full of interesting stories. She tells, for example, how she knew an old lady who claimed to have seen Napoleon land at Lulworth reconnoitering for a possible invasion site; the sort of rumour that might well have increased the recruitment in Calcraft's yeomanry. She recounts how she attended the excavation of a barrow and the discovery of a perfect burial urn; the lack of comment by Marston suggests that if this was a barrow near to Rempstone then he had not heard of the opening of it. She tells of the quarreymen's peppercorn rent:

At one time the quarriers had the privilege of coming down from the quarries straight to the sea; I think on Easter Monday; and kissing every woman they met. Civilisation and the advent of the policeman have put an end to that custom, but still they meet on Easter Monday at the town where the old charter used to be kept. Here the new freemen 'take up their freedom' and keep open their right of way to the water by kicking a football from the top of the castle hill to the quay [Ower], where nowadays the clay is shipped on its outward journey towards Staffordshire. A pound of pepper had to be paid as a quit-rent to the lord of the manor [Calcraft], who safeguarded yet other rights he had, by receiving a pepper-corn as rent from one of his tenants, who had to bring it himself to the manor accompanied by a one-eyed dog! When this unfortunate beast could not be found, a compromise was effected by tying a handkerchief over the eye of an ordinary dog; he could then only see out of one eye, and therefore answered enough to the description of a one-eyed dog for the purpose; at any rate in these very prosaic days of ours; which, by the way, are so prosaic that I daresay the one-eyed dog tradition has been given up, and the lord of the manor contents himself with the pepper-corn. I wonder why he had that pound of pepper as well as the pepper-corn? In seems a curious article to present to any one even as a quit-rent. I believe at one time the whole of London was paved from that district, just as many of the finest cathedrals have specimens of the local marble; but the trade is 'not what it was'; and at any rate one can sit on the shore nowadays, and know nothing at all about what was once the 'raison d'etre' of the little place [Ower Quay].

Jane Panton might be pleased to know that the squire of Rempstone still receives this peppercorn rent, although one-eyed dogs have been rare in recent years. Panton also tells a story of how the Mansels were almost tricked out of possession of Smedmore by old John Clavell's housekeeper, Elizabeth Churchill, and her daughter, Frances, who forged the old man's will in about 1836. But perhaps Panton's most daring tale concerns an amorous Dorset squire who was in the habit of visiting the very pretty wife of a tenant-farmer:

Some one gave the farmer a hint, and he returned home in the middle of the afternoon. The wife saw him coming, and the Squire had only time to climb up the wide chimney and put himself across the iron from which the pots were suspended over the open hearth. The farmer looked all round the room, saw nothing except his wife very busy, sweeping and dusting and singing, and he explained that he had returned home for a drink. She advised him to go and get it, and as he went into the dairy she saw the Squire's legs were hanging down. Without changing the tune of her song she sang 'Tuck up thee lags, Sir John, Sir John, tuck up thee lags, Sir John', and the unhappy Squire tucked up one and left the other in view, and she had only time to sing out, 'Tuck up the other lag, Sir John, Sir John', before the husband returned, quite satisfied that he had been misled. Then he departed to resume his work, and the Squire descended very black and very irate at the ignominious position, and he never again went after that special farmer's wife. They certainly had fine times in the good old days.

Edward Clark comments opposite this tale: 'This is a story told of Sir John I'Anson, Rector of Corfe Castle, who is reputed to have been a man of easy virtue. Only one life stood between him and the heirship to the Kingston Lacey Estates, and that was a boy, Henry Bankes, whose family took every precaution that he should not be brought into contact with Sir John I'Anson otherwise it was feared Sir John would poison him'.

Jane Panton has some favourites among the gentry. One such, identified by Clark as Lady Selina Bond, wife of Nathaniel Bond of Creech Grange, she describes as 'my dear little lady of the flowing curls and the flitting pony-phaeton'; 'very different' says Panton 'from the stern mistress of the hall' (Lady Caroline). Panton condemns Lady Selina's father-in-law, the Rev.

Nathaniel Bond, however, as 'one of the old fashioned squarsons...squire and rector all in one' and 'deserving of all that the worst Radical could say of their caste. '

Panton also writes about the Scotts of Encombe: – 'It is sad indeed to see the empty shuttered mansion that once teemed with life...here the old man (Lord Eldon) used to come after his fierce Parliamentary fights to rest with his beloved wife and children and with his almost equally beloved dog...'. It seems that in the early 1900s Encombe, Creech, Smedmore and Rempstone were all let to tenants: none had their squires in residence. Leeson House, once lived in by the Stillwell family, Clark notes, is 'now (1909) a girls' school kept by Miss Knight', and the family of Mr W. H. Bond were about to move out of Tyneham.

7

SIR HENRY CALCRAFT

(1836-1896)

Henry George Calcraft [see Plate 25] was the youngest of John Hales Calcraft's three sons. He went to Winchester and then straight into the Board of Trade at the age of sixteen, at a time when Britain was the greatest trading nation the world had ever known. An autobiographical note at the end of a surviving exercise book states:

> Received appointment in Railway Department of Board of Trade on 28 February 1852. Wages £90 per annum. Went there for first time on 1st March 1852.
> January 1853. Go to live at No.26 Upper Grosvenor Street, Grosvenor Sq. (with family). May 1852 go to live at No.99 Piccadilly lodgings. Received an increase of £10 per annum from 1st April 1852. £15 Increase to take place on 1st April 1854...

Henry stayed in the Board of Trade his whole working life until his retirement in 1893. From 1859 to 1874 he was private secretary to a succession of Presidents of the Board of Trade including the great radical John Bright. In 1874, during Disraeli's ministry, he was made head of the Railway Department at the Board of Trade, a post he held until 1886. During these twelve years the Government took an increasingly active part in regulating the affairs of the various railway-companies, laying down guidelines as to safety and efficiency. In a satirical cartoon from *Moonshine* 17 September 1887, Henry Calcraft is portrayed as making special arrangements for 'the unprotected female on the railway', apparently an allusion to the provision of 'ladies-only' compartments. Whether or not Henry was responsible for the introduction of lavatories on trains, or the communication-cord, is uncertain but both have been suggested. Henry's main influence at this time was probably his Department's power to allow or to refuse plans for new lines.

In 1886 his wisdom and efficiency were rewarded by his promotion to non-political head of the whole Board of Trade as Permanent Secretary. This was at the end of the Gladstone era and at the commencement of Lord Salisbury's Conservative Government. Henry was knighted in 1890, retired from his post in 1893 after falling victim to 'the demon typhoid' and became a director of the Suez Canal.

Two years later he spent Christmas with the Duke of Devonshire at

Chatsworth, then paid a visit to his brother William at Rempstone, returned to London, developed signs of pneumonia whilst dining at the Beefsteak Club a few nights later and, on 22 January 1896, quite suddenly died, aged only fifty-nine.

Henry seems to have been a popular public figure of his day; a friendly and elegant bachelor, a 'society swell', but also a hard worker and a discreet confidant. His obituaries in the national papers ring his praises:

For many years Sir Henry was one of the best known and most highly respected among the prominent Civil servants of the Crown, and his connexion with the Board of Trade forms an honourable and useful record of official work gratefully appreciated by the great commercial world in whose interest it was undertaken.'

As a young man his acquaintance lay chiefly in the Old Whig world, but as London society became larger, less exclusive, and less split up into political sections, he changed with the times and was constantly to be seen in the choice circles of all political shades. He was everywhere equally welcome, and his bright sparkling eye and kindly, cheery manner will long be remembered. Such was the man as he appeared in society; his intimates knew that behind all this there were sterling unobtrusive qualities of both head and heart. To his friends he was a true, discreet friend, and no man was more trusted or more frequently consulted in delicate matters requiring sound judgment and tact.

The Prince has lost a dear friend in the person of the late Henry Calcraft, whose death removes from Society one of its most deservedly popular members, and deprives our youthful patricians of their most cherished mentor, adviser, and guide. Everybody loved Harry Calcraft – in fact, it was impossible to do otherwise. But, speaking in a broad and general way, it may be assumed that the two persons who will miss him the most will be the Prince of Wales and the Duchess of Devonshire, for it may safely be averred that neither of these illustrious individuals have, during the past five-and-twenty years, taken many important steps without having previously consulted with, and obtained the advantage of, the shrewd and kindly common sense of Henry Calcraft. But, apart from the Heir-Apparent and the Lady of Chatsworth, there will this coming Season be a legion of people who will deplore no longer having Henry Calcraft to advise them what to do under difficult and delicate circumstances.

Outside of the Board of Trade office, however, Sir Henry Calcraft was anything but a dry official. He was the most fascinating of companions, an envied guest at dinner parties, and was always welcome in the smoking-room, where his frank criticisms on men and things conveyed in the crisp terms that he could not help using, always kept the conversation lively.

Many years ago Mr Delane, the editor of The Times, described Mr Calcraft, as he then was, as one of the most 'acceptable' men in London society. His popularity as a society man was certainly very high; but he was more than that. He was one of the ablest and most diligent of public servants, full of zeal for the work of his department, and untiring in carrying it out.'

Henry had been more than forty years a civil servant. During this period he had served no less than nineteen Presidents at the Board of Trade including Bright, Cardwell,Derby and Dudley Ryder (2nd Earl of Harrowby), becoming in many cases their 'official crammer or coach' and had, apparently, an exceptional knowledge of the politicians of his day. He was clearly on quite good terms with Disraeli (Lord Beaconsfield) and Lord John Russell, and probably was acquainted with Palmerston, Gladstone and Salisbury. An article entitled 'The Last of an old Social School', by T.H.S. Escott, gives some indication of this:

From a box in the Lyceum Theatre, at the very height of his popularity and prestige, Lord Beaconsfield sat watching the best of all melodramas, The Corsican Brothers, as it was played by Mr., still to become Sir, Henry Irving. The Prime Minister's companion was a gentleman at that time bearing in face and figure a noticeable resemblance to the heroes of Thackeray's novels, as seen in the engravings that used to illustrate the monthly parts in which they first appeared. The interest manifested by the audience in the statesman himself was reflected also upon the partner of his box, whose identity, perfectly familiar to the occupants of stalls, may have been unknown generally in the pit and dress circles. His name, however, would have been a household word to all those who, when the play was over, were returning by train to their homes. Even at this late date Henry Calcraft was comparatively a veteran among the officials of the Board of Trade. Nor were there many who could recall any other signature than his appended to the railway notices which flanked the wall just outside the booking office.

If there were one individual seeing, as it were, from a stage-box the evolution of the social drama from day to day, and intellectually qualified to rival Greville as a diarist, that man had for decades been Henry Calcraft. With the exception of Mr Gladstone, England has recently had no Prime Minister nor many high officials of State with whom Calcraft had not lived on terms of intimacy. He was among the few survivors of those to whom during his retirement Lord John Russell's house in Richmond Park, Pembroke Lodge, was always open. Here, or elsewhere, he met those illustrious remnants of a bygone order which have lasted even into these latter times. As a member of Brooks's Club, Henry Calcraft may have been reputed a Whig-Liberal, and possibly, advanced as were some of his views, his Whiggism was not of a much more levelling nature than that of the erstwhile Clerk of the Council. Probably, on most public affairs, he thought and felt after the usual manner of high and seasoned officials in the public service, who believe in vested interests, and who have enjoyed facilities for observing the human gullibility of parliamentary chiefs, from whichever side they may be drawn. Henry Calcraft had also during his vacations studied political life on the Continent from behind the scenes, and could have narrated much more than he ever cared to tell of some very remarkable episodes in the politics at least of France and of Spain.

Another paper states that 'there have been few of the notable political and social events of the last thirty years of which he did not know more than was generally known to others'. Several obituaries report that Henry Calcraft had kept a diary and that this was expected to be published and to be the cause of interesting revelations:

> *'We may soon expect to hear that the contents of Sir Henry Calcraft's note-books are to be prepared for publication. He was rather too free in his method of expressing himself to make that possible during his lifetime, but for some time he has been regarded as one of the shrewdest chroniclers of the Victorian era, and a man whose record of events and estimate of individuals would throw a searching light on many social and political events in which he had taken part.*
>
> *Sir Henry Calcraft's diary should be a work of exceptional value and interest. He has been the chronicler of life and manners in the present period of the Victorian era. Sir Henry was dependent for his social successes almost entirely on his agreeable manner, united with which were rare conversational gifts and a discretion that was never caught napping. He had, however, many influential relatives, among them the Duke of Manchester, so that he had opportunities of studying all sorts ond conditions of men, from the highest to the lowest.*

What has happened to this diary remains a mystery. Its discovery could still be of great historical interest. The Department of Trade and the Public Record Office could find no reference to it in 1975. It seems likely that whichever of his papers were not left at the Board of Trade, came to William Calcraft at Rempstone, as another newspaper clipping suggests:

> *Administration of the estate and effects of Sir Henry George Calcraft, of 101, Mount-street, C.B., for forty years in the Board of Trade, and for seven years Permanent Secretary, a director of the Suez Canal, of the National Telephone Company, and of the London, Chatham, and Dover Railway Company, who died on Jan. 22 last, aged 59 years, intestate, a bachelor, without parents, has been granted to his brother, Mr William Montagu Calcraft, of Rempstone, Dorset, by whom the gross value of the late Sir Henry Calcraft's personal estate has been sworn at £8,012 7s 2d, and the net value at £552 10s 1d.*

The only document resembling a diary which survives is Henry's Winchester exercise book. This contains a few brief jottings of events in 1853-54, and records the outbreak of the Crimean war: 'Declaration of War between England with France and Turkey against Russia: Lord John Russell postpones indefinitely the 2nd Reading of his new Reform Bill. The first forces taken by Sr C. Napier's fleet in the Baltic are 5 merchant vessels laden with salt'.

One of the most interesting essays in this book, dated 3rd July, 1850, while he was still at Winchester, is young Henry's comparison of the Country Gentleman of the sixteenth gentury with that of his own day. We can perhaps glean some idea of the young Henry's view of his own father, Squire John Hales Calcraft of Rempstone:

We should be greatly mistaken, if we were to suppose that the country gentleman of the sixteenth century was at all like the country gentleman of the nineteenth. The 'squire' of the present age, generally receives a superior education, goes to one of the Universities and becomes to a certain degree a scholar. He often travels through most of the countries of the Continent and not unfrequently proceeds as far as India or America. But the Country Gentleman who witnessed the Revolution was an illiterate and badly educated man, most probably had never been to college, had very rarely if ever visited the capital, and certainly had never been out of his native land. The great reason why he lived so much at home was that the expense of moving about from one part of the country to another, was so far greater than it is at present, and on the other hand he was not in the receipt of more than one fourth of the income which his acres now bear to his successors.

The heir of the family passed most of his time with grooms and gamekeepers; and his chief employments were the sports of the field, and in those he certainly excelled. His opinions as they were only derived from tradition, were of course bigoted; he was a Tory, and hated Frenchmen, Welshmen and Irishmen, Papists and Presbyterians, Baptists and Quakers, Jews and Londoners. He was a great drinker and as he was in the receipt of too small an income to buy canary or claret, he drank strong beer in large quantities.

The females of that chap in those days were very much like the housekeepers and cooks of the present time, and were therefore very unlike the refined and graceful beings of the present generation, who are a glory and comfort to all those with whom they have anything to do.

The rural seats of the English Country Gentleman have also undergone a great change during the last three centuries. In 1650 they were little better than the Farm houses of the present day, now they have all the refinements and comforts of the capital combined with the varied delights of the country.

So Henry's idea of a modern (mid Victorian) squire was a man of education and refinement. Like most Calcrafts, Henry was quite a Whig and, indeed, under John Bright's tutelage became even something of a Radical in his younger days.

Henry was buried at Corfe Castle alongside his mother, Lady Caroline Calcraft, who had died in 1892. The service was conducted by Canon Eldon Bankes, and was attended by Henry's brother, William Calcraft, his brother-in-law Dudley Ryder of Westbrook Hay and the latter's two sons Major

Dudley and Captain Cyril Ryder. One small bundle of letters to Henry have survived. Three quarters of these date from the years 1869-71, the vast bulk of them being short friendly notes from John Bright who, although still in office, is quite ill and writing from Rochdale, Llandudno or Scotland. There are also short letters to Calcraft from Hartington, Northbrook, George Duke of Cambridge, Kimberley and one from Gladstone which scarcely seems to be an affair of state:

10 Downing Street,
Whitehall
Ap 15. 69

Dear Calcraft,
The inclosed has been sent me by an acquaintance who assures me that tho'
anonymous, it is bona fide. It is merely an appeal for allowing marriage with
a deceased wife's sister, and requires no acknowledgment.
Yrs.

W.E. Gladstone.

There are a few letters to Milner Gibson (President of the Board of Trade during Palmerston's 1859 Administration) from Gladstone, Argyle and Somerset. Miscellaneous other papers include a letter from Lord Salisbury and two detailed notes on the export of cotton goods (in Bright's handwriting) and concerning the duties on glass imports (probably in Gladstone's hand). The fact that three-quarters of the extant letters are dated from just three years out of Henry Calcraft's long career of over forty years, suggests that only a small fraction of all the letters which he kept have survived.

In one of the Gladstone notes to Gibson he is worrying about 'the question of a duty on transparent soap' and another reads as follows:

11 Downing Street,
Whitehall
March 20.60

My dear Gibson,
I enclose a letter of complaints about the Portuguese Tariff from Mr Sandeman
an eminent member of the wine trade. It would be very well if you could move
the Foreign Office to weigh upon Portugal the duty of amending her ways.
Yours sincerely,

W.E. Gladstone.

However, among the thirty or so letters from John Bright are several of interest. It must be remembered that Bright was the leading Radical of his day, founder of the Anti-Corn Law League in 1845, a great reformer and Gladstone's partner after 1865 in the inspiration of the Second Reform Bill (1867). In a letter from Rochdale the ailing Bright asks Calcraft's advice on whether he must accept an invitation to visit the Queen:

Rochdale
Nov. 14.69
Private

Dear Mr Calcraft,
Is it necessary for me to go to Windsor on Saturday? I did not intend to return to Town before the 6th December, and this invitation is most unexpected and inconvenient...
...I rely on your experience and tact in this matter – and hope to hear from you Tuesday morning.
Yrs sincerely,

John Bright.

Writing from Llandudno 19 May the following year, he refers to a topical political event: 'Thank you for the Ballot Bill – these old and troublesome questions get settled one after another – and we are, in some things, becoming a more rational people.' This was early in Gladstone's first and greatest Ministry of 1868-74; it was the birth of the Liberal party and an unprecedented period of reform. A few months later Bright is still ill and clearly off his food: 'As to the Venison – you may have the gift, if you like, for yourself, or your friends, or for the Heads of the Office Mr. Farrar, Sir L Mallet and – in fact to do what you like with it, and I will pay the fee if you will tell me what it is. The newspapers write and look thunder and lightening – but I hope we are not always rightly re-presented by them.'

The comment about the newspapers probably refers to rumblings in the Balkans between Russia and Turkey. In a letter a week earlier, Bright had referred to the precedent of the Crimean War: 'I am told the Papers are warlike – what is said in "Society" on the Black Sea Question? The Country paid 100 millions and 40 000 lives or nearly so for the Turk 15 years ago – does it want to play the game over again at the same price?'

On 18 December 1870 Bright writes to tell Calcraft that his health has forced him to resign his Presidency of the Board of Trade and he thanks Calcraft for his kindness and assistance. Nevertheless he continues to write to Calcraft, as on 28 February 1871: 'Governments seem always more in danger from their good deeds than from their bad ones – or the House would agree to their Army reform in the main, and reject their reckless waste of public money in the increased Military Estimates. Whenever there is any special news of the interior of the H of C, I shall be glad of a line from you. I am well enough to look on and criticise, tho' not to take part in the fray.'

In due course, Bright did recover his health and political fervour and rejoined Gladstone's Cabinet in 1874. The following year he supported Lord Shaftesbury's move to pass legislation to control vivisection. In 1886 his opposition to Gladstone's plan for Irish Home Rule was a key factor in the fall of Gladstone's Administration, and the allusion in Calcraft's obituaries to his poor relationship with Gladstone may indicate that he continued to be closely allied to Bright, at least socially, and so was affected by this schism between the two veteran reformers. It is sad that further written records of Calcraft's relationship with Bright appear to have been lost.

Henry Calcraft was the last of the male Calcrafts to have been a public figure. Not since the days of his grandfather had a Calcraft cut such a dash in London society and in the government of the country. He was described as 'the moving power' in the Board of Trade. Funeral services were held simultaneously in Corfe and Mayfair. At the latter there were many members of both House of Parliament and wreaths from, among others, the Prince and Princess of Wales, the Duchess of Devonshire, the Roseberys, the Londonderrys and the Rothschilds. Blinds were drawn 'out of respect' in both Wareham and Corfe where the rector, Canon Bankes, officiated, and the chief mourners were William Calcraft, Kate Marston, three Ryders and a Waldegrave. Henry's nickname 'the Hangman' was an allusion to the official flogger and executioner, William Calcraft (1800–1879), a retired butler, who was no relation:

> A society favourite, Sir Henry Calcraft, has died this week, a man who was one of the leaders of the little band of wits whom the Prince gathered around him in his younger days. The late Sir Henry Calcraft – known amongst his intimate friends as the 'Hangman' – entered the Home Office at the early age of seventeen, and he therefore reached, in the natural order of things, a high position much before the time that is generally the case...
>
> ...The death of Sir Henry Calcraft removes one of the best-known figures in the West End in our day.

8

WILLIAM MONTAGU CALCRAFT
(1834-1901)

The last male heir of the Calcrafts was Henry's elder brother William Montagu Calcraft (1834–1901) *[see Plate 28]*. He went up to be educated at Caius College, Cambridge in October 1852 (although according to Burke's Landed Gentry he obtained his B.A. in 1856 when at Trinity College, Cambridge), and became squire at Rempstone after the death of his father John Hales Calcraft in 1880. He was a Justice of the Peace and High Sheriff of Dorset in 1898.

Not much is known of William other than the description of him in Jane Panton's book. But a delightful diary survives, kept by the twelve-year-old William in 1847, and it gives a picture of the leisurely uneventfulness of the life of a little boy born into the privileges and rigours of the early Victorian country gentry.

William's Diary
The Diary itself (*Rees' Improved Diary and Almanack for 1847*, price sixpence) contains interesting printed tables of political, metrical and other information, no doubt considered to be useful for a well educated man. There is a wages table which runs from one to twenty pounds per year. Porterage from Inns is set out in detail... 'parcels by waggon to be delivered within 24 hours, or the innkeeper to forfeit 20s.' Post Office Regulations state 'Letters not exceeding half an ounce, are charged one penny.' There is a list of Sovereigns of Europe and Foreign Ministers. The population of England is 14 995 508, Wales 911 321 and Scotland 2 628, 957. Dorset boasts only 174 743 souls.

Many of the references recorded in William's spidery hand are to Mr Windle. Windle seems to come and go and is very often cross. He was probably William's tutor. On January 16th William writes 'Went to the farm. Mr. Windle cam. I have had very nasty holy day.' During the week of 8th-14th of February quite a lot of snow falls and on the 11th he writes 'Went out made an *enormous* snowball.' On the following day, what must have been a great event occurred – 'Snow. Went to the pond and Windle tumbled in.' Obviously there were disappointingly no serious ill effects from this accident for the next day Windle accompanies William to Bushaw. The cold bath may not, however, have improved Mr. Windle's temper for he seems to have been in an exceptionally bad mood for the remainder of the month. On the 16th, William notes 'Windle very cross xx' and he was in the same frame of mind on the 22nd on a ride to Ower. Indeed, Windle was observed to be still 'xx' on a trip to Agglestone on March 17th. The code 'xx' seems to be necessitated by the risk that Windle might see the diary. Entries stop when 'Windle went away' on 7th April and recommence just before he returns on 6th May, the day before lessons begin again; the diary may well have been an educational exercise in itself. On 31 May, Windle is cross again. 'Fine. Windle very cross. Was to have bathed with him but too cross so did not.' Next day William had a day's holiday – 'no thanks to Windle.' Poor Windle is cross in June as well, and the blank pages of the diary throughout the summer and most of the autumn suggest a welcome seperation for all the parties concerned.

William seems to have little to do with himself in his spare time except to 'ride about the place', shoot at sparrows and rabbits and be moderately blood-thirsty. On 7 January he notes 'Fine, rode with Car to Newton. In afternoon went to farm made bullets with John Macdonald.' A few days later he rides to Challow Wood to see 13 hares and two rabbits 'killed in the net'. The following week he spends a couple of days cleaning 'one brace of pistols.' On the 25th, he goes out shooting with Pappa and kills '20 head of game'. About equal numbers of hares and rabbits are killed in February and at the end of the month he has to make some more bullets. The dogs are several times mentioned and on one occasion he spends all day with the puppies.

Riding expeditions are regularly reported to Corfe, Studland, Bushaw, Foxground Common and 'to Downshay with Papa' and 'to Worth by ourselves'. On March 22nd they visit the Cape of Good Hope; according to Christina Bevan, this was an old name for Devil's Dyke.

The Baillie family are cousins. Lady Georgiana Baillie was a sponsor at the baptism of William's eldest sister Kathy in 1830 and William's first entry in his diary for Jan 1st 1847 is 'Bailies came end of November 1846.' Throughout the ensuing pages there are references to 'Willy Bailie', 'Car B', 'Mary B', 'G.B.' and 'Georgy B'. On 18th Feb. the entry reads 'Showery. Went to the wood and about the place with Car B and Susy C'. The latter is presumably his 14 year old sister Susan Charlotte Calcraft. On March 23rd William records 'Fine. Kathy and Car Baily were confirmed. Went out with Papa.' Another relative is mentioned on 10th November when 'Georgy and Susy went to Southampton to see Aunt Eliza', presumably John Hales Calcraft's eldest sister Elizabeth.

William quite often mentions death and illness. 'Papa had a bad headache' on February 10th and on 11th May, after several days of picking cowslips, Willy has a headache himself. 'Old Shetler died suddenly' on May 21st and 'Old Rolls died suddenly' the very next day.

Despite aches and pains, William's father, John Hales Calcraft manages to get about the country, visiting the neighbouring gentry at Encombe and Crichel. Mr Mansel comes to dinner on February 4th and is at Rempstone the following day to ride to Studland with William. Mamma (Lady Caroline) also pays visits. On 25th May, William goes with her in the pony carriage to visit Major Bridges: 'disliked all 3 children. Boy conceited', he notes. On

June 1st 'the Girls went to Swanage for a week with Madmoissell' and the following Saturday William went to see them there – 'went in the carriage to Swanage with Mamma, had a bath Papa began mourning,' – for whom is not recorded.

An entry which gives quite a clear picture of a day at Rempstone in 1847 is that for May 26th. It reads: 'Fine. Rode to Bushaw in the morning. From two to three went to the wash pond. 3 to 5 did lessons. Half past 5 went missionary meeting in the pony carriage. Came home in the dogcart. Came home at ten.'

Sundays were, of course, especially religious and Willy records going to church sometimes 'both times' to "hear Wood preach.'

Towards the end of the year William gets less meticulous in diary-keeping, perhaps because of Windle's absence. One event which does, however, galvanise him into once again recording history is the brief visit home of his eldest brother John Montagu Hales Calcraft, aged 16. It seems that John may have been a naval cadet or midshipman at the time. On October 21st William writes – 'Johnny came home with a cold'. He no doubt attended the Guy Fawkes celebrations a fortnight later – 'had a fine bonfire, somebody set Furzy Island on fire' – and the next day Johnny goes away again 'to the Sidon at Portsmouth', whither Papa and Kathy go the following Tuesday 'to see Johnny off.' On the 11th William writes of the family's movements: 'Georgy and Susy came back. Papa, Kathy and George came back. Johnny sailed today on the Sidon'.

Henry, William's little brother, is clearly mentioned on 6th February: 'Showery. Rode to Encombe with Car B and spent a halfpenny without Henry knowing it'. (One of the few occasions on which the future head of the Board of Trade was duped, no doubt.)

One of the few exciting events recorded is when Gypsie, probably a horse, plays up on the road to Bushaw: 'Fine – Rode to Bushaw with Georgy. At the farm Gypsie kicked and jumped and ran away with M.'Georgy may either be the 'Georgy B' referred to elsewhere – presumably a Baillie – or could be his sister Georgiana Calcraft (subsequently Georgiana Ryder).

The only other adventures appear to be gastronomic when Papa brings home some Valencian sweetmeats on March 12th, and in the delicious entry for February 3rd: 'Snow. Did not go out. Made some barley sugar... the girls will not let us have any. Had some punch because rent-day at Wareham.'

Harry Clark recounted how his forebear had been a young soldier in the Napoleonic Wars, had several times faced a court martial and been sentenced to the lash, had lost an arm at Waterloo and then set up business in Dorset. He became a most successful merchant in Wareham (the Calcraft papers include some reference to transactions for coal from a member of the Clark family), and then became an agent for the Drax family. According to Clark, this forebear was one of those who used various methods to prevent Calcraft voters from voting, including the drastic device of shutting freeholders down their wells until the election was over. It was only in the 1880s that the Clark family came over to work for the Calcrafts. On his first visit to Rempstone to visit the Squire, Edward Clark was ushered into the drawing-room which was so full of smoke that it took some time for him to locate the whereabouts of his new employer, William Calcraft. It seems that the chimney smoked even in those days as it still does more than a century later! On another visit to see William Calcraft, there was a moment of farce. While in conversation together the two men became aware that there might be someone listening at the door. Calcraft indicated that, while he continued to talk, Clark was to investigate. Clark tiptoed to the door, suddenly pulled it open, and into the room fell the butler whose employment was, needless to say, instantly terminated.

William died at Rempstone on 29th April, 1901. So ends the Calcraft saga. At least one of William's sisters, Georgiana, lived on till war brought the dawning of a new age of machines and destruction; she died in 1915. Jack Ryder, her grandson, recalled her as an aloof old lady, rather disapproving of the disorganised and unpunctual Ryder family she had married into and multiplied.

Like his mother and his brother Henry, William Calcraft was buried at Corfe and not in the family vault at Wareham. Maybe nobody alive knew of its existence. The church was draped in purple and 'a posse of police' kept a watchful eye on the cortege. The chief mourners were Lord Radstock and Dudley Henry Ryder (brothers-in-law), and the service was attended by fellow members of the gentry including a Mansel, a Cavendish-Bentinck, a Pinney, two Bankes and three Bonds. No less than nine clergy were in attendance. Five members of the Ryder family were present. Edward Clark was described as Steward of the Manor, G. Linnington as Hayward and J. Bridle and Mr Toman as Bailiffs. The Mayor of Wareham and the Town Clerk were, of course, also there. William's obituary of 1901 reads:

The deceased was educated at Trinity College, Cambridge (BA in 1856), was Sheriff of Dorset three years ago, and Deputy Lieutenant and a JP for the county. Mr Calcraft was also the County Councillor for the borough of Wareham, which he has represented since its formation and has been a most regular attendant, and was Lord of the Manor and Chairman of the Rural District Council. He took a keen interest in the affairs of the county, and, as lately as April 11th, he presided at a meeting of the Tax Commissioners at Wareham.

Much consternation and regret were felt in Corfe when the death of the Squire became known. For many years the family has been honoured and esteemed in Dorset, where their lands in Purbeck occupy a large area, and much of Wareham was possessed by the late beneficent and considerate landowner. Mr Calcraft passed most of his time at Rempstone Hall among the tenantry and workpeople, who loved and respected him. Many of the men have worked all their lives on the estate, and several can proudly say that they have worked for the good old family for more than 40 years. Their master was pleased to retain such faithful servants, and they did yeoman service for him.

The late 'squire was one of a fast disappearing type, the good old English gentleman, whose word was his bond, and whose pleasure was the elevation and well-being of those around him. He was always ready to support any measures for the welfare of the community. As a member of the Wareham Board of Guardians he was most attentive and painstaking in its proceedings. Although one of the oldest magistrates on the Wareham Bench he rarely adjudicated. This makes the third magistrate removed from the division within eight months by the hand of death, namely, Mr L W Pike, Colonel Cambridge, and Mr Calcraft, in addition to the resignation of Mr Anderson. He was also patron of the rectory of St Mary's, Wareham, St Mary's, Swanage, and the vicarage of St Nicholas, Worth Matravers. The Corfe Castle Parish Council chose him as its Chairman, and he was also one of the School Managers. In matters political, Mr Calcraft was no strong partisan, his strong commonsense preventing him from rushing to extremes. For some years he had been a Liberal Unionist, and at the late election spoke and advocated the return of the Hon H Sturt. Many around this neighbourhood will miss the unostentatious liberality which sought not the applause of men. Mr Calcraft was unmarried, and, to the regret of many, this branch of the family expires. The flags on the Wareham and Corfe church towers are at half-mast, and many houses have the blinds partly down.'

What better epitaph could William have had than 'good old English gentleman.'

Ryders attended the funerals of both Henry and William in some force despite the fairly long journey from Hemel Hempstead to Corfe Castle. A newspaper report of William's death records that the relatives staying at Rempstone when the end came were Lord Radstock (brother-in-law) and Major and Miss Dudley Ryder. (Of course, most of them were possible heirs to Rempstone.) Furthermore, when Cyril Ryder had married Isobel Douglas-Hamilton a few years earlier, the honeymoon couple had gone straight from the wedding to Rempstone 'lent by Mr William Calcraft, uncle to the bridegroom'. Rempstone, it seems, is where their honeymoon began.

Unlike the Pitt-Rivers family from Cranbourne Chase, some of whom became pioneers of the new science of archeology, there is little evidence that the Calcrafts were ever aware that they owned some of the most interesting archeological and geological sites in the country. In the early 1800s a surveyor called William Smith was instigating, in Purbeck, the geological revolution that led to the realisation that the world was millions of times older than the Bible indicated, and also to the theories of Charles Darwin himself. Lady Caroline would not have been amused.

9

AFTER THE DYNASTY

As a child, Mrs Riddle had lived at Keeper's Cottage halfway up the road to Corfe and she could recall one day collecting sticks in 1901 when the butler from the Hall had galloped up to her father and herself in a terrible hurry. 'What's up?' her father had enquired. 'The old squire's dead!' the butler shouted as he sped by. That was the end of the dynasty. William Calcraft, the last of the Calcrafts of Rempstone, was no more. As a bachelor, he left no immediate heirs. So the estate passed successively to the offspring of his two oldest sisters: Katherine Calcraft who had married the Rev. Charles Dallas Marston and Georgiana-Emily Calcraft (1832–1915) who had married in 1857, Dudley Ryder of Westbrook Hay near Hemel Hempstead, the old seat of Richard Ryder who had been Home Secretary in Napoleonic times.

So what happened to Rempstone in the twentieth century after the Calcraft name had disappeared? During the next one hundred years there were only three squires of Rempstone: Guy Montagu Marston (1871–1927), Douglas Claud Dudley (Jack) Ryder (1901–1986) and his son James Calcraft Dudley Ryder (born 1934). All were blood descendants of the Calcrafts: Marston being a grandchild of Lady Caroline, and Jack Ryder a great grandchild.

Guy Montagu Marston (1871–1927)

It was Katherine Calcraft's third son, Guy Montagu Marston, who inherited first, in 1901, his older brothers Charles and William having died in 1870 and 1896 respectively. Sadly, very little is known of this interesting man. Outwardly, he was very correct – a typical country gentleman *[see Plate 33]*. Harry Clark, for many years Rempstone's solicitor, and Mary Spencer-Watson, the sculptor, of Dunshay Manor (repaired by Marston in 1906 for his bailiff to live in and manage the Worth side of the estate) could just remember him. On the surface, he struck them as being typical of his breed. Clark recalls that Marston could seem rather fierce, but then all squires could be fierce in those days. He recalled one occasion at the Court in Wareham where, when the magistrates entered, Marston barked 'Hats off!' so loudly that people jumped. Yet Marston's library reveals a much more complicated man: there are early editions of Sigmund Freud, Kraff-Ebbing and Havelock Ellis – all books about sex that heralded the sexual revolution of the twentieth century. There were also many tomes about comparative religion, philosophy, anthropology and magic.

Marston was a friend of Rupert Brooke *[see Plate 35]* and there were first editions of the poet's work, and three or four books by the notorious black magician Aleister Crowley, one of them signed 'G.M. Marston from Aleister Crowley, Rempstone, April 10' *[see Plate 38]*. Both Brooke and Crowley are reported to have stayed at Rempstone during Marston's squireship, Crowley leaving behind, allegedly, energised and disturbed denizens of the spirit-world. Marston was in love with his first cousin Daisy Waldegrave (the daughter of Susan Calcraft and Lord Radstock) and this love continued after her marriage to Edwyn Bevan. Marston, a naval officer until his retirement in 1921, was often away and so, for years, let most of Rempstone to the Bevans. A General Alexander was another pre-First World War tenant. It is sometimes said that Marston, a bearded sea-dog, had no interest in his landed inheritance, but this seems doubtful. He did repairs to the house in 1906 and 1919, for example, as can be seen by his dated monograms upon various Rempstone drainpipes. It is rumoured that he banned all hunting and shooting and fishing on his land. Meanwhile, the Bevans had improved the gardens and the lake and constructed a small courtyard and pool on the north side of Lower Rempstone. Yet Marston started to sell off his assets. First, the southern part of the estate including Worth Matravers in 1919 and 1921, and then a famous portrait of Kitty Calcraft by George Romney through Christies in 1923. It seems that Marston had lost touch with his other relatives who had married Calcraft women – the Rochforts and Burkes. Families are not very good at keeping in contact with their collaterals.

Why Marston sold off the southern part of Rempstone estate is a puzzle, but after the Great War many country families believed it was the end of the gentry: sons and heirs had been killed in the war and social revolution was in the air. The same feeling would be there in 1945 after the Second World War; then there would be a Socialist government, everybody felt poor and there were few available servants. Many landowners believed that their time was up and Jack Ryder would sadly contemplate selling Rempstone as premises for a school. Strangely, in the early twenty-first century landed estates are back in fashion. To some, Purbeck seems remarkably unchanged over the last one hundred years. The Bankes have handed over to the National Trust, the Bonds may have gone from Creech Grange, and the Scotts from Encombe, but the Mansels have hung on at Smedmore, at Lulworth the Welds are thriving and the Calcrafts' heirs are still at Rempstone.

It is possible to trace the relationships the Calcrafts had with the other Dorset gentry over the course of a hundred and fifty years. They were always on particularly good terms with the Dorset Pitts (originally the owners of Encombe, which they sold to the Scotts as late as 1807) although, by the end of the nineteenth century the Pitt family name, single-barrelled, had disappeared. On the whole, the Calcrafts also got along well with the Bonds and, especially with the Mansels. Relationships with the Scotts improved steadily from the days of the first Lord Eldon onwards. Only the relationships with the Bankes and Drax families remained cool. In the early twentieth century some of the Calcrafts' descendants probably had little idea that this was due to the long-forgotten political disputes of their ancestors in previous centuries.

Some of the correspondence with Guy Marston in 1909 over the Panton libel case reflects these relationships. Guy was somewhat a stranger in Purbeck but seems to have inherited his uncle's good-will locally. Mansel of Smedmore writes:

Dear Guy,
Yes, you may rely on me as a witness... the book is so very scurrilous, as well as untrue. I think the description of poor Mrs Sturdy... is almost the worst thing..

The book referred to, Jane Panton's *Fresh Leaves and Green Pastures*, was a volume of late Victorian Dorset gossip (see Chapter 6).

Writing from Morton's House in Corfe, F.C. Bentinck states:

Dear Guy
I quite understand your annoyance and indignation for the statements made in it are as offensive and impertinent as they are false and ill-natured...

but urges Marston not to sue:

Do you not think it would be better to treat her [Panton] *with the contempt she deserves? I cannot help thinking that your uncle Willie, who was a very dear friend of mine and whom I knew intimately from my boyhood, would have taken this course.*

Dudley Ryder of Westbrook takes a similar line of restraint. On the other hand Gerald Bond of Holme (a son of Nathaniel Bond of Creech), was all for action:

Dear Marston
...I am very glad to hear that you are going for Mrs Panton and her iniquitous book, and I shall be very pleased to assist...

Marston had recently been acquitted at a naval Court Martial after a ship he commanded ran aground. Yet he seems not to have lost his enthusiasm for litigation – egged on by his solicitors Clark and Pemberton.

There are several unresolved mysteries about Guy Marston and one is his motivation for taking this libel action. A note from Marston in the bound copy of the legal papers claims that he has made a 'curious discovery', namely, that the mistress of the publisher, Eveleigh Nash, a Mrs Ffoulkes, who apparently financed his publishing company, had been introduced to Marston's pretty tenant, Daisy Bevan, 'by a mutual friend and represented as a much misunderstood lonely woman.' In consequence, so Marston claims, and out of kindness, Daisy had invited Mrs Ffoulkes to stay at Rempstone in July 1908, 'but since then they have ceased to be friends'. Mrs Ffoulkes was, it seems, an authoress in her own right, having published the memoirs of 'many famous personalities' and having been the secretary of Douglas Sladen the originator of *Who's Who*. What a coincidence! Or was it? Who was this 'mutual friend'? Surely this carefully arranged visit to Rempstone was nothing less than a spying operation by an investigative author and publisher who had been tipped off that there was something worth reporting on. Panton's book was, presumably, already being prepared for publication by Nash at the time. There is clearly more to all this than meets the eye. Could it be that Nash, Ffoulkes and Panton operated more or less as a team, feeding off society scandal and gossip, and that Marston had something to hide which he did not want them to discover and expose? In 1911 Nash would publish the anonymous *Recollections of a Society Clairvoyant*; maybe Guy had been due for inclusion. In order to fire a shot across their bows this naval officer may have decided to take a libel action against them at the first opportunity. That turned out to be the next book that Nash published: Jane Panton's *Green Leaves and Fresh Pastures*. But was Marston still under the threat of blackmail? Is this why he had to sell so much of his estate, including Worth Matravers?

There is little doubt but that Jane Panton was harshly treated by Marston. To make matters worse she had recently been the centre of a well-publicised tragedy when her son had been found dead on the Cornish coast with his hands manacled. Was it suicide or murder? Or what? Could the boy's death have been connected with the libel action in any way? Or was he even the victim of black magic?

The libel case concluded in December 1909. Only four months later Crowley and his Scarlet Woman were staying at Rempstone with Marston (and the lovely Daisy Bevan) and practising sex rituals. We don't know if Daisy and Edwyn were involved in these ceremonies but they must have known about them. To make matters even stranger, Eveleigh Nash was also Crowley's publisher. Furthermore, the peculiar Mrs Ffoulkes published occult works as well as society gossip. So was Crowley in on this blackmail scam? Did he deliberately involve Marston in sex magic in order to blackmail this outwardly respectable naval officer? Around 1910 Crowley was, arguably, at his most creative, lascivious and dangerous.

Guy Marston was certainly vulnerable to blackmail, not least because he was ambitious. At the very same time that he was pressing forward with the libel action, in July 1909, Winston Churchill was appointing him to be a member of the Board of Trade's inquiry into Pilotage Law under the chairmanship of Sir Kenelm Digby. So Marston was obviously well thought of, but he was leading a strange double life. At sea, Captain Guy Marston appeared to be entirely orthodox as he commanded the Royal Naval sloop HMS *Blanche [see Plate 33]*, but when ashore, so it seems, he was sharing his beloved cousin Daisy in an unusual *menage á trois* with her husband at Rempstone. What is more, some or all of this menage were participating in Crowley's sex magic orgies, the taking of drugs and the black magical raising of the spirit of Mars, the god of war. Adultery alone was enough to ruin a naval career at that time. It was, therefore, essential for Marston to keep his private life well hidden! It seems he was successful, for by 1915 Guy Marston had been given far larger vessels to command. Every year from 1919 to his death in 1927, however, Marston steadily sold off some more of Rempstone's best assets: around two thousand acres of land, the village of Worth Matravers, Dunshay Manor, various properties in Corfe, the stunning Romney portrait of Kitty Calcraft, and possibly, a second Romney portrait of a Calcraft boy. If it was not for blackmail, then where did all this money go? He had no immediate family to support.

Years later Jack Ryder recalled that 'I found it diffcult to be completely at ease with Guy Marston'. When he visited Rempstone in the 1920s his cousin Guy had met him at the station in a chauffeur driven Wolsey and they had walked all the way from Rempstone across the heath to a boat at Goathorn that took them to Sandbanks for lunch.

Guy's well illustrated naval log books of various vessels including HMS *Imperieuse* and *Black Prince*, show that he had travelled around the world and visited the Sahara, the Middle East, India, Singapore, China, Japan and the East Indies. So, like Crowley, he had had a chance to discover the mysteries of Eastern magic and sorcery. Like Crowley, too, he was the child of deeply religious parents and his secret life can be seen as a reaction against their religious fanaticism and anti-sexuality. Crowley was the climax of that reaction; the most flambouyant destroyer of all that high Victorian morality (and Lady Caroline) stood for. 'Do What Thou Wilt' was his creed.

Guy left behind some Rupert Brooke papers in a deed box together with an unpublished poem about a divinely ordained 'barrier' to love – 'this great and aching love of mine, that ever yearns to know and to be known'. Was this written by Brooke or by Guy about himself, the solitary seafarer? 'I stand alone, a stranger at a gate'.

Looking at the photographs of Daisy Bevan and reading her history, one can see why Guy adored her. Daisy wrote a memoir of her life, apparently for her daughter Christina in 1926 *[see Plate 34]*. In it Daisy comes across as a warm, level-headed and adventure-loving woman. She describes an unhappy childhood with parents who showed her no affection or approval. Her father, Lord Radstock, exuding 'moral superiority', was a Plymouth Brother and had a strong sense of a personal divine mission. He had little interest in his children as individuals but drilled them as a platoon of Christian soldiers, with a fierce discipline. Most of the family silver, furniture and paintings were sold on religious grounds. 'I was brought up' writes Daisy, 'to be neither heard nor seen and every effort was made to suppress me'. No photographs of her were permitted to be taken. When told the facts of life as a teenager, by a Danish girl, she felt she had been 'poisoned' and for years went about haunted by this 'guilty secret'. Gradually, however, Daisy found ways to escape her psychological prison. She went with her handsome 'gypsy-like' aunt, Elizabeth Waldegrave (who warned Daisy never to trust a man who does not wear his hat on a tilt), and her companions, including, on one occasion, the incognito Queen of Sweden, to visit the ordinary naval seamen on board the ships at Portsmouth in order, ostensibly, to raise their moral standards. (Today we might suspect these Victorian ladies of 'slumming it' but without any insight into their own sexual motives). Daisy also found freedom on two long visits to Russia. On the second, in 1890, she went to live with Princess Galitzine and was surrounded by the flamboyant and mysterious Russian aristocracy – the women like men and the men, or at least some of them, like women. One day they paid a visit to Count Tolstoy, and Daisy found herself sleeping in his study on a little bed next to his desk on which were piled his pens and manuscripts. Tolstoy came in to talk to her and they chatted about the American authoress Mary Wilkins.

Daisy dreaded her return to England - 'the land of hedges and conventions'. She found the two countries as different as 'wild sad music' from 'a neat tune on a musical box'. At the age of twenty-one Daisy left home and went to live for three years in the East End of London among the poor Jewish community. Somehow, she was rescued from this exile by Millie and Edwyn Bevan who invited her to their villa in Cannes where she and Edwyn became engaged. They were married at St Mary Abbotts, Kensington, in 1896, and went to live in Somerset at the haunted Banwell Abbey, before moving to become her besotted cousin Guy Marston's tenants at Rempstone from Christmas 1906.

In seventy pages of memoirs, however, Daisy never mentions Guy and hardly refers at all to her ten or so years at Rempstone. They remain a mystery. Yet it seems clear that Daisy was something of a rebel and a romantic. She adored bathing, sometimes in the nude, and often in dangerous and exotic places – in a snow storm in the Baltic, in Bosnia, or in the Danube. She tells of swimming in a gale off St Albans Head and in the swell at Winspit, on one occasion with an obvious male admirer, the famous Edwardian neurologist Sir Henry Head. She clearly reciprocated the admiration.

Daisy ends her memoirs, dated New Year's Day 1927, by quoting some strange and suggestive lines by the poet Archibald Campbell:

I do not like disease and vice!
*I do not **want** to be immoral,*
*And yet **some** habit that's not nice*
Seems necessary for the laurel.

Jack Ryder, meeting her in her fifties, described her as 'a Venus' and 'very alert'; Edwyn as being 'tall and scholarly'. Edwyn read Sanskrit, had travelled widely in the Middle East and published several books on Greek philosophy and German politics. There had been some strange goings-on at Rempstone before the First World War among these intellectuals.

Jack Ryder (1901–1986)

When Marston died in 1927 the estate passed to Jack Ryder *[see Plates 39–41]*, Georgiana Emily ('Georgy') Calcraft's grandson by Cyril Ryder and his wife Lady Isobel Douglas-Hamilton, the sister of the 13th Duke of Hamilton and Brandon *[see Plate 32]*. Just as the Calcrafts had been moderate Whigs, so the Ryders were moderate Tories – Cyril's great grandfather being the Earl of Harrowby *[see Plate 12]* who had sat for thirty years in the Cabinet doing rather little except repeatedly refusing invitations to become Prime Minister, but ending his Parliamentary career, as we have seen, by leading the Waverers – those Tories in the House of Lords who supported the Great Reform Bill against the wishes of the Duke of Wellington. The Calcrafts and the Ryders had, together, helped the passage of the Bill quite significantly. Perhaps this had upset their Ultra Tory neighbour Lord Eldon at Encombe and the Drax squires at Charborough Park.

The Ryders and the Calcrafts had been acquainted since the 1750s, had been friends since the 1820s, and had intermarried in 1857. Georgiana Emily had had her fourth Ryder child in 1863: Cyril Ryder, a good looking young army officer, seems to have met the Duke of Hamilton's family sometime right at the end of the nineteenth century. The current Duke, Angus Douglas-Hamilton, has a photograph of Ryder and his army friend, the forceful Bertie Poore, posing with the sisters of the 13th Duke whom they married. Lady Florence, who married Bertie, thus became the Ryder's Great Aunty Flo. She lived on into very old age in Wimborne, wearing the lavender-scented lace shawls and little boots of the 1890s, surrounded by the unaltered jumble of screens, pictures, pianos and upholstery typical of her Victorian youth, well into the 1950s. Her old chauffeur, Munsty, had been a groom, and so hissed soothingly as he cleaned her car. To complicate matters, geneologically, Bertie's sister Nina married the duke. She went on to become a leading Edwardian animal welfare campaigner. Like his grandmother, Angus Hamilton is today a champion of the animals, boycotting, with the keen support of his wife Kay, a Scottish store that stocked paté de foie gras, and banning pheasant shooting on his land. When a tenant queried this, Hamilton asked 'Have you ever been shot at while you were flying?' The tenant hesitated. 'Well, I have', went on the Duke, 'and I can tell you that it's not much fun!' (Hamilton had flown Canberra bombers in the Malayan campaign.)

Cyril Ryder and Bertie Poore had possibly met the Hamilton girls at Studland where the Hamiltons used to holiday at Knoll House during the Edwardian summers, long before it became a hotel. In those days the length of Studland's sandy beach was usually deserted, except for a few locals and the striding figure of Augustus John followed by several of his female friends. The Hamiltons and the Ryders used to bathe naked, perhaps founding today's nudist tradition at Studland. Cyril Ryder married Isobel Douglas-Hamilton in 1897. Her brother Douglas, although descended from the early Dukes of Hamilton, had inherited the title from a cousin. He was not only the premier peer of Scotland, and a triple duke, but could claim descent from Charlemagne, Alfred the Great, The Emperor Justinian, Robert the Bruce and several other Scottish royals including the Malcolm in Shakespeare's Scottish play. He was the head of the Douglases who had been the most powerful Scottish noble family in the middle ages and also of the Hamiltons, who, in the sixteenth century, would have succeeded to the throne of Scotland if Mary Queen of Scots' line had failed – as it nearly did. Not that the 13th Duke was particularly interested in such things. He had been an active sailor and, although only of small stature, had gained a proud reputation for strength and bravery in the Navy, earning himself the nickname 'Pocket Hercules'. Sadly, he had suffered paralysis, apparently brought on by diving under dreadnoughts and was, in the Studland days, an invalid. He was also remembered by Jack Ryder as a man of great charm and force of personality.

His wife, Nina Poore, Bertie Poore's sister, not only had to care for her invalid husband but also look after a large family of children and a complicated estate. Her good friend was Admiral 'Jackie' Fisher, the First Sea Lord, and increasingly, she relied upon him. It has been alleged that they were lovers although the evidence is weak. It was quite possible in Victorian and Edwardian days for men and women to love each other without ever consummating the affair. Love and sex could be quite separated in their minds. Gentlemen were half expected to find sex professionally while putting their well-born muses upon a pedestal. (Maybe the Victorians were right to separate love and sex in this way. Affection, sex and attachment are three fairly discrete behaviours, each linked to different neurochemical systems. Perhaps it has been humankind's mistake to try to lump them all together).

Poor Isobel Ryder's matrimonial happiness did not last long. Cyril Ryder developed signs of his family's disease, tuberculosis, and had to be invalided out of the Army. His doctors sent them to live in Teneriffe where their children, Iris, Dudley (Jack) and Evelyn Ryder were born in the early years of the century. Not only did Isobel have to nurse her husband until he died in 1907 but, on a meagre budget, she had to care for a loving but headstrong little son and a youngest daughter who turned out to be suffering from a serious thyroid deficiency that retarded her mental development. When they came home from the Canaries the bereaved family bought a house in the New Forest near Burley. Years later Jack described himself as 'as tiresome and unsympathetic son'. Isobel got Jack off her hands by sending him to boarding schools and to holidays in Scotland with the Hamiltons. There, he could tear around the spacious grounds and corridors of the massive Hamilton Palace with his cousin Douglas, the future 14th Duke (and destined to be the first man to fly over Mount Everest and, amazingly, in an open cockpit plane), and Douglas's tribe of fascinating sisters. One of these, Margaret, led a wild life in the 1920s and 1930s with many famous admirers, including a cousin or two, before marrying the tall and dashing Jamie Drummond-Hay. Hamilton Palace certainly gave the children space for exercise, being larger than Buckingham Palace. Jack's mother, Issy, complained that it used to take her a quarter of an hour to reach the dining room from her bedroom.

Douglas and Margaret's younger brother, Nigel, the Earl of Selkirk, known as Geordie, also became a friend of Jack and, following a distinguished political career in Harold Macmillan's Cabinet, in which, among other things, he is reputed to have ousted the CIA from East Asia, retired to Wimborne and became a frequent visitor to Rempstone in later years. Jack Ryder, meanwhile, had excelled at rugby football. He played for Sherborne and later for Cambridge, where he read Forestry after the First World War. In the 1920s he played for Black Heath and was trialed for England, before an injury to his hip put paid to his sporting career. For the remainder of his life he felt that rugger was his outstanding achievement in life.

Dogged by dyslexia which, in those days, was taken as a sign of unintelligence, Jack felt he was intellectually a non-starter. In fact he was an excellent judge of people, secretly understanding and sympathising from behind his gruff façade. For a while he planted trees with the Forestry Commission in Wales and then helped another Scottish cousin run a wine importing business in London while he lived in a big house in Hornton Street. Jack was handsome in a Ryder rather than a Calcraft manner – fair hair, square face and blue eyes – and women in London pursued this tough young athlete. So, for a few years he enjoyed himself, sewing his wild oats. It was the *Brideshead Revisited* era and, in fact, he had known the Waughs when at Sherborne, perhaps giving Evelyn the idea of the Ryder name for his hero Charles Ryder, although not the character. Jack was quite dashing and once drove his Invicta the wrong way around Piccadilly Circus for a wager.

In 1927 he married the very young Nancy Baker of Dawlish in Devon *[see Plate 40]* – a vivacious and lithe blonde-redhead and, in quick succession, she had three daughters, Gay, Jennifer and Jacqueline, and twin sons, James and Ben *[see Plates 44, 46]*. The Bakers came from tough colonial stock. Little Granny Baker, when threatened by a man-eating tiger in India, had shoo-ed it away with her parasol.

In 1928 Jack's life changed when he inherited two quite separate estates – the Ryder estate of Westbrook Hay in Hertfordshire (land that had come into Ryder possession around 1715 by marriage to the Lomax family) and the Rempstone estate that came to him as Georgiana-Emily Calcraft's grandson, on the death of Guy Marston in 1927. By the terms of the various wills, Jack had to choose between the two. He could not have both. Some would have chosen the grand Georgian house and the increasingly valuable land on the edges of Hemel Hempstead. But Jack chose the heathland and trees of Rempstone. He chose rural rather than suburban, but not before he adroitly removed the chattels that were his at Westbrook including a Gainsborough portrait and the Ryder silver. The latter was promptly stolen from him, along with old General Sir Granby Calcraft's priceless gold medal of the Military Order of Maria Theresa, by his butler in Hornton Street. Interviewed in prison, the butler apologised to Jack Ryder but explained that this was merely a professional matter as far as he was concerned, and nothing personal.

The Rempstone estate, of course, came with death duties and, probably unwisely, Jack Ryder chose to pay these off by selling some of the estate's greatest assets including eight or so pubs, mostly in and around Wareham, for less than a thousand pounds each, to Strong & Co in 1931. Even allowing for inflation this was a mistake. But this tactic of selling off the assets to maintain the liabilities tended to continue. Round Island and Furzey Island were sold in 1935. The Old Granary in Wareham was sold for £7750 in 1964. Green Island was sold to Tim Hamilton-Fletcher in 1965. Jack was living on capital, selling year by year. Reproved by Ben Ryder's wife, Philippa, Jack sought to justify his tactics. His main adviser and solicitor, Gordon Redman, in 1965 wrote to reassure him that Rempstone was, in his opinion, 'one of the best run estates in Dorset.' Jack Ryder, in later years, regretted leasing so much to the Forestry Commission, but he knew he had done his best to improve the accommodation of his poorest tenants. He had put in baths and water closets, and built some new houses. Cottages and farms had been in a poor state when he had inherited. He would leave behind characteristically clumsy and ugly brick and concrete improvements.

So, in 1928, Rempstone had its new Squire. For several years tenants remained in the house. But, in 1931, Nancy and Jack began to supervise the refurbishment of its interior and the return of the Calcraft furniture that had been in storage. Jack was only in his late twenties and, for the next decade could not resist enjoying himself [see Plates 43, 44]. He built a concrete swimming pool under the pines at the bottom of the garden. He levelled the lawn on the north side of the house and made a tennis court where week-end guests, some from London, would desport themselves in long white flannels while maids in uniform served the tea. Jack was a keen and even aggressive player until well into the 1950s. Some of his old Cambridge friends such as 'Cocky' Cochrane, Bobbie Allenby, Bill Tucker (Dennis Compton's surgeon), Geordie Selkirk and Dick Strauss would turn up with their wives and women friends; Tucker in a Rolls. Elegant local brothers Eric and Geoffrey Warner would arrive in a Lagonda. Drinks parties out of doors were popular at Rempstone before the war. Jack's wife Nancy had to tolerate the flirtations. The children were banished to the nurseries and watched in silent awe from the upstairs windows.

In the late 1920s the athletic young squire regularly went skiing in the Alps with some of his Scottish cousins. They were among the pioneering British who introduced the sport of skiing (Jack pronounced it as 'she-ing') to the world. Back home, Jack's definition of 'country sports' was cricket, squash, tennis and golf. He never shot or fished and, of course, would never have dreamt of hunting. In the 1950s he was an active Captain of the

Studland cricket team whose fast-bowling star was Basil White. A star batswoman, who also played at Studland, was Molly Hession, wife of the film-making religious enthusiast Brian Hession, who rented from Rempstone the cottage at the end of the Goathorn peninsula. Known locally as the Bishop of Goathorn, Hession was a very good example of the muscular Christian – clean in thought, word and deed, he would condemn any light-hearted allusion to sex, however, mild or witty, as 'filthy German humour'. But he had his good points, bravely killing with a starting handle a fox dying in agony, its gangrenous leg caught in a gin trap. Wounded and sick wild animals, in those days, were never taken to a vet; but nor were they ignored. It was considered the proper thing to do to 'put them out of their misery', thus sparing them a great deal of the prolonged terror they often endure today while undergoing treatment.

Jack hoped his children would follow in his footsteps by being sporty. In this, he was to be disappointed. Vainly, he would try to coach them. A so-called gibbet was erected at the end of the lawn from which a ball was suspended on a piece of string and his sons were ordered to hit the ball with a cricket bat. They were not good at it. As one of nature's worst teachers, Jack became inarticulately furious with them. The more furious he became, the more incompetent became his pupils. Tennis and golf coaching failed for similar reasons. With his daughters, he became equally annoyed by their inability to learn how to play bridge. Sadly, Jack did not live long enough to see his granddaughter, Emily, running and swimming, nor his great grand-sons, Jack and Sam, enthusiastically playing every game under the sun. The athletic instinct had jumped a generation or two. Towards the end of his life, the only sport that Jack and his family could enjoy together was croquet on the front lawn: a game with a vicious streak in it that meant that friend-ships could be seriously tested.

Jack was not entirely old fashioned in his views. He was admired by, and tolerated the company of, several obvious gays – the writer Godfrey Winn (or Winifred God, as he was known to his friends) was one of them *[see Plate 45]*. Winn had strangely baggy old-fashioned tennis shorts beneath which, to the giggling excitement of some of the children present, he obviously wore no underwear. After the war, the twins naughtily clanked chains in the night outside the haunted bedroom where Winn was sleeping. Although far from gay himself Jack was well ahead of the times in accepting homosexuals, emphasising that they were often kind and creative people. He was not anti-Semitic either and, in a period when many Europeans, and not only the Germans, were openly and strongly disapproving of Jewish people, he fre-quently invited his friend Dick Strauss to stay at Rempstone. Nor was Jack an obvious racist. Fascism, however, was in the air in the 1930s. Few fully understood its ruthlessness or the implications of its anti-Semitism. Jack's sister, Iris, was a case in point. Sexually frustrated and unfulfilled, she had fallen under the spell of the British fascist leader, Sir Oswald Moseley and, with stars in her eyes, slavishly followed him around the country. Along with several other Dorset people, she was duly interned under Regulation 18b in 1940. After the war, paradoxically, she became a militant Zionist. Living in a small house at Bushey, on Rempstone, she then took up cats as a career, followed by flying saucers. She was a sweet natured eccentric who could believe in almost anything.

Jack's cousin, 'Douglo', the new Duke of Hamilton, had not been one of those Scottish aristocrats who had admired Hitler ideologically. But, like many, he had German friends and wished that war could be avoided. When Hitler's half-mad Deputy Führer, Rudolf Hess, had flown to Scotland in 1940, he said it was to see the Duke of Hamilton. Hess probably imagined that, as premier peer, Hamilton wielded some actual power. Hamilton, an RAF pilot, once told Jack and Richard how he was called to a police station where he was asked to interview the mysterious captured German flier. Hess then revealed, for the first time, his identity. When Hamilton queried this, Hess tried to prove it by showing a photograph of himself taken from his wallet. Uncertain of the man's sanity, Hamilton was eventually convinced that it really was Hess. Without revealing details, he telephoned Winston Churchill's office in London and immediately flew down to Northolt in a Hurricane. He found Churchill watching a film in the early hours of the morning. When he broke the news of Hess's defection, Churchill seemed unimpressed. Next day, Hamilton flew back to Scotland in the company of high ranking Foreign Office officials.

The Class Game

Many upper class people before the war thought in terms of 'breeding'. They honestly believed that they were upper class because their genetic make up or 'blood' was different from that of the lower orders. Like thoroughbred race horses or Guernsey cows they had the right stuff that made them socially superior. Money and good education were seen almost as the consequences of class and not the causes of it. They could not see that class was ultimately dependent upon wealth and income; for them, it was only birth that mattered. There was a sort of post-Darwinian logic about the racism and snobbery of Jack's generation. In the upper classes, women, too, were not regarded as inferior to men, merely as genetically different. In these circles, women often held the psychological, if not the legal, advantage. They were regarded as being innately more sensitive, caring and spiritual than men, while men were thought to be genetically braver, less emotional and psychologically as well as physically tougher. In consequence, gentlemen were expected to protect women, give up their seats to them on trains and generally to treat them with courtesy and respect. In the upper classes women more than held their own.

The great obsession of the English, however, was the class game. As classes, like sexes and races, were considered to be genetically quite distinct, nothing much could be done to change them. The last fifty years has seen a reversal in this way of thinking, as people have been struck by similarities rather than by differences, and have striven for equality of opportunity while, in the twenty-first century, the class obsession has been partially replaced by a celebrity cult, which is probably just as meaningless and trivial.

Before the Second World War, however, there were not merely the usual three classes in many people's minds, but a score of subtle gradations. Even among the titled aristocracy there were grades, with the dukes at the top, followed by marquises, then earls, viscounts, barons and baronets in descending order. More subtle criteria still were the antiquity of noble families and the dates at which the titles had been created. Some of the Hamilton maiden aunts, for example, looked down upon the Ryders because the Hamilton titles were centuries older than the Ryder titles. And so on. This obsession with class possibly helped the English to be less prejudiced in other ways. But to many, class seemed to be more important than almost anything else although, like sex and money, it was hardly a subject to be openly discussed. An aristocratic Englishman may have felt he had more in common with an Indian prince than he did with a Yorkshire miner. But the British aristocracy were also aware, by the nineteenth century, that they had to deserve their position in society. They could not allow themselves to become cut off from their people like the French aristocracy had done. That had led to the guillotine.

It was not the fault of the lower classes, so it was thought, that they lacked the right breeding; they should be cared for and treated decently. So it was that Jack Ryder took up his new position with a genuine desire to be a good and fatherly landlord to his Rempstone tenants. Jack recalled that he took over at a time when many in the working class 'looked up to and gained strength from an admiration of the upper classes'. Usually there was 'no visible envy and very obvious affection for their employers'. Many believed, said Jack, that the upper classes really were 'a superior race'.

Anyway, he preferred the rural working people to the clever mercantile middle classes of Poole or Bournemouth, and he exemplified that traditonal British feudal bond between lord and tenant that had united them for centuries against the aspirations of the bourgeoisie. In his youth, Jack Ryder had seen too many people 'trying to pretend to be what they were not'. He was suspicious of the nouveaux riches and of social climbers. In consequence, he was secretly ill at ease socially. He was only truly relaxed when at Rempstone, in its woods or garden, or in his study alone. One advantage of living in a large house is that people can get away from each other.

Mr Riddle

Rempstone garden in the 1930s was a paradise for the children, who ran about it stark naked in a way that would be frowned upon today and lead to Court orders from the local Social Services. Often, the adults' weekend parties were also in the garden and, on occasions, some of the guests drank too much cocktail or punch. One poor young man, showing off to the ladies, dived into a large clump of nettles instead of into the swimming pool and was badly stung.

Mr Riddle was the head gardener at Rempstone after the war. His head-quarters were in the dark and musky potting sheds in Rempstone's walled kitchen-garden, where he grew huge strawberries that were far more deli-ciously flavoured than any to be found today. When Jack and Vee Ryder unusually invited him on a visit to Stourhead gardens one day in 1950, he respectfully clambered into the back of the Daimler wearing his Sunday best suit, hat and, rather strangely, as it was a beautiful day, an old raincoat. It was, probably, the first and last time that the squire took 'Riddle' on an out-ing. The gardens at Stourhead were looking beautiful and the visit went well. After a few hours roaming around the lake the party reassembled in the car park but, much to Vee Ryder's sympathetic concern, old Mr Riddle appeared to be having difficulty in getting back into the car. 'Are you alright, Mr Riddle?' she enquired. 'Oh yes, madam, I shall manage it', the old man replied. But it seemed as though Mr Riddle had grown in size. He appeared bodily swollen and unable to bend his legs. For a few moments the Ryders feared that the visit had been too much for their aged gardener and that he had been struck down with a mysterious condition. Eventually, there was a 'snap' and a large bundle of cuttings fell from an inner pocket of his coat. On closer examination it was found that every pocket was similar-ly filled.

This had probably been standard practice. Competition between the gen-try in the matter of gardens had raged for centuries. Riddle obviously con-sidered that it was expected of him to continue this tradition. In Victorian times, when he had been a garden boy, there were no garden centres and only a handful of famous and expensive nurseries. As new plants were dis-covered and brought back to England, those with large gardens vied with one another to be among the first with the latest and most exotic specimens.

It is doubtful whether many of the cuttings stolen on this occasion ever took. The gardens at Rempstone certainly seemed to stay the same as they always were – rhododendrons, holm oaks, pines, gunnera in the lake and azaleas in the rockery. Snakes, too. Occasionally, Jack Ryder would open the gardens to the public for some charitable cause and, wearing his shabbiest clothes, collect the money himself from the visitors who imagined he must be a gardener. On more than one occasion, one such visitor, ashen faced, returned to the house having been bitten by an adder. None, as far as can be recalled, ever died. But Rempstone gardens in those days were a zoolo-gist's paradise: there were not only adders and grass snakes but also some of the rarest snake of all – the Smooth Snake.

Mr Riddle had come from north Dorset, but his wife was local. Mrs Riddle did wonderful sewing and tailoring, letting out the trousers, skirts and jack-ets of growing teenagers at the Hall. As a young woman she had gone to London to be a lady's maid. As she had stood outside Waterloo Station on her arrival, gazing in amazement at the great grey and black buildings of the smoke-filled metropolis – so entirely strange to a girl who had not previously been beyond Wareham – there were suddenly cries, and she turned to see a woman, a few yards away from her, run down by a hansom cab and killed. We sometimes forget how dangerous were streets filled by horse-drawn vehicles.

Sex and Class

One advantage of the old class system was that people did not feel personally responsible for their social positions. If you were born working class it was not your fault. You had no sense of personal failure. Whereas some of the gentry were taught to feel that their accident of birth was something for which they should feel humbly grateful to God, for the lower orders there was no sense of shame. In America, everyone might feel that they ought to get to the top and that, unless they become both a millionaire and the President, then they have been a failure. But in old England everybody knew their station. It was the way things were. If they were hard up they could blame the class system rather than themselves for their hardship. The class game, nevertheless, continued to be the national pastime – judging others' positions, finding one's own and, may be, trying to improve or exaggerate it. It was a way of establishing one's own sense of identity and self-esteem.

This continued throughout the 1950s. As in the First World War, so in the Second. The officers had, more or less, remained of a class. In both world wars they had led from the front and suffered disproportionately high casualties. Such self sacrifice had, for decades, helped to stifle class resentment. Yet both wars were socially disruptive. Women and the working classes had had glimpses of a new world. Class and gender freedoms seemed irresistible and, in 1945 a Labour government was returned. Yet, in many ways, despite the great reforms of the National Health Service and improved state education, things had stayed the same or slipped back a bit again. The 1950s resumed a wartime mentality. It was an era of suffocating orthodoxy and respect for authority. A strict dress code denoted one's position in the class system – braces and rolled up sleeves for the working classes and tweed jackets and grey flannels for the posh lot. Anything flashy or colourful was regarded with horror and suspicion. It was vulgar or the mark of a spiv. It was 'non U'. Spivs, cads and bounders were to be abhorred. Only the Teddy Boys defied the monotony by wearing drainpipe trousers, velvet collars and flamboyant hairstyles – an extraordinary working class phenomenon. But, then, the working class and the aristocracy could be closer to each other than either were to the bourgeoisie with their 'middle class morality'.

It was the 1960s that changed all this; they were a reaction against the grey dullness and inhibition of the 1950s. The social revolution of the 1960s defied class barriers, authoritarianism, militaristic machismo, conformity and, perhaps above all, the sexual suppression of the previous decade. The 1950s had seen an attempt to put the lid back on sexuality after the partial abandon of the war years: sex was not to be openly discussed, women's enjoyment of sex was to be absolutely denied; anything other than hetero-sexual relations within marriage – and only the missionary position, of course – were to be condemned.

The puritanism of the Victorian era had returned but without its redeem-ing hypocrisies. For young people in Dorset in the 1950s, and particularly for the middle and upper classes, sex became extremely difficult. Long, exhausting and furtive snogging sessions would often get no further. Young women would defend the edges of their brassieres and the hemlines of their panties with quite remarkable skill and perseverance. At Rempstone the young Ryders were no exceptions to this rule. On more than one occasion 'snogging' or 'necking' parties in dark cellars or haunted attics, well lubricat-ed with Merrydown cider, were broken up by Jack Ryder storming in at mid-night, hobnailed shoes grinding on the floor, switching on the lights and ordering the frightened guests to leave. Such events were denounced as 'damned poodle faking'.

Jack Ryder felt in two minds about sex. Part of him was tolerant and part of him was not. He could forgive homosexuals and those young women who 'got into trouble'. In an age where pregnancy outside marriage was widely regarded as a more serious failing than serial murder, he was forgiv-ing and even broad-minded. But he felt a guilt about his own sex life. After rugger in the 1930s he had, rather briefly, taken up women. Then, in an attempt to patch up his failing first marriage, he had invited his wife on a luxury cruise. This had turned out to be less than successful. After only a day at sea he had started an affair with one of the other passengers – and we have her word for this. In retaliation, Nancy Ryder took up with another fel-low passenger, the tall and handsome Ronald Graham, the brother of yet another duke – the Duke of Montrose. The huge scandal of a divorce ensued. Divorces were still relatively rare in the late 1930s. This one attracted head-lines in the national papers – 'Duke's nephew cites Duke's brother' was one. Dorset society was not amused – or, at least, pretended not to be. Soon, one divorce was followed by another. The attractive Vera (or Vee) Cook of Studland Manor was being divorced by her husband Mervyn Hamilton-Fletcher. They had been in Studland – only two miles from Rempstone – for a number of years, bringing up their four sons Robin, Tim, Nicholas and Alexander. Within months, Vee married Jack Ryder. Dorset gossip went into shocked overdrive. How long had Vee and Jack known each other? Had an affair been carried on for years? What sort of woman was this?

Jack and Vee
Vee, in fact, had long been associated with Dorset [see Plates 47, 48]. Her father, Sir Herbert Cook, an immensely rich London businessman and art collector, had bought Hillclose in Studland as a summer home at the turn of the century. In the winter he lived in Richmond where he housed his col-lection of Old Masters (including paintings by Poussin, Fra Bartolommeo, Turner, Dürer, Titian, El Greco, Rubens, Valasquez, van Eyck, Giorgione and

Rembrandt), or at his beautiful palace at Montserrate in Portugal. In Studland the young Vee had enjoyed her summers swimming in the sea, playing the grand piano (which she did extremely well) and meeting her parents' interesting friends. These included singers, artists and celebrities – including the notorious Robbie Ross, Oscar Wilde's first seducer and most loyal friend. Whenever Mr Ross came to stay at Hillclose there was, she recalled, an aura of excitement in the air. The Wilde scandal had continued to raise the eyebrows of Edwardian society for years after Wilde's demise.

Studland attracted interesting visitors including Ottoline Morrell and her lovers Augustus John and Bertrand Russell in the 1920s, and Googie Withers, the actress, in the 1940s. Her brother, Harry, an ADC in Purbeck during the war would clearly recall the visits from Eisenhower, Monty, Churchill and King George Vl, and that they used to meet and make plans at Rempstone. (They also met at Harry Warren house and at the World's End pub north of Wareham).

Vee was courted by several young officers during the First World War and one of them, her unofficial fiancé, Julian Gribble, had won a posthumous VC. Another early boyfriend was John Cobb the world land-speed record holder. Surprisingly, Vee had been permitted to visit Bovington Camp where, in 1918, she had been given a ride in a tank – surely one of the first women ever to do so.

Vee Cook was not, of course, allowed to pursue a career in music. After being taught by a series of governesses for herself, her sister Rachel and her brother Francis, she spent several years at Sherborne Girls School in its early days, under Miss Mulliner. When she married Mervyn Hamilton-Fletcher they had first lived with her in-laws at Leweston Manor not far from Sherborne. There, after the birth of her first son Robin, she had awoken one night to see a grey veiled lady sitting at the end of her bed. I am not ill, she thought, so why do I have a nurse? Vee spoke to her, but the figure did not reply. So Vee rang the bell by the bed. When a servant came with a lamp, the lady in grey had disappeared. Next day she was told that the ghost was well known at Leweston, but meant no harm. A year later, the butler fell off his bicycle in the park on his way back from Sherborne. He appeared very shocked and explained that he had 'ridden through' the Grey Lady.

Vee loved her sons, and almost to excess. But she was bored and frustrated in marriage. Highly intelligent and very talented as a musician and writer, she yearned for a more sophisticated life. Maybe this was the reason the Hamilton-Fletchers moved back to Studland – the scene of her childhood happiness. At Studland Manor (where her son Tim used to see the ghost of a man in black also seen by the subsequent owners, the Roses) they were near to the sea and to some of her old friends – the Andersons of Harry Warren house, the Mackworths, the Warners and the artist George Spencer Watson, his fascinating red haired wife Hilda, and artistic daughter Mary (they lived in Dunshay Manor that had belonged to Rempstone until sold in 1921). Vee became part of the Cowes yachting scene, and a big yacht was even named after her. She smoked Du Maurier cigarettes and was vivacious and accomplished: she played Debussy beautifully and painted in oils. Vee had inherited her artistic skills from her mother, Mary Hood, the daughter of Viscount Bridport of Cricket St Thomas – now a hotel and the location for the popular 'To the Manor Born' television series. The whiskery Viscount had had twins by a governess and an explosive affair with Lilly Langtry, the actress, whom he shared sexually with the Prince of Wales. The Hoods were a great naval family and were descended from Charlotte Nelson, Horatio's favourite niece. But the artistic talents probably came not from them but from Lord Bridport's wife, Lady Maria Fox-Strangways, the daughter of the Earl of Ilchester who lived at Melbury. Sadly, such talents, indeed almost any sort of talent, were rarely allowed to be channelled into a career for upper class young ladies in those days. So, Vee, like her gifted mother and grand-mother, was destined never to express her full creativity. Both Vee and her mother Mary (or Moë) wrote snatches of music and verse from which one can hear the quality that could have been developed. Vee's sister Rachel Lloyd became a writer and died many years later in Corfe, and their brother Francis, who inherited the Cook family fortune and the Old Master paint-ings, painted and composed with a natural yet untutored flair.

When Vee Hamilton-Fletcher became Vee Ryder in 1938 she took her four sons with her to Rempstone where they found themselves acquiring three Ryder stepsisters of more or less the same ages as themselves and two (twin) stepbrothers. Soon, to complicate the relationships even further, they were all joined by a new half-brother, Richard Ryder, who is the author of this book. But they were united in the glow of the scandal of the two almost simultaneous divorces that still caused tongues to click in prim Dorset par-lours. The imminent war would put an end to most of that, but not to all. The pious Joseph Weld of Lulworth Castle, for example, would never forgive Jack and Vee Ryder for their divorces and would, as Lord Lieutenant of the county many years later, as Lord Selkirk duly reported, refuse to agree that a lowly honour should be given to Jack for his forty years of unpaid and painstaking service to the community, to local government and as Chairman of the Poole Harbour Board. Jack saw a lot of Joe Weld. Weld, too, was a powerful personality and, like Jack, a magistrate. When Richard, in front of the Wareham magistrates, contested a parking fine dished out when he had parked outside the Bankes Arms at Studland one Sunday in the 1960s, Weld very properly stood down from the bench. Richard argued that the Highway Code implied that parking restrictions only applied on 'weekdays' and so was, surprisingly, acquitted. The police appealed, and the Lord Chief Justice, no less, had to quosh the case, ordering that the Highway Code be reword-ed. It duly was.

Divorce scandal or not, the large combined family, now comprising ten chil-dren, all got on surprisingly well. It is a tribute to Jack and Vee Ryder that they did so. Jack treated everyone with fairness, firmness and equality. Vee, however, could never feel the same tremendous love for her stepchildren that she felt for her own. In this respect she was a typical stepmother, but there was never any open falling out. Vee's mother, Moë, perhaps remarkably for a Victorian, went to some lengths to try to maintain contact between the departed Nancy and her rather deserted children. Moë was an unusual woman. She had supported the revival in English folk music and played the English concertina. She had also developed an interest in so-called Negro Spirituals and had, at her own and her husband's expense, brought over several black choirs to sing in England in the years before the First World War. One of the lead singers, John Paine, had stayed and lived near the house she had built at Looe in Cornwall, until some years after her death in 1943. At her expense he dressed and lived entirely like an Edwardian Englishman, complete with tweeds and gold watch chain. He was a well known figure. Of course there was gossip about his relationship with Moë, but who knows. Vee's parents had drifted apart in later years, her ailing father, Poë, a long-suffering and dependable man, spending more and more time at his little palace of Montserrate near Cintra in Portugal, attended by his mistress, Miss Heseltine.

The Two Cultures

Vee had brought to Rempstone a touch of the exotic. Her family were upper class Bohemians. This traditional clash of two cultures – the artistic and the down-to-earth – would be highlighted by E.M. Forster in *Howards End* composed, allegedly, while he walked along Nine Barrow Down above Rempstone, and later by C.P. Snow. The tender-minded and the hardheaded were now both represented at Rempstone. Vee found kindred spirits among the Woods family who rented Lower Rempstone (the eastern end of the house), and where filmmakers, musicians and authors, such as Lawrence Durrell, would come to stay in the 1950s and 1960s. Vee's grand relations, too, would sometimes visit. On one occasion old Lord 'Stavvy' Ilchester came to lunch and was amazed to see the Hogarth portrait of Henry Fox hanging over the sideboard where, over the years, it had been heavily splattered with gravy. It was, he said, far better than his own version of the same picture. Another cousin, Lord Bridport, also used to visit. Tall and completely bald due to alopecia, he seemed a frightening figure to the children. He told an amusing story as to how the police had let him off from a parking offence in Bridport out of deference to his title. (As late as the 1950s Wareham police had done the same for James Ryder, as the young squire; unwilling to interrupt his pleasure while in the cinema they had politely moved his car for him).

Peter Bridport also reminisced on how he had unexpectedly visited Vee's grandfather, Sir Frederick Cook, at Montserrate in Portugal in the 1920s, and found the old man surrounded by semi-naked and naked ladies. Vee, Jack and Richard had visited Peter Bridport at Horatio Nelson's estates in Sicily which Bridport had inherited, along with the fearsome local title, Duke of Bronte – literally Duke of Thunder. There, in 1965, they encountered maid servants still adhering to the same formal behaviour inculcated by the first British butler in the 1830s, and saw the estate's grapes being trodden by the bare feet of a shoulder-hugging ring of intoxicated men shrouded in a huge cloud of wasps, many of which were being trodden into the wine. When Richard innocently asked his austere cousin whether he had any trouble from the Mafia, he was met with a stony silence. Etna loomed in the background.

Meanwhile, in Upper Rempstone, Jack's spartan regime prevailed. While Lower Rempstone thought about Mozart, Jack concerned himself with the condition of the estate's drains, damp courses and cess-pits. He was obsessed with the problems of drainage. After the great Victorian sanitation reforms of the nineteenth century, it took decades for villages in rural England to catch up. Earth closets were still commonplace. Jack Ryder, like his son James, took trouble to understand such issues and to instal improvements. Jack was entirely down-to-earth and, in all things, eschewed squeamishness, whether about drains or anything else. On occasions, members of his family would react with disgust at finding a cooked caterpillar in their organically grown cabbage, or a slug in their salad. 'Don't be so damn stupid!' Jack would bark at them. 'Eat it up, it's all perfectly good protein.' If they still recoiled, he would angrily seize the offending item and eat it himself. This was all part of the macho, stiff upper lip ethos of the period. Jack professed indifference to any pain and insensitivity to all forms of fear. If a visitor showed that they were afraid of a wasp, for example, Jack would corner the insect against a wall or window and calmly place his thumb upon it. When he felt ill with a cold or a fever Jack's invariable remedy was 'fresh air and exercise'. He would put on his oldest tweeds, ancient raincoat and most dilapidated hat and proceed into the depths of Rempstone's woods, regardless of snow or driving rain, where he would cut away at the undergrowth with his brashing hook until utterly exhausted. He then dragged himself home for a hot bath. Doctors were full of misgivings about this approach. He survived, however, till the eve of his eighty-fifth birthday.

Jack found it hard to be sympathetic to any males who seemed to be exaggerating their illness. One spring, the tall White Russian, Tristram Yellin, came to stay and complained of feeling unwell. 'Well, get out and get some proper exercise', Jack urged gruffly. 'Walk to Corfe or to Studland.' Yellin tried. Three days later he was dead.

Jack rejected all luxuries. Even the discussion of good food was regarded as a foreign affectation. It was all very well for the French to discuss gastronomy but it was certainly not a British thing to do. Nor a manly thing. Food was simply to be eaten as a necessity for life, not as a pleasure. Jack's only concession to pleasure, after the war, was to allow himself a hot bath every night. The bathroom was, therefore, not allowed to become too comfortable and remained linoleum-floored and unheated. Indeed, as if to counteract the sheer decadence of having hot water on tap (although not always reliably), Jack installed an electric-shock machine beside the bath. Like some instrument of torture, this imposing piece of equipment, consisted of heavy duty cables, coils and red knobs. Jack used it to give himself painfully intense electric shocks, allegedly to treat his arthritis. There is a point, however, where the spartan life topples over into frank masochism. Jack was on the cusp.

The Ryders and the Hamilton-Fletchers

After Ronald Graham died, Nancy herself eventually came home in the 1980s to die at Rempstone, moving into a flat at the far end of the house. Touchingly, her ex husband Jack, who had not spoken to her for decades, used to bring her flowers. Divorces in pre-war days were far more terrible than they usually are today. Once divorced, partners were expected never to meet again, never to be on terms of friendship, and never even to be mentioned. Amazingly, the Rempstone children survived the divorces more or less undamaged psychologically, relying upon each other's company, Jack's strength and the enduring stability and presence of Rempstone itself.

After the 1960s people found they could begin to talk about divorce and even about sex. The opening up of topics such as these has continued to the present day. In a few ways, however, sex has become more, rather than less restrictive. Fifty years ago, children were expected and even allowed to be sexual among themselves. If six year olds wanted to play 'doctors and nurses' they were often permitted to do so, within reason. Today, even though female puberty is reached five or six years earlier than it was in Victorian times, sexual intercourse is illegal until three years later than it was, perhaps four or five years after puberty, and marriage is almost unheard of until even later still. Centuries ago marriages took place between twelve year olds and grown men unashamedly declared their love for, and consummated their marriages with brides who were scarcely pubescent. Nobody was shocked. These things were considered to be perfectly normal. Today's unhealthy and cruel hysteria about paedophilia was unheard of until the 1980s. The social disapproval of childhood and pubertal sexuality, between peers as well as with adults, nowadays compounds the psychological trauma affecting abused children. It is mainly fear and guilt that disturb children, not sex.

A big house like Rempstone with its distant bedrooms and spacious shrubberies gave childhood sexuality a chance for healthy expression. Visiting cousins, so it seems, often filled this role. Rempstone's children were then, of course, sent away to single-sex boarding schools where, from the ages of eight to eighteen, sexual experiences were likely to be with the same rather than with the opposite sex, marking another difference between the social classes. The psychological abuse suffered at public schools of the period was often extreme, but was accepted as part of the necessary 'toughening up' of the upper classes.

Like many upper class children of the 1930s, the little Ryders seldom saw their parents; they were handed over to the care of the servants. At Rempstone, the nanny was Mima Grey and she was assisted by a nursery maid. The children lived their lives upstairs, on the first floor, sleeping in the Night Nursery and eating in the Day Nursery. They had lessons in the School Room at the west end of the house. Governesses came and went rather rapidly, one leaving in tears after being found in a compromising position in the garden with one of the guests. The little twins, James and Ben, were pushed around in a smart double pram with a canopy embroidered with a big 'R'. But like many other children in similar circumstances they received very little affection, except perhaps from the servants. In charge of the indoor servants were the cook and the friendly butler, Morgan, in his green apron. He was a splendid old man although nicknamed Monkey Gland by Tim, for some forgotten reason. Gardeners brought fruit and vegetables daily, leaving them in the back passage for the cook to use.

In the late 1930s, after the divorces, the combined Ryder and Hamilton-Fletcher children would crawl around the tiny passages under the eaves and through the attics, with lighted candles and boxes of matches, oblivious of the risk of fire. They called it the RSPCA – the Rempstone Secret Passage Association. Perhaps because it was a group of boys (the Hamilton-Fletchers) joining a group of girls (the Ryders – the twins were too young to count) the combined family was a great success.

The Hamilton-Fletchers had received far more maternal affection and had been smartened up each day to be presented to the adults at tea time. Their stalwarts were their governess, Miss Northey, and Eva the nursery maid. Some nannies at Studland, however, had not been popular, hence a ditty composed by Robin:

There was an old witch,
Who lived in a ditch,
And her name was Nurse Pott.

They found their new stepfather, Jack Ryder, very fair and a lover of outdoor life. Together, they built bridges and cut down trees. Jack was strict about early rising and would hammer upon every bedroom door – regardless of age or status of its occupant – at 7.50 every morning. Meals had to be on time – 8.30 a.m. for breakfast, 1.00 o'clock sharp for lunch, and after the gong was rung, 8.0 p.m. for dinner. He believed in regularity and self-discipline. Old films of Rempstone in 1939 show the newly combined family of Ryder and Hamilton-Fletcher children dashing about Rempstone's grounds, dressing up as Indians, riding ponies, swimming naked in the pool, swinging on the swing, and driving an old First World War lorry through the woods. It was all great fun.

Jack very rarely bicycled but he was invited to go on a spying holiday in Germany in the late 1930s with an RAF cousin, Malcolm Douglas-Hamilton. Together, they bicycled around Luftwaffe aerodromes committing to memory the numbers and types of the aircraft they could see. As Jack's memory was a poor one, RAF Intelligence may well have received an underestimate.

Wartime

Then, the war came. The Ryders were advised to protect the windows of Rempstone with sand bags, which they did. At the end of 1940 the Army requisitioned the west end of the house, pushing the family into the eastern end. Lady Caroline's big drawing room was filled with tiered bunks and became a dormitory for troops. The squash court was converted into a canteen and bren gun carriers stood upon the drive. This situation lasted throughout 1941 while Jack Ryder, now an officer in the Dorset Regiment, was called away to Yorkshire and prepared for the invasion of German-occupied Norway. Robin Hamilton-Fletcher, aged 17, joined the Home Guard and, on his AJS motorbike and armed with a shotgun, made it his special duty to be the first to arrive at the scene of any crashed German aircraft in the vicinity. There were quite a few. Dorniers were shot down at Blandford, Fleet and Weymouth in July 1940. Messerschmitts crashed at Lulworth and Swanage and a Junkers 88 at Portland. Heinkel 111's came down at Sturminster Marshall, Branksome, Studland and West Bay. Bf110's peppered the ground at Kimmeridge, Lulworth, Piddletrenthide, Middlebere, Tyneham, Iwerne Minster, Tarrant Gunville and Owermoigne. Together with his younger brother Tim, Robin collected choice pieces of wreckage as souvenirs. These were carefully stored in a tuck box in the Rempstone attic, each piece carefully labelled, such as 'Magneto from Messerschmitt 109' or 'Piece of windscreen of Heinkel 111 that dived into the ground near Wareham. N.B. pilot's hair and blood'. Some of these items were eventually returned, long after the war, to German survivors and relatives keen to have mementoes. One night in 1940 when Tim and Robin were alone at Rempstone with the elderly housekeeper, the telephone rang to say that the church bells were being rung and that invasion was therefore imminent. Robin loaded his .300 Canadian rifle.

In Rempstone's garden there is a little folly built in the eighteenth century grotto style. It was originally positioned so as to be viewed from across the lake but, by 1940, it was hidden in the trees and rhododendrons. Vee and the bailiff secretly buried under its floor a large metal dustbin filled with tinned food for the family to eat under German occupation: spam, bully beef and baked beans.

Bombing raids increased on Poole, Bournemouth and Sherborne. Portland was frequently a target for enemy action. Spitfires and Hurricanes from RAF Warmwell led the counterattack, assisted by the secret experimental radar and jamming station at Worth Matravers. Throughout the summer of 1940 the Battle of Britain raged overhead and a few bombs dropped near Rempstone as the Germans tried to destroy the munitions factory at Holton Heath. Instead, they hit Goathorn, Arne and Vitower. Baby Richard Ryder, in his pram atop the cliffs at Studland (while his mother visited her friends the Andersons at Harry Warren), was machine-gunned by a low flying Messerschmitt, or was it a Focke-Wulf, while another dropped a bomb on Swanage, killing the bank manager. Later, an experimental high-altitude

Spitfire disintegrated over Keeper's Cottage, the pilot's body falling into the copse opposite – 'every bone broke' said Keeper Witt lugubriously, – 'but skin unbroken'. (He took a professional interest in death). Then a Catalina crashed on Long Island and a Liberator came down, killing all its American crew, at Vitower. Their bodies were laid out overnight in the farmhouse.

Suddenly, in 1942, Vee Ryder was given only two weeks notice to quit the whole house. The north side of Purbeck had become one of the leading battle training areas in the country. Furthermore, the long sandy beach at Studland and Shell Bay still needed to be heavily defended as a possible German invasion site. With great efficiency, Vee found and bought a large house, Millbrook, in the north Dorset village of Childe Oakford and moved her large family there, putting most of Rempstone's furniture and family portraits into storage in Bournemouth for the duration of the war. The Army then moved into the whole of Rempstone [see Plate 49].

After the war was over, tourist coaches would stop on the main road and guides would inform their passengers that this was the house where Eisenhower, Montgomery and Churchill had planned the D-Day landings. There is probably no written proof of this. It is true, however, that those men and King George VI, as well as Generals Bradley and Alexander, had on more than one occasion, visited the area to view the preparations for invasion. Wearing heavy make-up to conceal his strained features from the newsreel cameras, the King had inspected the Royal Marines. At Studland, various new techniques such as smoke-screens, floating airfields, flame throwers and setting the sea on fire were tested, and observed from Fort Henry at the bottom of Studland Manor's garden. Driving from Rempstone towards Studland the king is supposed to have remarked that this was one of the most beautiful places in his kingdom. Rempstone Hall, as the local Army headquarters, appears to have been visited by some or all of these wartime leaders, if for no other purpose than to provide them with a reasonably comfortable lavatory (see page 132).

The Ryders were not much interested in such celebrity. But there were certain names that did mean a lot to Jack and Vee: Winston Churchill, Dame Nellie Melba, Charlie Chaplin, Jack Buchanan, Noel Coward, Kaiser Bill, Rupert Brooke, General Smuts, Velasquez and Queen Victoria. Whenever in the vicinity of Bovington, Vee and Jack would reminisce about Lawrence of Arabia who had died there on his motorcycle. He had been a tremendous cult figure locally.

In 1941, Jack was posted to Basra to defend the oil wells for a short time, before being sent on to Burma where, because of his age (early 40s), he was appointed to air reconnaissance analysis and, later, to being a liaison officer with the Americans. He would have been much better suited, as an ex rugger forward, to a front line job. As it was, he tended, as did many of his generation, to judge the Americans by British standards and, so, found them seriously wanting. They seemed to him to be brash, vulgar and trigger-happy. The only time that Major Jack Ryder ever fired his gun was to put out of its misery a seriously wounded pig in India.

In Burma, away from his new wife and family, Jack became quite depressed. Being part of a successful campaign that eventually drove back the Japanese army was some consolation, but he was never to talk about it freely after the war. His only happy memories were of walking up the Himalayas and into Tibet, from where he brought back some beautiful bells for his children. When he heard the little twins had been very naughty during his absence he sent orders to the Rempstone bailiff to beat them (he never did).

It had not been an outstanding war for Jack, unlike for his cousin Robert 'Red' Ryder, who had won a VC at the St Nazaire Raid. Later, on several occasions, Robert anchored his yacht off Goathorn and visited Rempstone for tea. He was a poised and polished man with typical Ryder-type good looks. Two of Jack's new stepsons, Robin and Tim Hamilton-Fletcher, also saw war service. Tim was in the Navy in Ceylon. Robin went from tanks to secret and heroic action with the SOE and SAS in France and Italy, nearly dying in a crashed aircraft at Middle Wallop. Returning home to Childe Oakford, wounded and with bloodshot eyes, he never told his mother what had happened. She looked at his SAS beret and read the motto on his badge. 'Who cares who wins', he joked.

Peace at Last

After the war Rempstone continued in military and then naval occupation (renamed HMS *Purbeck*) as the long and difficult process of bomb disposal was carried out. Rempstone Heath and woodlands were still full of unexploded bombs and shells. Some of its deserted cottages at Goathorn had been used as targets and were flattened, never to be rebuilt. Not all the explosives were successfully removed from Purbeck. In 1953 several of Richard Ryder's old companions from Forres School were blown up and killed by an allied mine they had discovered on Swanage beach.

During the war the land had been maintained by the estate bailiff or foreman, Reg Spiller, who was in the local Home Guard with Keeper Witt and Fred Simpson (who was also in the secret branch of it, the Auxiliary, with orders to kill anyone who discovered the whereabouts of his underground base). Farmers, gamekeepers and students were classed as 'reserve occupations' and so were not called up to join the Regular Army. In the event of invasion, however, they would have formed the core of the Resistance. A big burly Dorset man, Reg Spiller was later supplied with German prisoners of war to dig ditches and cut hedges. One, a Waffen SS corporal, had immediately identified Spiller as his new führer and had commanded his German squad with ruthless zeal and efficiency. Spiller was to say years afterwards that in the months immediately after the war more Rempstone ditches were dug and trackways mended than for years. Spiller and the ex SS man remained in touch until well into the 1960s. A track, nicknamed 'the autobahn', built by the Germans, still carries estate traffic.

From 1946 until 1948 the Ryders and Hamilton-Fletchers had to live at Vee's house, Hillclose, in Studland. A lovely Voysey building with a beautiful view of Poole Harbour and Sandbanks, it was perfectly situated. In its then large garden (now built upon by three new houses) were a handful of wooden bungalows where members of the family could enjoy a degree of teenage and early twenties independence, and huge bamboo clumps allowed the youngest member of the family to play doctors and nurses with various girlfriends of the same age, including the daughter of the cook. (On many occasions bamboo clumps turned out to be very useful for childhood naughtinesses). The remarkably cold winter of 1946–47 temporarily put paid to such high jinks. Jack Ryder built a large igloo out of ice blocks on the drive as, for weeks, the snow lay thick upon the ground.

In the days before television, the long winter evenings were enlivened by listening to the BBC's Home Service on the wireless. The children had favourite programmes according to their age. There were Uncle Mack on Children's Hour, Tommy Handley in Itma!, Larry the Lamb, Mr Growser and Dennis the Dachshund on Toy Town, and the sheer excitement of that prototype James Bond – Dick Barton, Special Agent, that Richard listened to each night with the cook and her daughter. Later, came In Town Tonight. Richard did not read very much, he always felt too busy, but he enjoyed the adventures of Biggles and the Arthur Ransome stories. Vee read him tales about the Norse Gods.

At last, the Navy withdrew from Rempstone and the family returned in 1949 to find a trampled and battered interior. Military boots had destroyed the wooden floors, and the panelling and linoleum were punctured with bayonet holes. Compensation was minimal. At a time when materials and labour were scarce it was a daunting challenge to put Rempstone Hall back to its old condition. The bay windows had to be rebuilt and the roofs restored. Frugally, Jack replaced the stolen brass door knobs with no-nonsense bakelite. Lower Rempstone was separated internally from the western end and let to tenants – Bill and Kato Woods, an American novelist and his gifted Hungarian-born violinist wife.

With few servants, it was now possible for the depleted Ryder family to fit in to Upper Rempstone. Nobody thought of installing central heating and no log fires were lit until tea-time. In bitterly cold weather the only thing to do was to keep active and wear more clothes. The children would, in consequence, sometimes wear three or four sweaters, one on top of the other, and go for vigorous long walks. Such tactics helped, but did not prevent the itching and throbbing of painful chilblains and chapped legs. For Jack, this was all part of the ascetic life – like his occasional swims at Winspit, Cannon's Cove or Dancing Ledge, where he would dive off the rocks into the deep cold swell even at unseasonable times of the year. Living in such chill conditions in the winter certainly added a spice to life – one relished a hot bath and the crackling comfort of an open hearth, preferably with roasted chestnuts or tea and crumpets. A good log fire could toast one side of one's body while the other side remained quite frozen. Jack was not only spartan, he was also thrifty and installed a call box as Rempstone's only telephone, to teach his children not to be extravagant. It required three big pennies and the pressing of Button A to get through. One then had to shout.

Parts of the interior of Rempstone were dark, cold and deserted. There was a sense of the past. The attics contained numerous glass cases of stuffed birds and animals that had, in the old days hung upon the walls in the hall. There were also some broken eighteenth century musical instruments (possibly Georgiana Bellamy's or Elizabeth Bride's, perhaps even used by John Calcraft's friend David Garrick), General Sir Granby Calcraft's stiff red uniform jacket, Napoleon's lace ruffles in a frame, innumerable portrait prints of ancestors, various African clubs, several pith helmets to ward off the tropical sun and a silk top hat in a box. What happened to all these? Jack and Vee had no idea of their historical or monetary value and all were gradually smashed and destroyed by children. Dressing up and fighting imaginary battles were still very much in vogue as juvenile pastimes.

The Calcraft's library, however, was better protected and, under the advice of the famous bibliophile, Alan Thomas (whose wife had died under mysterious circumstances), Richard had carefully oiled the leather covers of the better books – Edwards' Birds, Cook's travels, a first edition of Ricardo, Parliamentary Reports and so on. The Calcrafts' tastes covered politics, natural history, economics and travel. The contents of the house were nothing but the best and had been put there by the early Calcrafts. The furniture, now largely dispersed, was mostly dated from 1770 to 1820, suggesting it was mainly purchased new by John the Younger or the Lefebures. The inhabitants of Rempstone in the twentieth century accepted what was there, not realising its value. After the war, an odd job man had come to the door to sharpen all the kitchen knives. Looking at the walls he also offered to clean the pictures. Stupidly, Jack let him do so. He badly damaged most of them. There were paintings by Hogarth, Reynolds, Gainsborough, Romney and Cosway.

Many ex servicemen found it hard to find work after the war. Some knew only how to fight and sabotage, and so tried to turn such skills to constructive use. Several attempted to persuade Jack that the felling of trees in future should be done by the use of explosives rather than with saws or axes. They demonstrated on a couple of large oaks at the edge of Foxground, bringing them down with charges placed around their trunks. But the explosives splintered and destroyed some of the best timber in the trees, and so the technique never caught on. Many of the trees at Rempstone were already riddled with embedded bullets and shrapnel that posed great dangers for the saw mills.

There had been an increase in poaching during the war and, afterwards, the old local tradition of smuggling was revived by unemployed ex-servicemen, some of whom were convicted of importing contraband on to the deserted islands in Poole Harbour. Smugglers, poachers and pirates all became confused in infantile minds and at least one Rempstone child lived in fear of meeting men with parrots and black eye patches upon the moor, as dusk descended.

In the grey and boring decade of the 1950s Robin had married and fled the nest, becoming one of the peacetime Army's youngest acting Lieutenant-Colonels at twenty-eight. Tim had motorcycled all around the world on a Norton Dominator, settling eventually at Mau Narok in Kenya with his beautiful wife Mary and establishing a new Rempstone Farm there. The others, who had been at boarding schools during the war, mostly Sherborne or St Swithans (Winchester), were now leaving and doing secretarial courses or national service. The girls were expected to marry and the boys to have some sort of careers. But in those days no planning or advice was given by the schools themselves. All was left to chance and opportunity, as if careers were considered to be slightly vulgar. The gentry should either have no need to work or should follow the age-old formula: the eldest inherits, the second goes into the Army or the Navy, others help to build the Empire, and the youngest goes into to the church. It more or less turned out this way. Nicholas became a regular soldier, James and Ben went to agricultural college and Tim was improving the Empire.

The Ryders had scarcely had to work for their livings for six generations and so were not very good at it. The eldest Ryder boys, James and Ben, after National Service in the family regiment, the rather toffee-nosed Green Jackets (their great uncle Dudley Ryder had been Colonel of the regiment), and having gained agricultural qualifications, began gradually to take over the running of Rempstone. The youngest Ryder son, Richard, did the modern equivalent to going into the church by reading Psychology at Cambridge and, after a short sojourn in the United States, took a job in an Oxford psychiatric hospital.

There was a certain dullness about Dorset in those days that the younger generation tried to remedy. Much-needed life was injected into a stodgy social scene in West Dorset by the likes of Jerry Moeran, Arthur Watson of West Bay, Susie and Rosie Young the famous Biba twins from Bridport, and by some of the Pinneys, Chamberlains and Grove-Whites around Dorchester. Careers, too, became more of a priority: Michael Scott, for example, becoming a successful general after the Falklands War; Richard Eyre, a most distinguished theatre and film director, and Arish Turle, a decorated military man.

Rempstone remained very much a well loved family headquarters at this time. However far away, sons and daughters paid regular visits. Gay Ryder, was now married to the charming Sir Toby Coghill, outstanding headmaster of Aberlour House preparatory school in Scotland; Jennifer Ryder was married to the handsome Jeremy Browne of Houghton near Blandford; and Jacqueline Ryder to the wealthy stockbroker Tom Winser. All continued to visit, and with growing numbers of children.

For a brief few months before war loomed it had been a happy time at Rempstone. The old order held. After the war it would never be quite the same. The complement of servants was then reduced to a live-in cook and two domestics who visited daily. Jack had lost his handsome dash and become despondent. Manfully, he struggled on, bearing the heavy responsibilities of the family and the estate.

Christmas at Rempstone

Christmasses continued to be the highlight of the family's year, when everyone came home. A huge Sitka Spruce or Norwegian Fir would be dragged into the drawing room from the Rempstone woods and, despite the extraordinary risk of combustion, covered with lighted candles. The big hallway was transformed into a wildwood with great boughs of holly and mistletoe, and with ivy all up the stairs and crowning the stuffed head of the Highland bull hung high up on the wall. The outdoors had come indoors. There was the smell of wood fires and candles. The atmosphere was magical.

The house at Christmas might contain some thirty members of the family and, as each was supposed to give a present to all the others, several hundred brightly wrapped bundles would form a small mountain at the foot of the big tree. Christmas dinner was at lunch time. The turkey was carved on the sideboard and served with thick gravy, bread sauce, roast potatoes and brussel sprouts. After the crackers, the blazing Christmas pudding and the brandy, Jack would insist upon healthy exercise, and so all members of the family, wearing paper hats, had to play a dangerous game of hockey upon the lawn, armed with lacrosse sticks, cricket bats, old tennis racquets or anything else with which to hit the ball. A furious rough and tumble ensued, usually ending when one of the children got hurt. Honour satisfied, the family then had hot baths, followed by Christmas cake and tea out of one of the family's beautiful Georgian silver teapots, and at Jack's signal, and not before, they were then allowed into the drawing room for the opening of the presents. Father Christmas had, of course, come the night before, so children had no new toys from breakfast time until the evening. They had to wait. It was worth it: the opening of gifts before a huge blazing log in the ornate fireplace, the coloured lights and tinsel.

After Christmas the snows sometimes came. When they were heavy, Rempstone could be cut off from Corfe and Studland for a day or so. Tim and others would rise to the challenge and start the big estate tractors – Caterpillar or Fordson Major – on which they charged the deep snowdrifts at high speed, rearing and roaring like knights on warhorses. Getting stuck was part of the fun. It was easy to get stranded in a mere car. Vee's Lea Francis was certainly not up to Arctic weather and Jack's Perkins diesel-engined shooting-brake was not much better. The object of the young drivers, said Tim, was to go out courageously to buy stores from the shops in Corfe and then to get stuck as near as possible to a pub.

At Christmas, Rempstone ordered a whole ham, a whole turkey (one of Mr

Dean's largest) a whole tongue and a whole Stilton. By the twelfth day of Christmas, when all the holly and ivy boughs had to be out of the house, and after most of the guests had departed, there was usually plenty of food left over in Rempstone's larder. Jack and Vee, both of whom detested waste of any sort, would heroically continue to chew their way through this cold Christmas debris, at least until the meat had gained a slightly green tinge, and long after what would today be called its sell-by date. Jack would liberally water the hollowed out Stilton with port until it had become a purple quagmire which could be easily ladled out with the silver cheese-scoop.

Every Christmas the Salvation Army band would pay a special visit to Rempstone to play carols on the drive. Jack always had mixed feelings about this. He surreptitiously did good himself but slightly disapproved of 'do-gooders'. He could recall from childhood the irritating fervour of the old Victorian salvationists and quietly regarded religion as a load of 'medicinal' tommy-rot. Vee had a more sentimental view of it – indeed, almost a poetic one. It was left to Vee, therefore, to put money in the collecting box and to thank the trumpeters and trombonists from Swanage and Corfe. Gradually, over the years, religion disappeared from Rempstone Christmasses and fewer and fewer visits were made to Corfe and Studland's beautiful churches.

In the 1950s Jack used to visit poor families on the estate as Christmas approached and leave them a Christmas hamper. This consisted of an old cardboard box filled with fruit, sausages, butter and other essentials, packed by the cook at Rempstone under Jack's direction. It seems an amateur and rather patronising gesture to us today but these Christmas boxes were well received.

Also at this period Vee often used to visit the little cottage where the Paynes lived in the hamlet of Bushey. She used to buy some of their dark golden heather honey and old Mr Payne would play folk tunes for her on his concertina. Little Mrs Payne, in her flowered apron, would tell stories of seeing William Calcraft in his beaver hat and Lady Caroline riding past in the 1870s in her 'Victoria carriage' accompanied by the bailiff on horseback. The cottage smelled of tomatoes, Gumption polish and Lifebuoy soap. There were lace curtains, lace antimacassars and an aspidistra on the table.

Social Life
Little seemed to happen to jollify the countryside in the 1940s and 1950s except for the flower shows, the gymkhanas and the regattas. Studland was a good place for all three. The flower shows were held on the cricket field and the competitive exhibits of parsnips, cauliflowers, sweet peas and beetroots were housed in a big tent. Vee would enter roses and prompt Riddle to produce exhibits of fruit and vegetables, sometimes successfully. Other than the egg and spoon race there was not much for the children at a flower show. It seemed to be all village gossip. The regatta was more fun, being held on the beach. Besides the sailing races and the swimming, which all looked

grand against the backdrop of the white chalk cliffs of Old Harry, there were sandcastle competitions and a beauty parade. Gymkhanas could be fun, too. Not because any of the Ryders were particularly horsey but because it was a good place to ogle at young women. Nearly all the ponies were ridden by girls. Boys and men showed no desire to ride a horse. If they wanted speed they would choose to ride an Ariel or a Triumph motorbike or an MG sports car. Pony riding was something to do with burgeoning female sexuality. At gymkhanas, spotty youths could be seen furtively eyeing the multitude of bejodhpured bottoms on parade, bouncing up and down on saddles.

The younger and single members of the Rempstone clan would try to enliven the boredom of the period by doing the rounds of Dorset parties. These were still supposed to be limited to those of the right class. There were enjoyable parties with the Scotts at Encombe, the Bonds and Moseleys at Creech Grange, the Welds at Lulworth, the Turles at Kingston, the Sturdys at Trigon and the Mansels at Smedmore. Of the local landowners, only the then shy and disabled members of the Bankes family failed to participate socially. Some of the young Scotts were great favourites with the Ryder children: David and Vereena at Encombe, and Veronica and Michael at Bucknowle, and there were the Reids and Outrams at Church Knowle, where the lovely Nicky lived. Nicky Outram founded her Daring Deeds Club at Newton Manor School and was, for several years, a star of Purbeck society. Everyone adored her. She, in turn, adored Jack Ryder, in a granddaughterly kind of way. Later, came the exciting Sewells of Osmington, and the Michies of the Manor House in Wareham.

The young James, Ben and Richard Ryder's main interest was, quite naturally, in girls. These were to be found at Hunt Balls, Pony Club dances in Dorchester or in and around Newton Manor School in Swanage. Shameless (in those days) heavy drinking in the beautiful surroundings of Athelhampton, Bryanston, Handford House or Milton Abbey, followed by reckless and drunken driving, and as little dancing as possible, relieved the monotony of country life, but yielded little in terms of actual sexual gratification. The Ryder brothers would sometimes steal each other's friends. This happened once at Creech Grange where James developed a nose bleed while dancing with a sister's Danish au pair girl. On his return from the bathroom he found that the Dane, and his treacherous brother Richard, had both disappeared. German, Austrian and Scandinavian au pairs, however, proved a reliable source of romance. On the whole they lacked British inhibitions.

Later, in the 1960s, the success rate improved considerably as female resistance, aided by the advent of the pill, began to crumble. The black tie and ball gown dances of the previous decade gave way to less formal events. Foxtrots were replaced by jives or rock'n roll, black ties by blue jeans, cocktail parties by barbeques. Parties in London, of course, tended to be far more productive sexually than those in Dorset. But, however much the adult generation objected to hippies, beatniks and long hair, things were definitely changing. Furthermore, the Knoll House Hotel in Studland, booming under the management of Colonel Fergusson, now started to employ dozens of single girls in the summer months and so became a honeypot for Dorset's bachelors. To make it even more erotic, the girls who cleaned the hotel's bedrooms were known as 'bedders'.

The 1960s' fascination with sex was due not merely to the release of previously inhibited passions. It was actually intensified by those inhibitions. It was time to overthrow mindless religious guilt on the subject. Even in Dorset, contemporary morality seemed to focus upon sex to the exclusion of almost all other issues. Poverty, cruelty and oppression were ignored while parents, teachers and religious leaders could, apparently, find little else to disapprove of morally than the perfectly natural activities of sex. There are three good reasons why sex needs some control – jealousy, pregnancy and disease. But these are practical reasons and not unexplained moral ones. Why was the Church so obsessed with sex? Jesus Christ himself had not shown this obsession with the subject. So why was everybody apparently against it? This was the burning yet unspoken issue at the heart of many a wild Dorset party of the period.

The adults at Rempstone, however, still maintained a far more formal social life based upon a sense of propriety rather than pleasure. Once or twice a year a large drinks party was held in Lady Caroline's old Drawing Room at Rempstone. The lists of invitees would be drawn up by Vee and Jack Ryder, accompanied by frequent sighs and comments such as – 'Oh, do we really have to invite those awful people?' and 'I suppose he'll bring his frightful wife!'. Tim, overhearing these groans one year, asked, quite innocently, – 'If you hate all these people, why do you invite them?' The answer appeared to be that, well, one just had to do these things. Vee, in fact, was very good at parties but Jack tended to resent the expense. Driven by such considerations, he devised a strategy that involved ordering in bulk the cheapest possible sherries and whiskies that he could find. A vintner in Poole or Dorchester would supply him, very discreetly, with Moroccan sherry and Algerian whisky – or the other way around. Jack would then immediately decant these shamefully improper liquors into the most beautiful cut glass Georgian decanters that had been in use at Rempstone since the eighteenth century.

On one such occasion things went hilariously wrong when Jack, grumpily preparing for the ordeal, muddled the two sets of decanters. Nearly all the men, when presented with the choice of either sherry or whisky, chose the latter, with water. Nearly all the women chose sherry. Too much in awe of Jack, who appeared particularly fierce that night, to complain or suggest that there was a mistake, the men obediently consumed their watered sherries while the women, some apparently convinced that they were drinking a rare vintage amontillado, consumed three or four large glasses of raw Algerian whisky. When it began to snow outside, the guests started to leave. But first one, then another, overdressed matron found it extremely hard to get up from their chairs. Lady so-and-so then fell right off the end of the sofa. Everyone commiserated and her husband explained there was something wrong with her shoes. And so it went on. The party ended with a score of all too sober husbands supporting strangely unstable wives as they zig-zagged their ways to awaiting Bentleys on the drive.

Barring happy mistakes such as this, adult parties tended to bore the younger generation. Nevertheless, the latter were expected to hand around the stale cheese biscuits and to make polite conversations about absolute trivia. It was not considered quite proper to talk about anything actually interesting like politics or geology or physics or philosophy. Foreigners did that sort of thing. Instead, the British had to talk about the weather, or the end of rationing or, at a stretch, their children's school certificates. One could admire the sheer genius of the British at being able to prattle away endlessly, quite happily, about practically nothing.

Some of Jack and Vee's cocktail party cronies were, however, genuine friends. Vee felt sincerely fond of various Debenhams, Ross-Turners, Digbys, Leeses, Bonds and Keils, for example, while Jack got on well with the Inges, Scotts, Corytons, Mansels, Redmans, Selkirks and Hinchinbrokes. Both were amused by Harry Clark of Wareham – the urbane Rempstone lawyer – who always had good stories up his sleeve, and often about the Draxes, one of whom, according to Clark, had wanted his ashes to be shot into space. Jack liked Eric and Geoffrey Warner, the bachelor headmasters of Spyway School, while Vee preferred their musical brother Philip and his lovely wife Pam who had once won the Studland Beauty Competition. Both enjoyed the company of Charles and Jane Turle, the parents of Richard's friends, Arish and Gillies. Nevertheless, both Vee and Jack found it hard to be intimate. Vee had discussed some of her worries with Olivia Durham, a glamorous pre-war socialite (with whom she had once been locked in a church in Bergamo by a religious fanatic), and with Nora Backha, another Russian emigrée, but she lacked any 'best friend' or confidante. Neither Jack nor Vee had friends with whom to closely share their interests.

One thing that the real gentry at the time were certainly not interested in was foxhunting. It seemed that none of the old landed families in Dorset regarded hunting as anything but a rather absurd vulgarity. They considered it a sport for the urban nouveaux riches, as indeed it was. Its chief motive was snobbery. Most foxhunts had been started only in late Victorian times but, skilfully promoted by nineteenth century advocates such as R.S. Surtees, Charles Apperley and Henry Dixon, who were trying to raise funds for the new sport, the myth had been put about that it was an ancient and aristocratic pastime. In fact, unlike some other sports, the old aristocracy looked down on foxhunting as being uncivilised. This has now largely been forgotten thanks to the clever spin of the Countryside Alliance in the late twentieth century. Certainly, no member of the Calcraft dynasty of Rempstone Hall had ever hunted, nor would have dreamed of doing so. Indeed, no foxhunt met upon Rempstone land.

The Calcrafts had shot game, of course, but only occasionally. Until the 1960s Rempstone was replete with guns: various muskets, a Manton flintlock rifle of about 1820 (still loaded more than a century later), two brace of duelling pistols, a tiny pocket pistol of 1790, a modern BSA repeating rifle, a long Arabian gun, a massive blunderbuss (for defending the house against invasion), a 16 bore, and two venerable double-barrelled 12 bores, one made by Holland & Holland, and the other by Coggeswell & Harrison. There was also an arsenal of swords – a score of militia cutlasses, several cavalry sabres of the period of the Napoleonic Wars, foreign swords of assorted types, a couple of rapiers and a number of dress swords. Many, no doubt, had harrowing stories attached to them, now, thankfully, forgotten. One, apparently, had been General Granby Calcraft's sabre at the Battle of Talavera, where he had led the charge of the Heavy Brigade.

In the 1950s Rempstone continued to have its own gamekeeper at Keeper's Cottage. Old Keeper Witt, with a permanent drip at the end of his beak-like purple nose, was a man of few words. He was a survivor of the Battle of the Somme, and still had a large lump of shrapnel moving around inside him. His job was killing, and always had been.

Rempstone had a lot of wonderful wildlife. In addition to the rare snakes and lizards there were scores of species of water birds and duck around the edges of the harbour. The deer were mostly Sika but later Roe predominated. Keeper Witt, on orders from Jack, showed young Richard how to shoot rabbits and took him to see the badgers at Bushey one night. There were rabbits and squirrels galore, but otters, hares and even foxes (because not hunted), were quite scarce. Buzzards, owls and woodpeckers frequented the woods around the house itself and there were snipe upon the moor. Arish and Gillies Turle shot one of these in the 1950s and, naughtily, put it in Gay Ryder's bed. It was a sort of love offering. She was not particularly amused.

The fishing at Wareham was famous. Some of the largest salmon ever caught in England have come from the Frome. Many disputes about the fishing rights occurred over the years but the Calcrafts retained the right to net them. This practice continued until the 1950s. The Calcrafts had agreed the fishing rights on both the Frome and the Piddle with the Pitt and Bankes families in the 1760s. The fishing issue was the subject of an action in the High Court taken by William Calcraft and Elizabeth Kittoe against Montague John Guest and Sarah Ernle-Erle-Drax as late as 1896. This records that John Bankes had sold to John Calcraft in March 1769 his fishing rights in both rivers at Wareham.

Neither Guy Marston nor the succeeding Ryder squires were interested in shooting or fishing. They let the shooting rights to a syndicate, in later years run by Jack Inge and his children John, George and Susan. One or two other old retainers maintained their ancient rights and would pay for them by dropping a haunch of venison, a lobster or a large salmon on the front door mat at Rempstone. Vee Ryder detested this habit. 'Oh, not another ghastly salmon' she would exclaim indignantly as she tripped upon a huge sack-clothed carcase. Pheasants arrived in a similar manner. These were destined to be hung in the Rempstone larder until almost putrid, and eaten green, by Jack.

Animal Friends

Animals, of course, were good ice-breakers at Rempstone. You could always find an obliging dog or cat to bring into the conversation if it began to flag. Both Jack and Vee were very fond of animals and the house always had several dogs. They were well known in the neighbourhood. If the squire's dog decided to make a journey over to a nearby farm to visit a bitch, he was always recognised and treated with respect. Toby, a black and curly mongrel was one such. He was a cheerful fun-loving dog who lived for food, bitches and a good run through the woods in pursuit of a deer. He adored life and people. He died of a heart attack after making love in old age.

Dogs and cats lived in the house, the dogs sleeping upstairs in their owners' bedrooms. Much of Vee's shopping in Swanage was to get bones from butchers and fish-pieces from fishmongers. Huge saucepans on the Aga would cook evil smelling chunks of offal and fish that would end up in the dogs' and cats' big glazed food bowls. Tinned pet food only became popular in the late 1950s.

Vee used to visit the Zoo department at Harrods whenever she went to London to look at the parrots, monkeys, snakes and other exotic captives. There, on two successive visits, she and Richard found themselves alone with one other customer – Charlie Chaplin. The elderly Chaplin mysteriously dogged their lives, once sharing a first class compartment with them on the Orient Express. Although they travelled right across Europe together, they never spoke a word to each other. They had not been introduced.

As Vee's children grew up and spent more time away, so her strong maternal instincts had to find an outlet. She turned, increasingly, to animals. An aviary was built and filled with budgerigars and love-birds. The dogs and cats increased in number. A minah bird arrived and sat in a large cage in the kitchen where he conversed with the cook, May Mayell. He imitated Vee's voice calling 'Mrs Mayell! 'Mrs Mayell!'. His conversation was not a lot more interesting, but not much less so, than that of many people one could meet at drinks parties in Dorset in those days. 'Good morning'. 'How are you?' 'Very well thank you'. 'Nice day,' and so on. Egbert could say the same things but in a range of entirely different voices. To this extent, he had the edge on them. He tended to live in the kitchen during the day and was transferred to the drawing room in the evening. The kitchen was not a bad place to be. Mrs Mayell was always there gossiping to the cleaners or to the gardeners or to Reg Spiller. Before the days of dishwashers all members of the family were expected to do the washing up. There was a constant coming and going. In the centre of the kitchen was a large elm table with a white scrubbed top nearly four inches thick. At the end was the Aga.

Then, one day, a monkey arrived. Bimbo, a very excitable and affection-ate Capuchin, was accommodated in Richard Ryder's bedroom. This was not considered strange at the time. But much to Jack's alarm, Vee would allow Bimbo to jump around the picture rails and curtains. That is why the walls and Calcraft family portraits had to be cleaned once in a while. Bimbo dis-covered fairly quickly that he could arouse the interest of his rather stodgy human companions by turning off lights and twiddling the knobs on the wirelesses and televisions while they were in use. Finally, after months of aggravation, he smashed a valuable Georgian glass punch bowl and his movements were subsequently curtailed. Shortly afterwards, he died of dia-betes. Almost at once, however, he was replaced by a succession of further monkeys. There were, for example, Bernard and Ethel, who had very pink parts of their anatomies. They were, to Jack's relief, moved outdoors to a heated revolving Edwardian summer house in the garden. The animals now seemed to take precedence over humans at Rempstone and several guests were firmly reprimanded by Vee for helping themselves to fruit from the Chien Lung fruit bowl. The fruit, it was explained, was for the monkeys and the minah bird. Not infrequently, animals were fed off valuable antiques. After some years of this simian soap opera, Vee wrote a book about it enti-tled *Living with Monkeys*. She later published her childhood memoirs – *The Little Victims Play*.

Animals have always been a support for unhappy teenagers who feel them-selves cut off from other humans. Animals are unconditionally affectionate and forgiving. Vee had considered that animals should be better treated and was outraged by their cruel predicament in factory farms and zoos, and she transmitted this concern to Richard, her youngest child. But Vee had no idea how to put her concerns into effect. This was something that Richard would try to remedy. Consumed with growing guilt about shooting for sport, he gave it up and, from 1969, began to write and campaign political-ly for animals' rights. He saw animals and humans in the same light. He eventually published several books on the subject, became a modernising chairman of the RSPCA, set up the European animal protection initiative, was closely involved with various successful reforms including new legisla-tion to protect laboratory animals and farm animals in Britain and saw the outlawing of hunting with hounds when the Hunting Act was passed in November 2004. One of his first campaigns had involved his confrontation with the Buckinghamshire and Courtenay Tracy otter hounds when those hunters, dressed in blue knickerbocker uniforms and red hats, had held a meet on Rempstone land at Wytch in 1970. Photographs of Richard with a gun under his arm, facing the hunters, appeared on the front pages of the national press on the following day under the headline – 'Gun-toting Psychologist'. Richard went on to organise a national campaign against otter hunting that ended when it was banned in 1977. As the Director of the Political Animal Lobby Richard conveyed large donations to all the main political parties in the 1990s and ensured that each began to take the issue of animal welfare seriously. Like his ancestors, the Calcrafts, he stood for Parliament on a couple of occasions, as a Liberal Democrat, and introduced two new words (and theories) into philosophy – *speciesism* and *painism*. Although living in Oxford or in Devon, he would visit Rempstone for family events together with his children, Emily and Henry Ryder.

Jack and the Exotic Visitors
Life at Rempstone continued much as it always had done throughout the 1950s, 1960s and 1970s. Vee had her sons and her animals to think about and became more involved in music, cooperating with Kato Woods (Havas) in founding the Purbeck Music Festival and in playing the piano at their concerts. She continued to bring to Rempstone's rather philistine milieu some touches of her own exciting and artistic temperament. Various distinguished musicians, such as Sir Arthur Bliss, came to Rempstone at this time. Her brother, Sir Francis Cook, would also occasionally visit. A complete Edwardian with moustache, aromatic cigarettes and black velour hat, he was a total contrast to Jack. Before the war he had driven pink Rolls Royces. After the war he made do with a specially painted purple Rover. Francis was proud to be, in the words of the *Daily Mail*, 'Britain's Most Married Baronet', and to have beaten Henry VIII in this regard. One or two writers also came to stay, such as Anya Seton and Lewis Namier. Both visited to do research: Seton into the story and atmosphere of Corfe Castle and Namier into the history of the Calcrafts.

An amusing visitor to Rempstone was the Australian entertainer Archie Campden who would accompany himself as he sang his own strange little ditties:

> *Algy met a bear*
> *And the bear met Algy,*
> *The bear was bulgy*
> *And the bulge was Algy –*
> *All because he didn't take care.*

> *Bessie met a bus*
> *And the bus met Bessie,*
> *The bus was messy*
> *And the mess was Bessie –*
> *And all because she didn't take care!*

There were other verses that were less innocent.

In the 1970s some more colourful people chose Dorset as a place to retire. An elderly gay couple settled in Corfe, for example. When asked at a Rempstone cocktail party how they intended to spend their declining years, one replied archly: 'We hope to be enlarging the circles of our friends!' Things were looking up in the Dorset repartee department.

Another exotic visitor was Vee's old friend Prince George Chavchavadze [see Plate 50] – a member of Georgia's deposed royal family. His parents, Prince and Princess Troubetskoy, had been helped by the Cooks (Vee's parents) after they had escaped from the Russian Revolution in 1917. They now lived in a squalid wooden bungalow near Harman's Cross. Occasionally, the old princess, Mooshka, would come to tea at Rempstone and, much to the delight and amusement of the Ryder children, proceed to eat whole pots of strawberry jam. 'Just a leetle bit of jam, my dears' she would murmur as she did so. Her sons, George and Paul, were fascinating. Paul, a novelist married to Princess Nina Romanov (from the Tsar's family), lived in America where he was invited to translate the writings of Stalin's daughter Svetlana who came to stay with him on Cape Cod. Paul wrote to Vee Ryder at the time – 'There have been only two great loves in my life – one a Romanov and the other a Stalin!' It was the younger prince, George, however, who was Vee's favourite. Witty and urbane, he was one of the best Chopin pianists in the world. With rings on his fingers and wearing a velvet smoking jacket, he would play effortlessly on the Rempstone Bechstein. He told wonderfully risqué stories and was that old fashioned thing, a virtuoso conversationalist and raconteur. Married to a rich Belgian heiress he lived in a small chateau in Burgundy from where he could keep in touch with the White Russian colony in Paris. Young Richard Ryder was sent on visits to Burgundy and taken by George and his one-eyed Italian chauffeur (a reader of Dostoyevsky) to Paris cabaret night clubs, plied with Green Chartreuse and shown naked ladies. On one occasion, they were due to have tea with Prince Youssopov, Rasputin's murderer, but George had to divert to buy a tin of special cat food and the visit had to be aborted. In Venice, however, where Vee and Richard went to stay with George in his crumbling palace, they met the mad remnants of the old Italian aristocracy, sat upon some huge golden sofas that had once belonged to Wagner and visited the most eccentric members of Venetian society. La Dolce Vita! This was really the life that Vera craved – witty, artistic and exciting.

On return to Rempstone everything must have seemed a bit dull. Jack represented the opposite virtues: understatement, moderation and stolid British common sense. Yet he tolerated the occasional appearances of Mooshka, George and Francis, with a very good grace. Somewhere, deep beneath the tweed, there was a spark of fellow feeling with such exotics. Another entertaining visitor was the American millionaire, Paul Walter, from New York.

Unlike for the Americans, there is a sense of longevity in British life. Almost every house or pub or hostelry has a history if you care to know it and, even if you don't, you feel it. People, too, see themselves not only in the round but in the 'long'; they are the living and breathing outcome of a family line stretching back hundreds of years. It helps to know this. It creates a sense of security and purpose. So, whereas the British feel little need for religion (finding meaning, magic and morality in secular things), the Americans seem all too credulous. Whereas in Britain an adult's rationality and seriousness are measured by their scepticism, in America the reverse is true: they will claim to believe in almost anything in order to be taken seriously.

Jack Ryder was in every respect the typical country squire *[see Plates 51–53]*. He wore clothes that were made to last. And they did, some of them, for forty or fifty years. An old tweed hat with a few jay's feathers inserted under the band, a woolly shirt with a slightly frayed collar, a brown tie, a gold tie pin holding the collar together underneath the knot, a moleskin waistcoat worn shiny in places, a tweed jacket with leather patches on the elbows and a silk handkerchief spilling from the top pocket, khaki cavalry twill trousers that were so thick they might stand up on their own, and great hobnailed shoes – 'like boats' James said. Jack was a study in browns, buffs and khakis, with an occasional touch of moss green. He seemed to merge with the countryside itself; he was a part of nature. (Clothes, for all the family, had to be fairly clean but never too tidy or too new. It seemed proper to look slightly frayed and dishevelled.) *Time* magazine, having interviewed Jack over the Wytch farm oil discoveries, described him as 'Hobbit-like'. So did the *Spectator*. He was, however, too fierce and too large for a hobbit, being about five foot ten. Yet he lived much of the time in his study which was, indeed, hobbit-like. After the war he had papered the walls with ordinary brown paper which made the room very dark. An old oak desk with a raised top full of drawers and pockets further cut off what light there was coming through the heavily curtained window. Two walls were entirely covered with the Calcrafts' leather-bound books on old book shelves edged with numbered strips of brown and gilt material. Another wall, only dimly visible from the door, boasted a black Purbeck marble fireplace, on either side of which were two great Georgian wing armchairs, covered in dark green leather. There was a mahogany drum table in the centre of the room on which were piled old maps, pieces of broken Crown Derby, a jam jar full of used nails and several balls of twine. Jack, himself, could be located by the cloud of pipe smoke in the area of the desk, where he sat in his Chippendale chair glaring at his papers through half-moon spectacles. The study was certainly a den – indeed, almost a burrow.

Another interesting room at Rempstone was the old Muniment Room on the ground floor which Jack had converted into the downstairs WC. It also housed the telephone and its coin box. The room had a vaulted ceiling and its window was defended with solid shutters secured by a heavy iron bar. Its third fixture was a great Chubb safe the size of a kitchen cupboard that was hardly ever opened. One night in 1960, however, Jack suddenly opened it and took out a mass of gleaming Calcraft silver which was taken into the Morning Room, filling the room with a strange musty smell, as tureens and teapots and spoons and salvers were removed for the first time from their green baize wrappings into which Rempstone's last butler had carefully folded them before the war. The room glowed like Aladdin's cave. 'If you want anything, take it!' Jack said to his children, tersely. So each, rather awestruck, chose in turns: one going for the heaviest items, another for the most practical, a third for the most lovely.

In Jack's case, appearances were, on the whole, consistent with character. Hard working, self-disciplined and peppery, he favoured the simple things of life. He loved his pipe, read the *Daily Telegraph* and refused to watch television. (Later he did.) Although he publicly condemned the estate oil as 'a damned nuisance', privately he felt it was his patriotic duty to acquiesce with the oil industry's demands. He also felt a great sense of duty to his estates and tenants. Jack was fiercely unselfish and was a fair and conscientious father who, nevertheless, found it hard to show the affection for his children that he felt. He coped with his severe arthritis with stoicism – creating a stir by abruptly sacking his posh private surgeon at the King Edward VII hospital in London when the man inadvertently broke his femur. Jack was thrifty but lacked a business flair. Being dyslexic he found his office and committee work extremely taxing. Nevertheless, he persevered out of a dogged sense of duty: these efforts, combined with the almost constant pain of his old rugger injuries, making him, on occasion, irascible. Young men tended to fear him. Young women, innately designed to deal with the male temper, often found him sympathetic and lovable. He could certainly be intimidating to poachers, trespassers or errant tenants. One of the latter, a tall and powerful man, had the fright of his life one day when the squire drove his Daimler straight at him and at increasing speed. Fortunately, the tenant jumped into the hedge in the nick of time. 'What was all that about?' enquired an alarmed passenger. 'Oh, he knows' was Jack's grim reply. No more was ever said.

Fierceness and bad temper were far more acceptable fifty years ago; such traits were expected in males and were often the cause of affectionate amusement. Jack met an equally fierce man in Admiral Charles Turle of Tolpuddle Manor and, on the strength of their fierceness, they became the best of friends. Both were men in the Victorian sense of the word. Waiting at the white line for the railway crossing at Wareham to open one day, Turle was angered by a young male driver who drove his car in front of him. Ignoring his seventy years, Turle got out and knocked on the driver's window. When it was lowered he calmly punched the young man on the nose. A few years later Jack fell asleep in his car while waiting at the same white line, causing consternation to the drivers behind, some of whom assumed he had died. Although he had been a magistrate for a time, Jack would sometimes drive through the red traffic lights at Wareham. He had opposed their installation and was damned if he would put up with them. Jack could be a fine example of a grumpy old man. As he grew older his driving became erratic: there were, one suspected, only two positions in which his arthritic right leg was comfortable; either with his foot flat on the brake or flat on the accelerator.

He was a familiar figure to motorists: sitting low in the driving seat, his hat over his eyes, often with a dog on the passenger seat beside him. Some of these canine companions would occasionally give Jack a respectful lick on the cheek. From behind, as viewed by a following motorist, especially if the dog had curls, this could give the impression of a well coiffured young woman becoming affectionate. On more than one occasion, rumours of this sort were circulated.

Some families grow cantankerous in old age and others tend to mellow. Both Calcrafts and Ryders are in the latter category, and Jack certainly mellowed as the years went by. His loves were Rempstone, his family, rugger and trees. Towards the end he radiated a sad and kindly tranquillity.

So, what was a typical day for Jack in the 1950s? He rose early, washed and shaved with one of a series of cut-throat razors that he kept sharpened with the leather razor strop which hung in his dressing room among the fading rugger caps and photos. He used a badger hair shaving brush and a stick of shaving soap, the lather mixed up in a shaving bowl. (The results were not always perfect and Jack frequently had stubble on his chin.) He then went downstairs in his dressing gown to use the lavatory and to open the shutters and the curtains in the Drawing Room and Morning Room and check in the kitchen to make sure Mrs Mayell was cooking the bacon. The dog, Toby, Ching or Sandy, who had slept in a big basket in his bedroom, would come with him and would be let out of the front door. Jack would then return to his dressing room to dress, choosing from a series of almost identical woolly shirts and brownish or greenish ties. This accomplished, at 7.50 a.m. sharp, he would start his round of the occupied bedrooms, hammering on each door and shouting – 'Time to get up – ten to eight – time to get up!' He would then go downstairs again, let in the dog and sit at his desk in his study planning what he would say to Spiller that morning. At 8.30 a.m. Mrs Mayell would knock furtively on the study door and call – 'Breakfast's ready, Mr Ryder' and Jack would arthritically limp into the Dining Room, his hobnails crunching on the flagstones. If there was nobody there, as was all too often the case, he would turn angrily to the gong and give it one or two violent swipes, before helping himself to whatever was on the sideboard: bacon and scrambled egg in the silver entrée dish, occasionally fried mushrooms and, even more rarely, large and succulent kippers from the fishmonger in Swanage (Toby, the dog's, favourite). In later years the diet grew more spartan and cooked breakfasts became a rarity. He then sufficed with grape nuts, porridge or wholemeal toast and bitter marmalade. Perhaps a Rempstone apple or two, preferably half rotten, would serve to end the meal which had been washed down with tea, or coffee on Sundays. By this time, Vee and the children had, grumblingly, come down, mumbling 'good mornings'. Jack by now would be reading the *Daily Telegraph*, or if it hadn't yet arrived, a *Country Life* or a *Countryman*. The former was destined for the Morning Room, the latter for the downstairs WC. At about three minutes to nine, Spiller would knock loudly on the outer door of Jack's study. Sometimes, if Spiller was too early or if a point had to be made, this was initially ignored. Jack would eventually rise and go back to his study, closing the door behind him so that those in the dining room could not hear what was being discussed. Occasionally, however, Jack's raised voice could be heard fulminating angrily as he thumped his desk – 'No. I am not having it... I don't care a damn... I will not put up with it...' Needless to say, Spiller always acquiesced. 'Right, Sir, I'll see to that then.' They were a good team; not highly creative but you knew where you stood with them. Rempstone business was slow, solid but dependable. It often did not make sense financially but there was nothing flowery or untrustworthy about it. The two of them together, Spiller, at least four inches the taller, commanded unarguable respect locally. Spiller would not have been a good man to fall out with. Undominated by the Squire he could have become despotic.

Jack would either spend the mornings labouring with his paperwork in the darkness of his great desk, its pigeonholes stuffed with papers, old seals and pieces of sealing wax, or he would drive off to Wareham for 'meetings'. What these were was often unknown to the family, but they seemed to be mostly the local Council, the Poole Harbour Commissioners, or to do with his business interest at Hyde Sand and Gravel on Worgret Heath. Wareham was where Jack went. Vee, on the other hand, shopped in Swanage. Jack was usually back for Earl Gray tea at five, often with fruit cake and scones, too rarely with crumpets. After tea in the summer there would be a chance for good exercise of some sort, then, as always, his bath at seven and down for dinner at eight. By the 1950s, dinner had lost its formality unless there were guests. Food was simple and mostly consisted of cold ham, cold beef, cold lamb or cold salmon and salad. The larder always housed hunks of cold meat of one sort or another, usually leftovers from the hot joints of Sunday lunches. Soups became a feature and Jack would add a glass of sherry to his and grind into it hard Dorset biscuits, using the edge of one of General Braddock's old silver soup spoons. Baked potatoes with butter and marmite were a favourite standby. In season, there were wonderful broad beans, peas and tender carrots from the garden. Desserts, always referred to as 'puddings', became rarer as the years went by, but sometimes consisted of cooked Rempstone rhubarb or apple pie. Drink was rarely wine in those days; more often beer, cider, barley water, ginger beer or just plain tap water. After dinner, Vee and Jack would separate, Vee to watch television in the Drawing Room or to play the piano, Jack to sit in his winged armchair in the Morning Room where he soon fell asleep behind a newspaper with the BBC's Home Service on in the background. His slumbers increasingly interrupted by family members coming in to say goodnight, he would eventually give up and go to bed around midnight. Jack and Vee slept in separate but adjoining rooms.

About once a year Jack and Vee would go to London; Jack to attend a rugger dinner and Vee to visit her sister Rachel in Chelsea, shop in Gorringes or Harrods and take Richard to the conjuring at the Fortune Theatre. Jack would stay at his club, the RAC, and Vee in an old fashioned hotel like the Rembrandt or the Basil Street Hotel. Both would take several suitcases, hats and coats. In 1960 Jack was sworn at by a porter at Waterloo; he had tipped him sixpence, just as he had been told to do by his mother in 1910. London seemed another world from Dorset.

Jack, however old fashioned he appeared, did subtly move with the times. An example is how he became increasingly informal in his approach to employees. For forty years he had addressed his bailiff, Reg Spiller, as 'Spiller' and his cowman, Ernest Short, as 'Short'. But in his twilight years they became Reg and Ernie. Indeed, Reg would now sit down and enjoy an occasional cup of tea at Jack's breakfast table. Neither of them, however, ever called him Jack. To them he was still 'Sir' or 'Major'. Ernie had started his career as a footman at Smedmore in the 1930s and had then become Jack's batman in the army during the war. In 1949 he had returned as the manager of the home farm, had married the Hamilton-Fletchers' and Richard's old nanny, Eva, and settled into the accommodation at the far eastern end of Rempstone. Some servants stayed on for years. Vincent girls came and went generation after generation until the Second World War. After the war, the only resident servants were the cooks, Mrs Mayell and Mrs Brown. Mrs Browsea and the pretty little Marion Best, who looked like Snow White, came daily to do the housework.

Manners of Speech

The Rempstone yard accommodated an assortment of lorries, old tractors and concrete mixers. It had a Dutch Barn full of hay and a pigsty. Jack had arranged a home-made and creative draining system so that the output from the pigs could drain into a straw filled pit to create a useful slurry. After a few years it got hopelessly blocked and made the smell a lot worse. There was also a sawmill at the yard. Several saws would slice up the huge pines and oaks from Rempstone's woods, driven by a venerable single piston engine with a massive iron flywheel and a deep voice. Bong! bong! bong! thudded the great engine, sending giant smoke rings up its ten-foot exhaust pipe. You could hear the scream of the saws and the explosions of the engine echoing down the valley a mile away.

The estate gang, under Reg Spiller, was composed of old regulars: Fred Stockley the carpenter, Noel Churchill the mason, Ernie Battrick the labourer, Jim Wellman, the lorry driver from Tyneham, Gordon Linnington the builder and three or four woodmen – Percy Brownsea, Bill Christopher, Tom Caddy and Teddy Vincent. The gardeners, such as Fred Churchill, were a separate concern. So were the sawyers. Up till the 1960s all would touch their hats to the Squire, address him as 'Sir' and Vee as 'Madam', and refer to the children as Mr James or, if young enough, as Master Richard. The regular tenant farmers found the Squire fierce but fair, so they often stayed on for decades: the Deans at Rempstone Old Farm, the Pitmans at Wytch, the Hunts at Bushey, and the Simpsons at Claywell. Gradually, as the years went by, the old formalities of address softened, and after the 1960s, if they persisted at all, they became self-conscious and secretly resented – a slight source of embarrassment on both sides. In the old days conversation with estate workers tended to be limited to the matter in hand – drains or roofs or slurry pits and to the weather. Bad weather in Dorset was either 'wild' or 'sharp' – both adjectives ('woild' and 'jarp') sounding good in a strong Dorset accent. Sometimes the accent was too strong to be understood easily, particularly when words like 'snow' were constantly employed to mean 'you know'. Old 'Kipper' Witt said little, but when he did, it was hard to decipher. On occasions, he would add a 'compris?' – the extent of the French he had learned on the Somme. 'Thick' for 'that' was sometimes used and a 'w' inserted before vowels, such as 'wold' for 'old'. Old Harry Cattell in Corfe would say 'thick wold woak' for 'that old oak'.

Belief in traditional folklore was at a low level in immediate post-war Dorset but there was still a woman near Weymouth who believed she had been bewitched or 'overlooked' as it was called locally. Witchcraft in Dorset had, for centuries, been viewed, as it still is in parts of Africa, as the cause of much ordinary ill fortune. Any bit of bad luck could be blamed upon some neighbour's malevolence. Crop failures and animal diseases, in particular, were attributed to this cause. Although witches could be benevolent, providing cures for illnesses and love charms, just as often they would be feared as the main source of evil. In Dorset a witch could traditionally turn herself into a hare that could only be killed by a silver bullet. When questioned about witches in 1955, Harry Cattell replied: 'Witches? They be out o'date!' He had several cures for warts, however – 'Wurts? Jarm 'em away!' This could be done if you cut some elder, he explained, and 'put as many snotches in 'em as you'm got wurts and then throw 'em down the closet. '

The language at the Hall was somewhat different, but both Jack and Vee had some antique inflexions. The way people spoke, of course, still defined their class. Not only accent mattered, it was also a question of vocabulary. Both Vee and Jack used Edwardian and 1920s words and pronunciations, but neither had 'plummy' or affected accents, although Jack rhymed 'cloth' with forth and 'off' with Corfe. Occasionally, he would drop the initial 'h' from words like 'hotel'. He rarely swore but when he did it did not get much worse than 'dashed', 'damnable' or 'damned'. Occasionally, there was a 'blast' or a 'bother'. When he lost his temper he would thump the table or desk so that things rattled and spilt, rather than swear. 'By Jove', of course, was still around. Vee sometimes turned an 'o' into a 'u', as in 'Cuventry' (Coventry), 'Cumpton' (for Compton) or 'Oliver Crumwell'. She also said 'la(r)ndry' for laundry and 'la(r)nch' for launch. Both Jack and Vee played 'goff'' and not golf. Jack called toilets 'gents', 'WCs', 'cloaks' or simply, lavatories, while Vee called them 'aunts'. Swimming attire for both sexes was referred to as 'bathing dress'. Disapproving adjectives were 'foul', 'frightful', 'ghastly' and 'monstrous', and bad situations for Vee could be 'hideous'. When ill she sometimes felt 'piano' (with a long 'a'). People who had too high an opinion of themselves were called 'frightfully posh' or 'rather grand'. Those not of the upper class could politely be referred to by Jack as 'not out of the top drawer' or 'not quite pukka', and as 'rather mere' by Vee, although to comment at all about class was, itself, not quite 'the done thing'. People who were disliked were usually described as 'tiresome' or if really difficult, 'maddening'. Words of approval from Jack were 'splendid', 'good show', 'jolly good' and (to a relative) 'well done old boy' (or 'old girl'). For Vee, good things could be 'simply heavenly' or 'divine'. Adverbs were important for Vee and often sounded extreme: 'frightfully', 'utterly', 'hideously', 'awfully' and 'monstrously' were constantly in use, as in 'frightfully tiresome', 'hideously dull' and 'monstrously expensive'. New words were employed by the younger generation, like 'super', 'wizard', 'gosh', 'golly' and 'smashing'. Some very rich expressions could be heard in the fields, too. One Rempstone farm worker with a strong Dorset accent was overheard discussing his sweetheart: 'I do love 'er so much, I could drink 'er piss as beer!', while Spiller would 'bet my balls on an acre of swedes'.

There were certainly some characters around who said some wonderful things. Some old gaffers still wore waistcoats, brown corduroy trousers and collarless shirts, and spoke so broad that young people would try not to talk with them for fear of not understanding a word they said. There was Ginger Smith from Bushey who trimmed the 'rosydandrons' in the Rempstone garden and old Hookey Harris in the Bankes Arms in Studland who had shot off his hand when poaching rabbits – 'I 'eld 'im (the arm) up to the moonlight – and the bugger (the hand) were garn!' He was never slow to cadge a drink – 'The tide's come in, Sir.' Nor was his mate Old Dan'l, whose only known utterance was 'Argh!'. In the 1950s there were still gypsies on Wareham Heath, not only in caravans but still with barefoot children. Jack went out of his way to help them. They, too, spoke broad.

The End of an Era
Both Jack and Vee, although constantly being seduced into activities by the local Conservatives, remained quite independent in their political views and both told Richard, at various times, that they preferred the Liberal Party. Like most who are not professional politicians they could get away with being politically inconsistent in their views. Most of us enjoy this luxury of being a bit of a Tory on one day and a Liberal on the next. Neither Vee nor Jack liked Mrs Thatcher, thinking her to be both extreme and vulgar. (Geordie Selkirk, still an influential Tory, hung her picture in his downstairs lavatory). Harold Macmillan seemed to them to be the most reasonable of the Conservative leaders; both had come across him socially before the war and knew of his wife's sexual adventures with Lord Boothby. Vee's sister, Rachel Lloyd, remembered Macmillan's 'ghastly teeth and dreadful breath' and having to entertain him while his wife misbehaved elsewhere.

In 1972, Jack employed his gifted architect stepson, Alexander Hamilton-Fletcher, to design and build a house half a mile west of Rempstone Hall, and

Jack and Vee moved in to Bushey House two years later. In 1980, after an afternoon playing piano duets at Morton's House in Corfe, Vee drove home to Bushey House, had a heart attack and dropped down dead. She was buried at Studland, near her parents' grave, at a funeral attended by her children, stepchildren, grandchildren and great grandchildren. When Jack lay dying in a nursing home at Winfrith Newburgh some five years later, at the age of eighty-five, he had sweet fantasies, perhaps brought on by the painkillers. He believed that he had had tea with his two dead wives and was so pleased that they had got along well together. As a boy he had always wanted to go to the moon, and shortly before he died, he reported to his relatives that he had done so. Jack, at his request, was buried in an unmarked grave in Rempstone woods where, he said, his remains might do some good for the trees. Jack had cared about the countryside long before conservation became a fashionable subject in the 1960s and, as Chairman of the local planning committee, had resisted unsightly developments and encouraged organic husbandry. He had been Chairman of the Wareham and Purbeck District Council for seven years, vice Chairman of the Dorset and Avon Water Board for twelve years, vice Chairman of the Corfe Parish Council for fifteen, governor of a half dozen local schools, vice Chairman and Chairman of the Poole Harbour Commission for sixteen years, a magistrate for six, Chairman of the South East Planning Committee for seven, and a member of five County Council committees. He had outlived nearly all his pre-war friends. Only Geordie and Wendy Selkirk lived on for another few years, their funerals being held eventually in north Dorset near the old family home of Ferne, not far from Shaftesbury. Angus Hamilton read a lesson and the bagpipes played. Ferne still continued as the animal sanctuary that Nina Hamilton had founded with her formidable Swedish friend, Miss Lind-af-Hageby, many years before.

Jack had been born three months after Queen Victoria died and Vee could actually remember the old queen's funeral. She had been just two at the time. Both of them grew up as Edwardian children. In nurseries before the First World War the main threat to Britain was still felt to be France, and the bogeyman feared by Edwardian children was still the spirit of Napoleon Buonaparte. Both Jack and Vee could recall their nannies' threat – 'Behave, or Boney will get you!' No generation had seen more social, cultural and technological change than Jack's and Vee's, yet both had successfully coped with it. They had journeyed all the way from childhood fears of Bonaparte to the television age and the landings on the moon.

James Calcraft Dudley Ryder (born 1934)

When Jack *[see Plate 54]* moved into Bushey House in 1972, his eldest son James Ryder took over Rempstone. Alexander Hamilton-Fletcher, no doubt aided by the artistic skills of his wife Nichola, improved the interior for James, his wife Sally and their three daughters, Lara, Melanie and Emma. The interior was redecorated some years later for James' second wife

Georgina, whose own tastes were more sumptuous. Happily married, and for the last time, James and Hilly Ryder, early in the twenty-first century, prepared a house in Wareham for their retirement and old age. It would be the first time that an heir of the Calcrafts, Lords of the Manor of Wareham, had ever lived in that old Saxon town. Since Jack's death, James had become a jovial and popular squire and had run the two estates of Rempstone and Wareham with relaxed assurance, joining in enthusiastically with local customs such as the Court Leet in Wareham. He continued the family interest in politics through his chairmanship and presidency of the local Conservative Association.

Witty and affectionate, James had charmed many Dorset ladies over the years. Unlike his father, he found business decisions easy to make and his judgements were sound and practical. His younger twin brother, Ben, who also had had an interest in the estates, was his perfect foil. Whereas James was easy going, Ben has tended to be cautious. Ben's wife, Philippa Cunningham, too, was creative in her attitudes to business; for years, she tried to develop the estates in ways more appropriate to the twentieth century, by tapping the growing tourist trade and, with Richard Ryder, protesting at the rape of Rempstone by the oil industry. Meanwhile, Ben worked hard at farming Rempstone's land. He was thrifty and careful. In middle age he and Philippa took up golf and could afford a small house in Portugal. Their children all continued to live on Rempstone: Douglas, their eldest, at Rollington, Guy at Rempstone Old Farm and Vanessa (a gifted photographer) at Vitower. Guy Ryder duly became the estate's paid manager, based at the estate office in Cow Lane, Wareham. While James' eldest daughter, Lara Manningham-Buller *[see Plate 55]* and her husband Mervyn, lived in Lower Rempstone, his middle daughter, Melanie Moriarty, lived at Burnbake and his youngest, Emma, was often to be found with her mother in the North Mill house at Wareham. It was in 1996 that James and Lara toured the house with half a dozen occultists, eventually participating in the exorcisms. Politely James asked the ghost of his great great grandmother to leave. Maybe, at last, she has.

Shortly after James became resident at Rempstone a friend asked whether he could hold his new security company's first AGM there. Some twenty ex SAS and ex-Intelligence officers duly came to stay. Shortly after dark the local policeman turned up to explain that he had just received a warning that a Bournemouth burglar was planning to break into Rempstone that very night. James explained that the burglar was more than welcome to try! Sadly, he never did. Burglars are generally wary of houses full of dogs and shotguns. Adding the SAS would have been the last straw.

Final Thoughts
It is possible to look at families as organic units. They are creations of their times. The Edwardian Ryders were a good example *[see Plate 30]*. Dudley Henry Ryder of Westbrook Hay had six sons – one an Edwardian bon viveur with loud check tweeds and plus fours who gambled on the horses and spent

a lot of money on pretty ladies, another who died young, a third who died a missionary in Africa (perhaps eaten by cannibals), one, an army officer, dying of consumption and another who was a convicted 'homosexualist' and was, therefore, not very much talked about. They typify the age they lived in. They were described by Great Aunt Helena as 'the stupidest people I have ever met.'

In 1996 the revelations about the hauntings had amused the Ryders. Richard, as a child, had been afraid of the ghosts at Rempstone long before their presence was confirmed by the mediums. Going upstairs at night on to the dark landings and passageways had always been a terrifying prospect. Two areas upstairs were especially spine-tingling. These were eventually independently identified by the experts (Richard was abroad at the time) as where the shades of Lady Caroline and the abused servants were located. In broad daylight, things were not so bad. But alone, in the dark, on a wet and windy night, then everything changed. One of the experts, Michael Poynder, attributed Rempstone's spectral atmosphere to the flow of underground water beneath the house.

Richard had seen two white figures standing by his bed when he was ten, but, otherwise, there were no other reported sightings. Only strong menacing feelings – presences. Is it only sensitive and fearful people who 'imagine' such things? Or is it the other way around? Do children who grow up in haunted houses become sensitive and disturbed? All such topics were ridiculed by the Ryders at Rempstone – until the 1990s. Any child mentioning ghosts earlier in the century would have been laughed at – Jack 'pooh-poohed' such nonsense. But then Jack pooh-poohed many things – ghosts, astrology, most music, most poetry, most religion and the authenticity of many archeological finds. For Jack, the world seemed to be riddled with fakes, falsehoods and foreign affectations: all hysterical nonsense. For years, despite the opinions of distinguished archeologists, he even refused to accept the authenticity of the Stone Circle or of the Roman pottery found at Vitower. Jack, in a quiet way, was a great debunker of humbug, but sometimes it went too far. Perhaps such scepticism was a reaction against the spiritualism and quackery of his Edwardian childhood. Paradoxically, Jack created his own stone circle at Bushey House, as a folly.

The Calcraft story is full of mysteries: the mystery of the first John Calcraft's birth; the mystery of the Junius letters; the mystery surrounding the macabre death of John Calcraft (the Younger); the mystery of the reported murder of Captain William Calcraft in Portugal; the mystery of the real reason for Marston's libel action; the mystery of Jane Panton's son's death; the mystery of Aleister Crowley's visits to Rempstone; and the mystery of the hauntings.

By the year 2000, John Calcraft's living Rempstone descendants numbered thirty-seven, although none bore the surname of Calcraft. Of these, about two-thirds still lived in Dorset and still, to a large extent, depended upon the wealth that John Calcraft had invested in Wareham and the Isle of Purbeck some two hundred and fifty years before. A score of in-laws and step relatives, most notably the Hamilton-Fletchers, were also in the area. Attendances at family get-togethers, such as the celebration of James' and Hilly's wedding in August 2003, and of James' and Ben's seventieth birthdays in the following year, could be numerous.

So the story of a dynasty and its descendants closes. Looking back over three centuries, certain patterns can be seen. The first is that of family traditions. For example, the Calcrafts maintained for generations the traditional family interest in politics, and it lingers still among their descendants. Sex highlights a second pattern: the tendency for generations to alternate between suppression and expression – the profligacy of 'Crafterio' John Calcraft and his actresses is followed by the monogamy of his son, by the Parisian high jinks of his grandson, by the puritanism of Lady Caroline Calcraft and then by the indulgence in sex magic by her grandson, Guy Marston.

For the upper classes, women's sexual freedom was far greater in the eighteenth century than later. By the mid Victorian era this freedom had shrunk to zero, where it remained for decades, easing only fractionally at the start of the new century and during the Second World War. Eventually, it took off during the 1960s and has never yet looked back. The Calcraft story exemplifies these trends. Both Daisy and Guy (and, no doubt, many of the Victorian Calcrafts) had suffered from the lovelessness of puritanism. Yet it is sex that is still proving such a difficult thing to manage in the world today. It is at the root of the clash between Islam and Western values (and between Western neoconservatism and real liberty). If the late twentieth century has proved anything about how to live it is that the age-old fear that sexual freedom will lead inevitably to decadence is groundless and that, on the whole, the pains arising from a modicum of sexual freedom are considerably less than the pains resulting from sexual puritanism.

Finally, there is the tendency for children to attempt to realise their family's or parents' unfulfilled ambitions: the Rt Hon John Calcraft trying to gain the political respectability and title that his father craved; John Hales Calcraft seeking the rural peace of mind that his father clearly never enjoyed; Sir Henry finding the urban sophistication, excitement and success that his countrified family must have sometimes yearned for during the dull mid nineteenth century, and Guy Marston seeking the intellectual freedoms that his mother may secretly have wished for. There is also the overall 'natural history' of a dynasty – its rise through ambition and the making of money, its attainment of established national and metropolitan status, its marriage into the aristocracy and, then, its gradual decline into the rural mediocrity of the later Calcraft years.

It seems that human beings, as social animals, naturally tend to arrange themselves into a hierarchy where each level respects and tends to obey the levels above. In the long evolutionary battle for survival this has proved to be the most effective way for groups or troops of human primates to survive against external threats and for the requirements for food and procreation.

This is why most people, most of the time, are happy within a hierarchy of class, provided it is non-oppressive, reasonably fair and flexible. This tendency has been bred into us through evolution.

In peaceful societies, hierarchies are not quite so obvious as they are when a nation is at war. But they have always been a feature of armies and navies. For centuries, armed forces have tended to arrange themselves into hierarchies containing approximately seventeen ranks or rungs on the ladder. These seventeen ranks have usually been divided into three groups: officers, non-commissioned officers and men. Social class in Britain has been arranged on a similar basis although with more ranks lower down the scale than in the military model. The three major groups, however, are still there, and have been called by various names, most simply: upper, middle and lower. Karl Marx referred to aristocracy, bourgeois capitalists and workers. Like many theorists, however, Marx grossly oversimplified. He missed the nuances and complexities of the British system. Sociologists in general have also made this mistake. They have glossed over the grades within the three main groupings. Furthermore, they have blurred the essentially hierarchical nature of the class ladder by emphasising roles and occupations. Roles are certainly important but they are secondary to the essential hierarchy of respect, prestige and, ultimately, power: these are the qualities that are crucial to class.

The American Revolution consciously overthrew such a class system to produce an ostensibly egalitarian society – at least for white males. Each society arranges its hierarchy differently. Nevertheless, America continues to be, on the face of it, a remarkably classless society. But it is still hierarchical; respect, prestige and power in America depending chiefly on one thing: money. The British class system also ultimately depends upon wealth, but has disguised this fact, its upper echelons believing in birth as its defining factor. Occupations and behaviour (i.e. manners, accent, posture and dress etc) have been useful signals of class in British society but they have been mere labels for birth, although well known not always to be reliable labels. Although many Britons have been content to accept their class status, there is, of course, the somewhat contrary impulse of self improvement. This impulse, nevertheless, itself also implies some acceptance of the class structure and the rules of the game. Few individuals have consciously wished to reduce their class status and most would like to think of themselves as rising up the ladder. Wealth itself, as in the case of the Calcrafts, was the first step. The purchase of land was the natural next step, as it has been for centuries in Britain. Then came the Calcraft marriages into classes higher than themselves; then, finally, the passage of time. Horace Walpole once remarked that it takes three generations to become a gentleman. With the Calcrafts one can see this, too. It was third-generation John Hales Calcraft, the Squire of Rempstone, who could finally feel that he had arrived. He had acquired 'birth', as had his children. The Calcraft Dynasty had, finally, made it. Yet, paradoxically, the first two Calcraft squires were committed to social change:

to freedom of speech, to reducing the power of the monarchy and to extending the franchise. They challenged the very class system into which they had successfully climbed.

The nature versus nurture debate is one of the perennial but mainly unconscious dichotomies on which societies swing first one way and then another. Before Sigmund Freud, British culture had tended to emphasise the importance of an individual's physical 'nature', both in its effect upon the conduct of children and adults, and in its moral significance. It was 'blood' that mattered more than upbringing. Not only class, but such human qualities as criminality, courage and compassion were also considered to be based upon heredity. When someone's 'breeding' was questioned, it was their hereditary component, and not their education, that was at issue. Social Darwinism had encouraged such assumptions. Both the American and British ruling classes tended, therefore, to regard themselves as innately more able than other social and ethnic groups. A similar view continued through to the twentieth century, peaking, horrifically, under Nazism. The corollary, however, was that most decent upper class British people went on to assert that it was, therefore, their duty to bring order, justice and support to the less genetically fortunate, both at home and in the Empire. The assumption that they were genetically superior was, of course, wrong, and this premise was gradually exposed as being wrong during the latter part of the twentieth century, when environmental and educational factors, rather than innate hereditary ones, came to be seen as responsible for most of the differences between classes and races. Following the DNA revolution, and as the twenty-first century dawns, however, the pendulum is again swinging back to the 'nature' side of the debate as scientists search for genes allegedly responsible for a range of behaviours such as sexual preference, high achievement, and drug addiction.

Where are we today? Are we in what John Major called 'the classless society'? Probably not, although the rules have changed and there are now a number of competing hierarchies in Britain: the American-style hierarchy based on wealth, for example, and the hierarchy of celebrity (mainly based upon sport, politics and show business), as well as some lesser, but possibly far more deserving, hierarchies of science, professionalism, military and academic status. Strands of the traditional class system, however, still survive in Britain and, strangely, the more recent hierarchies tend eventually to key themselves into these. People of wealth and celebrity, for instance, still frequently end up aping, sometimes inaccurately, the traditional eighteenth century trappings of the landed gentry. Of course, class resentment and envy have always existed and the long struggle for Parliamentary reform and the widening of the franchise, in which the Calcrafts significantly participated, was an important reaction to this resentment.

As the twentieth century closed people who had made money still drifted back to the countryside to set themselves up as gentry. Some brought a welcome breath of fresh air. But there was a frightful heartiness about a minority of such so-called country people: women and men who shouted continually as if to proclaim to the world 'We don't care a damn about anybody or anything except ourselves!' The Dorset countryside, as Thomas Hardy knew only too well, was deeply steeped in cruelty to animals and humans alike. Some Dorset farmers of the 1950s could vandalise the landscape and exploit animals, often at the taxpayer's expense, and still complain. This was the old 'reactionary' character of Dorset that had been noted in the 1820s.

At the top of the social ladder for more than a thousand years has been royalty. But royalty has rarely, in England, been universally or slavishly respected. The Calcrafts politically opposed George III and quite probably, like many others of their class, tended to despise the foreign origins of their monarchs. Only from about 1880 until 1980 has modern royalty received widespread respect in Britain. The Calcrafts married into the aristocracy and became gentry, and the gentry of England often regarded themselves as being superior to the aristocracy. The gentry justified such arrogance on the grounds that they were in touch with the soil. Somehow, irrationally, perhaps even mystically, the soil seemed to matter. While aristocracy was aloof, urban and even cosmopolitan, the gentry believed that they belonged to the land. They were of the earth.

Today, we live in a world that would surprise nearly all of the Calcraft Dynasty although not, possibly, the broadminded John 'Crafterio' Calcraft nor his radical great grandson, Sir Henry. People do not take themselves, or their social positions, quite so seriously as they did in Victorian times, but today's ambivalence towards class is still bewildering. Right wing values and attitudes from lower down the social scale are now pedalled strongly by the British tabloid media (although most are foreign owned) which increasingly determine the course of public life, where more sophisticated liberal sentiments, as so often espoused by the Calcraft family, seem to be in decline or, at least, under threat.

The Calcraft story illustrates the complexities of English social life and the mixed feelings towards class. British class structures deny equality and only partially acknowledge liberty and justice. Yet, more important even than equality, liberty or justice is universal contentment, and many feel a sort of contentment with this peculiar British way of doing things. In the twenty-first century the British are still addicted, sometimes secretly, to the idea of class. Wealth and the cult of celebrity challenge but have not entirely displaced the traditional criteria. There is, however, a growing mythology about the old class system – that servants were always underpaid and downtrodden, that the middle classes were boringly conventional and that the upper classes nearly all lived in the countryside. Such views are stereotypes. In fact, servants often led contented and protected lives, some members of the middle classes showed unconventional originality and many of the upper classes lived mainly urban existences. Yet, for many who can afford it, although the ideal way of life is still imagined to be that of the old English country gentry, the characteristics of this class are all too often misunderstood, as the Calcraft story illustrates. It is not automatically true that to be counted a country squire one has to vote for a particular party or hunt foxes. In the present century, Britain is in danger of believing in a misleading caricature of what it has traditionally meant to be a country gentleman. For nearly two hundred years the Calcraft model of squiredom was quite different from this caricature; instead, it was liberal, was more proud of its library than its tack room, hardly indulged in blood sports, often challenged the establishment and was concerned for the wellbeing of the wider community.

So over the centuries, to what did people aspire? Most strove to fulfil what they saw as their fore-ordained roles in society and to lead a decent Christian life. But those who were ambitious sought advancement up the social class ladder. There are, thank goodness, competing forms of snobbery in Britain today. The traditional class system is ignored by many born after the 1960s watershed. They worship other gods such as celebrity, and seek personal fulfilment through money, exotic holidays or inner, more gentle, truths. Young people aspire to succeed in their chosen field, whatever it is. Fame, riches, beauty, power or goodness are all options. Only a few of today's ambitious people see the traditional class system as being relevant. Most have other ladders to climb. Of course, there were always heroes and heroines who were to be admired and emulated: saints, soldiers or statesmen. Today, sportsmen and showbiz stars top the bill. But the 'hero-system' used to run parallel with the class system. Today, it partially obscures it.

What then motivated the principal players in our dynastic drama? John Calcraft, the first, seems to have been driven by power and the lust for success. His son, by a desire to consolidate his father's achievements and, genuinely, to transform British society. Then came John Hales Calcraft who wished to live a dignified and contented life; his wife, Caroline, to do God's will and her son, Henry, to be on terms with society. But there were motives common to them all: sex, of course, is strong, whether expressed or repressed. For all of them the sense of dynasty is there: they are proud of their family and its position. But it would be wrong to write off the Calcrafts as superficial or mercenary placemen. They were, on the contrary, men of principle. Think only of the two most unlikely to fit this bill – the first two Johns. Both craved a title (they had expected to become the Earls of Ormonde) and, by the standards of their times, probably deserved one, yet both, at crucial moments in their lives, took principled decisions that they must have known would ruin this aspiration: Crafterio by attacking the king head on, and his son by standing out against his colleagues and voting, heroically, for parliamentary reform. History has shown both of them to be right, but both died at the height of their defiance of the establishment.

To see a family story as a dynasty that rises and falls over a century or two, is a satisfying way to view history. But, maybe, the Calcraft dynasty did not quite end when William Calcraft died in 1901. Perhaps, under a light disguise, it continues still.

ADDENDUM

Just as this book went to press the author was made aware by John Slingsby of some further evidence about the first John Calcraft's love life, contained in E.J. Burford's *Wits, Wenchers and Wantons* (Hale, London, 1986). From this we discover that Calcraft slept with at least four actresses. Two, Georgiana Bellamy and Elizabeth Bride, he lived with for a number of years, successively, as we have already seen. The other two were passing affairs. The first was Lucy Cooper (1733–1772), one of the 'great Impures of Covent Garden' (see page 50), and described by a contemporary as 'lewder than all the whores in Charles' reign'. Although kept by Sir Orlando Bridgeman she enjoyed having lovers. In Burford's words she was 'an irrepressible madcap' and the life and soul of every party. She died only a few weeks after Calcraft, in October 1772. (She had also been Sir Francis Dashwood's mistress and so knew a lot about his Hell Fire Club). The second was 'the lovely but very diminutive' Gertrude Mahon (1752–1809) who, as a teenager from the rival theatre company, was alluded to, tongue in cheek, as one of the 'Drury Lane Virgins' and, more specifically, as an 'Avian'. This referred to a group of actress-whores who all took bird nicknames, hers being 'the Bird of Paradise'.

Most of these little courtesans seemed to spend and drink with gay abandon, and came to unhappy ends. Some were highly intelligent like Bellamy and Perdita Robinson, who both published memoirs. Only a handful, like the dutiful Elizabeth Bride, ended up with money, social position or a stable marriage. The whole Covent Garden area in mid Georgian times was full of coffee houses, taverns, bagnios and brothels, and was known as the Great Square of Venus. The motives and behaviour of the young women earning their livings there varied. They ranged from straightforward whores, to 'posture molls' (equivalent to today's strippers and bondage experts), to (sometimes well born) good-time girls like Lucy Cooper, more selective courtesans looking for rich protectors, bit-part actresses like Gertrude Mahon who supplemented their wages sexually, and to serious stars of the stage such as Peg Woffington (Garrick's one-time flame) and her rival Georgiana Bellamy, who also liked to sleep around a bit.

John Calcraft was too busy making money and power-broking to be called a rake, but he was certainly an admirer of actresses.

SHORT BIBLIOGRAPHY

The Main Sources for Political Material:
Parliamentary History and Debates (Hansard).
Dictionary of National Biography (see Calcraft).
History of Parliament: The Commons 1754–1790, L. Namier & J. Brooke: 1964.
Reform: The Fight for the 1832 Reform Act, Edward Pearce, Pimlico, 2004.
The Grenville Papers, ed. W.J. Smith, 1852.

At the Dorset County Record Office, County Hall, Dorchester, there are various papers, including: Henry Fox: Private Letter Book, 1746–1754 (about 170 Letters). Henry Fox: Private Letter Book, 1754–1755 (about 25 Letters). Henry Fox: Unmarked Letter Book, 1746–1748 (about 190 Letters). John Calcraft: Letter Book, 1745–1746.

Sources of Personal and Social History:
Various Papers at the Dorset County Record Office, including Manorial Deeds, Estate Papers, Maps and Plans etc.
Marston v. Panton and Others, Court Papers, unpublished, 1909.
Family Bibles at Rempstone (three of which contain pedigrees).
An Apology for the Life of George Anne Bellamy, 1785.
Daisy Bevan: Odd Memories of an Ordinary Person, unpublished, 1927.
Enchanting Bellamy, Cyril Hughes Hartmann, Heinemann, 1956.
Fresh Leaves and Green Pastures, Jane Panton, Eveleigh Nash, 1909.
Garrick, Ian McIntyre, Penguin, 1999.
History and Antiquities of the County of Dorset, John Hutchins, 1773.
Rempstone Hall 1600–1975, S.A. Hamilton-Fletcher, unpublished, 1975.
The Calcrafts of Rempstone, Richard D Ryder, unpublished, 1975.

General:
Class in Britain, David Carradine, Penguin, 2000.
Dorset's War Diary: Battle of Britain to D-Day, Rodney Legg, Dorset Publishing Co., 2004.

INDEX

Alexander,
General 126
Allenby, Bobbie
125
Anderson (family)
132, 138
Animals (at
Rempstone) 23,
85, 96, 122, 126,
142, 150, 151,
152, 164, 167
Arne 138
Ashley Cooper
(family) 17
Athelhampton
146
Ayliffe, John 38-
40

Backha, Nora 148
Baillie (family)
112
Baker, Nancy 124,
125, 131, 134,
136
Bankes (family)
17, 37, 41, 42,
70, 71, 74, 85,
107, 110, 114,
117, 118, 133,
146, 149, 160
Bankes, Henry 25,
40, 63, 101
Bankes, John 25,
40, 149
Bankes,William 17
Banwell Abbey
121
Barnes, Anne 14
Barré, Colonel
Isaac 29
Barry, Spranger 43
Battrick, Ernie
158
Beaufort, Duke of

69, 84
Bellamy, George
Anne
(Georgiana) 3, 9,
24, 25, 27, 30,
31, 33, 34, 35,
38, 39, 40, 41,
43-59, 68, 69, 82,
86, 88, 90, 112,
113, 114, 116,
122, 124, 142,
169
Bentham, Jeremy
65
Bessborough, Lord
34
Best, Marion 158
Bevan, Christina
112
Bevan, Daisy (née
Waldegrave) 61,
82-84, 117, 119-
122
Bevan, Millie and
Edwyn 121-122
Bimbo 151
Blandford 25, 38,
64, 138, 143
Bliss, Sir Arthur
152
Board of Trade
103-106, 108,
109, 110, 113,
119
Bonaparte, Princes
s Pauline 11, 69,
83
Bond (family) 25,
41, 63, 85, 87,
101, 102, 114,
115, 117, 118,
128, 141, 146,
148
Boothby, Lord 160
Bournemouth 128,

138, 139, 162
Bovington 132,
139
Braddock, General
Edward 24, 49,
55, 157
Bradley, General
139
Branksome 138
Bride, Elizabeth 3,
10, 12, 19, 24,
31-35, 41, 42, 56,
59, 60-62, 76, 82,
91, 92, 142, 169
Bridport, Viscount
Peter 133, 134
Bright, John 103,
105, 107, 108,
109, 110
Brooke, Rupert
117, 120, 139
Browne, Jeremy
143
Brownsea, Percy
158
Bryanston 17, 146
Buchanan, Jack
139
Bucknowle 146
Bushey (Bushaw)
37, 111-113, 127,
145, 149, 158
Bushey House
160, 161, 163
Byron, Lord 11, 44

Caddy, Tom 158
Calcraft, Arabella
Margaretta 62,
71-72, 81
Calcraft, Bridget
10, 61
Calcraft, Lady
Caroline 3, 7, 11,
12, 13, 17, 45,

48, 61, 68, 69,
81-103, 107, 112,
115, 116, 120,
138, 145, 147,
163, 164
Calcraft, Caroline
Elizabeth 34, 35,
48, 59
Calcraft, Caroline
Jane 81
Calcraft, Colonel
Thomas 26, 36,
40, 60
Calcraft, Elizabeth
(née Hales) 62,
64, 81
Calcraft, Elizabeth
Mary 62, 81
Calcraft, Emily 35,
68
Calcraft, Fanny
Catherine 81
Calcraft,
Georgiana Emily
(Georgy) 82, 83,
90, 116, 122
Calcraft, Sir
Granby 3, 24, 32,
35, 41, 42, 49,
51, 53, 56, 58,
60, 62, 67, 71,
76-81, 85, 86,
125, 142, 149
Calcraft, Granby
Hales (b.1802)
62, 67
Calcraft, Sir Henry
3, 13, 35, 103-
110
Calcraft, Henry
Fox 9, 35, 59, 86
Calcraft, John
(The Older
1726–1772) 3, 5,
8-11, 19-59, 60,

61, 62, 64, 76, 80, 86, 93, 142, 149, 163, 164, 167, 168, 169
Calcraft, John (The Younger 1765–1831) 3, 5, 11, 60-77, 81, 93, 163, 168
Calcraft, John Hales (1796–1880) 3, 5, 11-13, 35, 58-64, 67-69, 81-103, 107, 111-113, 164, 165, 168
Calcraft, John Hales Montagu (1831–1868) 13, 82, 86, 87, 89, 93, 99
Calcraft, Katherine 87, 116
Calcraft, Richard 81
Calcraft, Susan Charlotte 82, 90, 112
Calcraft, Thomas 26, 36, 40, 60, 67, 76, 77, 80, 86
Calcraft, Thomas Hales 62, 81
Calcraft, William 35, 36, 62, 163
Calcraft, William Montagu 3, 58, 68, 85, 86, 88, 89, 93, 106, 107, 110-116, 145, 149, 168
Calne 25, 34, 86
Cambridge 108, 111, 114, 115, 124, 125, 143
Cambridge, Duke of 108
Canada 10, 24
Cannes 121
Cannon, Professor

John 4, 29
Cannon's Cove 141
Campbell, Archibald 121
Carter, Marion 14
Castlereagh, Lord 64, 66, 67, 70
Cattell, Harry 159
Cavendish-Bentinck (family) 114, 118
Chamberlain (family) 143
Chaplin, Charlie 139, 150
Chatsworth 104
Chavchavadze, Prince George 153
Chenton, Mary 14
Childe Oakford 139, 140
Christopher, Bill 158
Church Knowle 85, 146
Churchill, Sir Winston 69, 119, 127, 132, 139, 158
Cibber, Mrs 43
Clark (family) 113, 114
Clark, Edward 88, 89, 91, 95, 101, 114
Clark, Harry 88, 113, 116, 148
Clavel (family) 17
Claywell 37, 158
Cobb, John 132
Cobbett, William 65
Cochrane, 'Cocky' 125
Coghill, Sir Toby 143
Congreve, William 59
Conway, General

H. 29
Cook, Sir Francis 133, 152
Cook, Sir Frederick 134
Cook, Sir Herbert 131, 134
Cook, Mary Lady (Moë) 133, 134
Cooper, Lucy 50, 169
Coote, General Eyre 24
Corfe 7, 8, 26, 34-38, 40-42, 63, 64, 101, 107, 110, 112, 114-118, 120, 133, 135, 144, 145, 152, 159, 161
Corn Laws, The 65, 72, 109
Corunna 78
Coryton (family) 148
Cosway, Richard 142
Covent Garden 30, 31, 43, 46, 169
Coward, Noel 139
'Crafterio' (see Calcraft John (The Older 1726–1772)
Creech 101, 102, 117, 118, 146
Crichel 37, 112
Cricket St Thomas 133
Crimea, The 13, 109
Crowley, Aleister 17, 117, 119, 120, 163
Cumberland, Duke of 24, 74

Dancing Ledge 141

Darwin, Charles 115
Dashwood, Sir Francis 169
Dean (family) 158
Debenham (family) 148
Deens, Eliza 14
Denman, Thomas 67
Devonshire, Duchess of 104, 110
Devonshire, Duke of 103
Dickens, Charles 91
Dibben, Emma 14
Digby (family) 17, 148
Disraeli, Benjamin 103, 105
Dorchester 33, 36, 38, 63, 86, 143, 146, 147
Douglas, Duchess of 55
Douglas-Hamilton, Lady Isobel 115, 122, 123 (see also Ryder, Lady Isobel)
Douglas-Hamilton, Lord Malcolm 137
Douglas-Hamilton family (see Hamilton, Dukes of)
Drax (family) 17, 25, 26, 37, 93, 95, 96, 97, 98, 99, 100, 113, 118, 122, 149
Drax, Thomas Erle 25
Drummond-Hay, Jamie 124
Drury Lane

(Theatre Royal) 9, 10, 31, 43, 169

Dunshay Manor 37, 116, 120, 132

Durham, Olivia 148

Durrell, Lawrence 134

Edinburgh 19, 20, 22, 31, 55

Eisenhower, General D. 132, 139

Eldon, Lord (*see* Scott family) 64, 66, 69, 70, 74, 93, 102, 107, 117, 122

Ellis, Havelock 116

Encombe 17, 25, 89, 93, 102, 112, 113, 117, 122, 146

Eveleigh Nash (Publisher) 88, 119

Eyre, Richard 143

Fergusson, Colonel 147

Ffoulkes, Mrs 119

Filliter, George 61

Fisher, Admiral 'Jackie' 123

Fishing 11, 86, 117, 149

Fleet 138

Fooks, Ralph 86

Forres School 140

Fox, Charles James 19, 27, 38

Fox, Henry, Lord Holland 9, 19, 20, 22-27, 30, 33-42, 45-53, 58, 59, 67, 86, 126, 133, 134

Fox-Strangways, Lady Maria 133

Foxground 7, 37, 112, 142

Foxhunting 148

Frampton (family) 17

Francis II, Emperor 76

Francis, Philip 27-29, 34, 48, 60

Freud, Sigmund 116, 166

Frith, W.P. 87

Furzey Island 37, 125

Garrick, David 10, 30, 43, 49, 59, 142, 169

Gay, Jennifer and Jacqueline 124

George III 29, 167

George VI 132, 139

Ghosts 17, 132, 162

Gibraltar 33, 42

Gladstone, William 93, 103, 105, 108, 109, 110

Goathorn 37, 120, 126, 138, 140

Gordon, Jane, Duchess of 12, 82

Gordon, 4th Duke of 12, 82, 83

Gover, Eliza 14

Graham, Ronald 131, 136

Granby, Marquis of 24, 32, 49, 51, 56

Grantham 9, 11, 19, 21, 34, 36, 47, 48, 54

Green Island 37, 125

Grey, Lord 70, 73

Grey, Mima 136

Greyhound (public house) 42

Gribble, Julian 132

Grove-White (family) 143

Hales, Dr Stephen 12

Hales, Sir Thomas Pym 12, 62, 81

Hamilton, Angus, 15th Duke of 122, 161

Hamilton, Douglas, 13th Duke of 122, 123

Hamilton, 'Douglo', 14th Duke of 123, 124, 127

Hamilton, Nina, Duchess of 161

Hamilton Palace 123, 124

Hamilton-Fletcher (family) 4, 132, 136, 137, 141, 158, 164

Hamilton-Fletcher, Alexander 85, 87, 131, 160, 161

Hamilton-Fletcher, Giles 87

Hamilton-Fletcher, Mervyn 131, 132, 162

Hamilton-Fletcher, Nichola 161

Hamilton-Fletcher, Nicholas 131, 143

Hamilton-Fletcher, Robin 131, 132, 137, 138, 140, 143

Hamilton-Fletcher, Tim 124, 125, 131, 132, 137, 138, 140, 143, 144, 147

Handford House 146

Hardy, Thomas 167

Harman's Cross 153

Harris, Hookey 160

Harrowby, (Dudley Ryder) Earl of 64, 66, 67, 68, 69, 72, 74, 82, 105, 122

Havas, Kato (*see* Woods family)

Head, Sir Henry 121

Hell Fire Club 26, 169

Hesse, John 21

Hess, Rudolf 127

Hession, Brian 126

Hession, Molly 126

Hinchinbroke (family) 148

Hogarth, William 19, 134, 142

Holland House 9, 49, 58

Holton Heath 138

Honest Jack (*see* John Calcraft the Older)

Hood family (*see* Bridport, Viscount)

Huish Manor 61

Hunt (family) 158

Huskisson, William 71

Hutchins, John 8, 81, 87

Ilchester, Earls of 23, 133, 134

Inge (family) 148, 149

Ingress 10, 34, 35, 36, 41, 60, 61, 76

Ireland 42, 44, 53, 54, 58, 64, 67, 93
Iwerne Minster 138

Jamaica 42, 82
John, Augustus 123, 132
Junius 10, 24, 26-30, 88, 163

'Kaiser Bill' 139
Keeper's Cottage 116 139, 149
Keil (family) 148
Kimmeridge 138
Kingston Lacey 101
Kingston Maurward 17, 25
Knoll House 122, 146

Lane, Jane 14
Langton Matravers 37, 65
Langtry, Lilly 133
Lawrence of Arabia 139
Leeds Abbey 10, 34, 35, 60, 61
Lees (family) 148
Lefebure, Calcraft 35, 60
Lefebure (Lefebvre), Charles 35, 60, 61, 85, 86
Lefebvre, George 35
Lincolnshire 9, 10, 19, 24, 36, 61, 62
Linnington, Gordon 158
Lomax (family) 124
Long Island 37, 139
Lulworth 100,

117, 133, 138, 146

McIntyre, Ian 30
Mackworth (family) 132
Macmillan, Harold 124, 160
Magic 3, 7, 17, 116, 119, 120, 154, 164
Mahon, Gertrude 169
Manchester, 5th Duke of 12, 69, 82, 106
Mandeville, Viscountess 68
Manningham-Buller, Lara (née Ryder) 13, 87, 161, 162
Manningham-Buller, Mervyn 162
Mansel (family) 85, 87, 101, 112, 114, 117, 118, 146, 148
Mansel, Kitty 85
Marston, Rev. C.D. 87
Marston, Captain Guy Montagu 17, 87-93, 95, 97, 100, 110, 116-124, 149, 163, 164
Marston, Katherine (née Calcraft) 88
Maxwell, Jane (see Gordon, Duchess of)
Mayell, Mrs 150, 156, 158
Melba, Dame Nellie 139
Melbury 133
Metham, Sir

George 30, 44, 45, 46, 47, 51
Meynell (family) 88
Michie (family) 146
Middlebere 138
Milton Abbey 146
Minden 24
Moeran, Jerry 143
Montagu, Lady Caroline (see Calcraft, Lady Caroline)
Montrose, Duke of 131
Montgomery, Lord Bernard 132, 139
Moore, Sir John 78
Mooshka, Princess (see Troubetskoy)
Moriarty, Melanie (née Ryder) 87
Morley, Emily 14
Morrell, Lady Ottoline 132
Moseley (family) 146

Namier, Sir Lewis 33, 34, 152
Napier, Colonel 22, 58
Napoleon (Bonaparte) 11, 35, 72, 73, 76, 77, 78, 82, 83, 100, 142, 161
Nelson, Lady Charlotte 133
Nelson, Viscount Horatio 134
Newcastle, Duke of 25, 34, 73
Newton Manor School 146
Nine Barrow Down 7, 8, 134

Outram (family)

146
Outram, Nicky 146
Ower 7, 37, 100, 101, 111
Owermoigne 138

Paine, John 134
Palmerston, Lord 65, 67, 87, 105, 108
Painism 152
Panton, Jane 13, 87-91, 93, 95, 99, 100-102, 111, 118, 119, 163
Peel, Robert 65, 67, 69, 83
Pemberton (family) 88
Peninsular War 60, 62, 80
Perceval, Spencer 73, 74
Peterloo Massacre 72-74
Piddletrenthide 138
Pike, William Joseph 100
Pinney (family) 114, 143
Pitman (family) 158
Pitt, George 25, 36
Pitt, John 25
Pitt, William, The Edler (Lord Chatham) 10, 17, 25, 27-30, 34, 36-40, 42, 49, 50, 60, 63, 67, 81, 93
Pitt (family) 115, 117, 149
Poole 7, 8, 10, 26, 37, 40, 54, 58, 86, 128, 133, 138, 141, 142, 147, 157, 161

Poole Harbour 7, 8, 37, 133, 141, 142, 157, 161
Poore, Bertie 122, 123
Poore, Nina (*see* Hamilton, Duchess of)
Poor Laws 65, 66
Portland 138
Portugal 44, 60, 78, 108, 132, 134, 162, 163
Poynder, Michael 163
Purbeck, Isle of 7, 8, 36, 62, 63, 89, 93, 114, 115, 117, 118, 132, 139, 140, 146, 152, 154, 161, 163

Radstock, Lord 82, 84, 90, 114, 115, 117, 120
Redman, Gordon 148
Reform Bill 11, 69, 70, 71, 73, 74, 86, 107, 109, 122
Reid (family) 146
Rempstone Heath 7, 8, 140
Rempstone Old Farm 158, 162
Reynolds, Joshua 24, 142
Richmond, Duchess of 12, 83
Riddle, Mr 128, 129
Robinson, Perdita 169
Rochford, Countess of 53
Romanov, Princess Nina 153
Romilly, Sir

Samuel 67
Romney, George 60, 117, 120, 142
Rose (family) 8, 36, 90, 132, 145
Ross, Robbie 132
Ross-Turner (family) 148
Round Island 37, 125
Russell, Bertrand 132
Russley Park 40
Rutland, Duchess of 34
Rutland, Duke of 9
Ryder, Audrey 87
Ryder, Ben 87, 124, 125, 137, 143, 146, 162, 164
Ryder, Cyril 108, 115, 122, 123
Ryder, Douglas 162
Ryder, Dudley (*see* Harrowby, Earl of)
Ryder, Dudley Henry 68, 90, 114, 162
Ryder, Sir Dudley 22, 67
Ryder, Colonel Dudley 143
Ryder, Emily 126, 152
Ryder, Emma 161, 162
Ryder, Evelyn 123
Ryder, Gay 124, 143, 149
Ryder, Georgina 161
Ryder, Granville Dudley 68, 82
Ryder, Guy 162
Ryder, Henry 152
Ryder, Hilly 162,

164
Ryder, Iris 126, 127
Ryder, Lady Isobel 123
Ryder, D.C.D. 'Jack' 15, 78, 87, 114, 116, 117, 120, 122-129, 131-142, 144-163
Ryder, Jacqueline 124, 143
Ryder, James Calcraft Dudley 13, 87, 116, 124, 134, 135, 137, 141, 143, 146, 154, 158, 161, 162, 164
Ryder, Rt Hon. Richard (1766–1832) 68, 116
Ryder, Richard Dudley 68, 116, 133, 138, 140, 143, 146, 151, 153, 162
Ryder, Jennifer 143
Ryder, Lara (*see* Manningham-Buller)
Ryder, Melanie (*see* Moriarty)
Ryder, Nancy (*see* Baker, Nancy)
Ryder, Nathaniel, Lord Harrowby 67
Ryder, Philippa 125, 162
Ryder, Captain Robert 'Red' 140
Ryder, Sally 161, 162
Ryder, Vera (Vee) 15, 87, 129, 131-134, 138, 139, 141, 142, 144,

145, 147- 153, 156-161
Ryder, Vanessa 162
Russell, Lord John 67, 73, 105, 106

Sandford, Colonel 46
SAS 140, 162
Sawyer, Anthony 20
Selkirk, Earl and Countess of 124, 125, 148, 160, 161
Scott (family, *see also* Eldon, Lord) 17, 36, 69, 93, 143, 146, 148
Seton, Anya 152
Seven Years' War 10, 42
Sewell (family) 146
Sex 3, 7, 9, 11, 12, 13, 17, 48, 84, 116, 119, 120, 123, 126, 128, 130, 131, 136, 147, 164, 168
Shaftesbury 161
Shelburne, Lord 25, 29, 34
Sherborne 17, 36, 124, 132, 138, 143
Sherborne Girls School 132
Sheridan, Richard 43
Shooting 149
Simpson (family) 158
Smedmore 89, 101, 102, 117, 118, 146, 158
Smuts, General 139
SOE 140

Soho 9, 44, 57, 58
Speciesism 152
Spencer-Watson (family) 132
Spiller, Reg 140, 150, 158
Stoborough 37, 87
Stockley, Fred 158
Stourhead 129
Studland 7, 8, 112, 122, 123, 126, 131, 132, 133, 135, 137, 138, 139, 141, 144, 145, 146, 148, 160, 161
Sturdy (family) 118, 146
Sturminster Marshall 138
Sutton, Lord George 56
Swanage 37, 63, 65, 113, 115, 138, 140, 145, 146, 150, 156, 157

Tarrant Gunville 138
Temple, Lord 27, 28, 29
Thomand, Marquis of 41
Tierney, George 67
Tolstoy, Count 121
Tompin, Maisie 14
Trenchard, George 8
Troubetskoy, Prince Peter and Princess 'Mooshka' 153

Tucker, Bill 125
Tunbridge Wells 44
Turle (family) 146
Turle, Arish 143, 148. 149
Turle, Admiral Charles and Jane 148, 155
Turle, Gillies 148, 149
Tyneham 89, 102, 138, 158
Tyrawley, Lady 48
Tyrawley, Lord 43, 44, 51, 55, 59

Victoria, Queen 139, 161
Vincent, Eliza 14
Volter, Anne 14
Vincent, Teddy 158
Vitower 37, 138, 139, 162, 163
Vyvyan, Sir Richard 74

Waldegrave, Daisy (see Bevan)
Waldegrave, Elizabeth 121
Waldegrave, Mary 82
Waldegrave, Hon.W. 66
Walker, Selina 14
Wall, General 45
Walpole, Horace 25, 33, 34, 59, 165
Walter, Paul 153
Wareham 8, 10, 11, 25, 26, 28, 29, 35-38, 41, 42, 60, 61, 62, 64, 67, 70, 71, 74, 75, 78, 80, 81, 84, 86, 87, 93, 95, 96, 100, 110, 113-116, 125, 130, 132, 133, 134, 138, 146, 148, 149, 155, 157, 160-163
Warmwell 138
Warner, Eric and Geoffrey 125, 132, 148
Warner, Philip and Pam 148
Waterloo, Battle of 11, 12, 65, 72, 80, 83, 113, 129, 158
Watson, Arthur 143
Waugh, Evelyn 124
Wedgwood, Josiah 11
Weld (family) 117, 146
Weld, Joseph 133
Wellington, Duke of 11, 61, 62, 69, 70, 71, 72, 73, 74, 77, 78, 79, 80, 93, 122
Wellman, Jim 158
West Bay 138
West Digges 43, 55
Westbrook Hay 68, 107, 116, 124, 162
Wetherill, Lord 74
Weymouth 86, 138, 159

Wilberforce, William 66, 67, 82
Wilde, Oscar 132
Wilkes, John 24, 29, 34, 42, 85
Williams (family) 17
Winspit 8, 37, 121, 141
Winn, Godfrey 126
Winser, Tom 143
Witchcraft 159
Withers, Googie 132
Withers, Harry 132
Witt, 'Kipper' 139, 140, 149, 159
Woffington, Peg 169
Wolfe, General James 24
Wolverton 36
Woods (family) 141, 152
Worth Matravers 7, 8, 11, 14, 20, 28, 33, 34, 36, 37, 41, 42, 54, 88, 112, 115, 116, 117, 119, 120, 138, 144
Wytch Farm 8, 37, 151, 154, 158

Yellin, Tristram 135
York, Duke of 76
Young, Susie and Rosie 143